Volume 7

Econometrics
Reading Lists

Economics Reading Lists,
Course Outlines, Exams,
Puzzles & Problems

Compiled by Edward Tower, September 1995
Duke University & The University of Auckland

NOTE TO USERS AND POTENTIAL CONTRIBUTORS

These teaching materials are drawn from both undergraduate and graduate programs at 105 major colleges and universities. They are designed to widen the horizons of individual professors and curriculum committees. Some include suggestions for term-paper topics, and many of the reading lists are useful guides for students seeking both topics and references for term papers and theses. Thus, they should enable faculty members to advise students more effectively and efficiently. They will also be useful to prospective graduate students seeking more detailed information about various graduate programs and to librarians responsible for acquisitions in economics. Finally, they may interest researchers and administrators who wish to know more about how their own work and the work of their department is being received by the profession.

The exams, puzzles and problems include both undergraduate and graduate exams contributed by economics departments and individual professors. They should be especially useful to professors making up exams and problem sets and to students studying for Ph.D. exams. They may also serve as the focus for study groups.

From time to time, we will reprint updated and expanded versions. Therefore, we welcome new or updated teaching materials, particularly those which complement material in this collection or cover areas we missed. Potential contributors should contact Ed Tower, Economics Department, Box 90097, Duke University, Durham, North Carolina 27708-0097, U.S.A., **tower@econ.duke.edu**

While Eno River Press has copyrighted the entire collection, authors of the various parts retain the right to reproduce and assign the reproduction of their own materials as they choose. Thus, anyone wishing to reproduce particular materials should contact their author. Similarly, those wishing to make verbatim use of departmental examinations, except as teaching materials for one's own class, should contact the department chair concerned.

Associate Compilers for this series are:
Ömer Gökçekuş, Visiting Lecturer, Duke University
Chao Jing, Graduate Instructor, University of Colorado
Wells D. Tower, Senior at Wesleyan University

Dan Tower helped produce the volumes with creativity and energy. Nancy Hurtgen and Tom Hurtgen advised on many aspects of the project. Members of the Duke Economics Department have been helpful from the inception of the project, and belated thanks go to Allen C. Kelley, who suggested in 1980 the usefulness of collecting syllabi.

Eno River Press
115 Stoneridge Drive
Chapel Hill, North Carolina 27514-9737
U.S.A.
Fax & Phone: (919) 967-8246

3 2280 00514 1403

ISBN for the volume: 0-88024-187-X
ISBN for the series: 0-88024-160-8
Library of Congress Catalog Number: 95-061333

ECONOMETRICS READING LISTS

Contents

***

U = Undergraduate, **G** = Graduate
RE = Reading Lists with Exams, Problems and/ or Term Paper Topics

Introduction to the Econometrics Volumes
Richard A. Piccirillo, Jr.
Duke University

Econometrics is a crucial link between macroeconomics and microeconomics. Autoregressive unit roots and cointegration are a few of the concepts of econometrics that are applied to macroeconomic models such as asset pricing models and ARMA models. Yet, econometrics is the core of several microeconomic fields such as labor economics and health economics, embodied in standard regression analysis, panel data estimation(i.e. tobit and logit models). and duration models. While econometrics is sometimes criticized for being inexact, it must be emphasized that it is the best technique economists have to obtain estimates of the effects of certain significant independent variables on a dependent variable. Moreover, it allows for improvement in the fit of the regression by correcting for heteroskedasticity, endogeneity, and misspecification of the model. These two volumes cover all of the various concepts of econometrics in the form of reading lists which enable the reader to understand the theory and problems and exercises which test the reader's ability to apply his knowledge to particular models.

Volume 7 contains reading lists and syllabi as well as a few exams from a selection of econometrics courses taught at the nation's top universities. These courses range from basic econometrics to applied econometrics to advanced econometrics to time series analysis. The recurring themes in this volume are standard regression theory, non-spherical errors, limited-dependent variables, ARMA and ARCH models, and duration models.

While numerous authors are mentioned, there are a handful whose work is considered required reading in most courses. This group contains: Dr. McFadden on estimation of discrete response models; Dr. J.L. Powell on estimation of the Tobit model; Dr. Amemiya on advanced econometrics; Dr. H. White on misspecification estimation; Dr. Heckman on discrete panel data models; and Drs. Greene, Maddala, and Berndt on foundations of basic econometric analysis.

In addition, this volume includes forecasting, indirect inference, and competing risk models. It also includes a course in econometric research and a course using STATA for forecasting.

In Volume 8, there are large number of qualifying examinations, midterm and final exams, and even some homework assignments from the same types of courses as in the previous volume. Standard regression theory and its empirical application are strongly tested in many interesting examples, such as the estimation of Cagan's model. While parametric estimation is the principal focus, this volume is peppered with semi-parametric estimation. It also contains exercises in hazard models, autocorrelation, and distributed lag and time series models.

In sum, the first volume gives the reader a strong foundation in econometric theory while the second one allows him to apply this knowledge empirically to various models. These two volumes are tailored for graduate students who wish to become well-rounded in the study of econometrics, but it can also inspire undergraduate students who desire to enter the field of economics and have strong backgrounds in mathematics and economics.

Professor Mark Y. An

man@ping.econ.duke.edu

Fall 1994   Economics 345

Applied Econometrics

Course Description: This course covers several econometric topics which have been widely used in applied economic research. It provides the students with hands-on *necessary* tools to read research articles in their fields and to conduct empirical research of their own. It focuses primarily on the applications of those tools. However, we will, on several occasions, also address issues such as the source of a specification problem, or the theoretical foundations behind what we are doing. The students are expected to use SAS computing language.

Prerequisites: The prerequisites for the course are the first-year graduate level econometrics Econ 341 and Econ 343.

Course Evaluation: The students' course grades will be based on a midterm (30%), a comprehensive final exam (50%), home assignments (10%), and a term report (10%). The midterm exam is closed-book while the final is open-book. Both exams are in class. The students are encouraged to work in group for the homework. Each student is required to submit a term report on an applied and empirical research topic. The report should be no more than 12 double spaced pages. The students should consult the instructor on the topics chosen as soon as possible but no later than October 14, 1994. The report is due on the last day of class, December 2, 1994 (an absolutely firm deadline).

Textbooks: The main texts for the course is Greene (1993). Maddala (1983) is an excellent reference book dealing with limited dependent variables. For a comprehensive survey on the economic applications of most of the topics of the course, the students are referred to Berndt (1991).

Berndt, E. (1991): *The Practice of Econometrics*, Addison-Wesley.

Greene, W. (1993) (**required**): *Econometric Analysis*, 2nd edition, McMillan.

Maddala, G.S. (1983): *Limited-Dependent and Qualitative Variables in Econometrics*, Paperback Edition, Cambridge University Press.

Topics:

I. Preliminaries (Greene: Chapters 3 and 4)
      1.1 Probability (I): Basic Concepts
      1.2 Probability (II): Sampling Distributions
      1.3 Statistics (I): Estimation
      1.4 Statistics (II): Hypothesis Testing

II. Nonlinearity (Greene: Chpaters 8, 11, and 12)
      2.1 Nonlinearity in Variables
      2.2 Nonlinearity in Parameters: NLS
      2.3 Nonlinear Optimization: Hill Climbing Algorithms

III. Non-spherical Errors (Greene: Chapters 13, 14, 15 and 16)
      3.1 GLS in General
      3.2 Heteroskedasticity
      3.3 Autocorrelation
      3.4 Panel Data Models (I): Model Selection
      3.5 Panel Data Models (II): Fixed versus Random Effects

IV. Limited dependent Variables (Greene: Chapters 21 and 22 and Maddala's Book)
      4.1 Introduction: An Example of Female Labor Supply
      4.2 Qualitative Response Models (I): Binary Choices
      4.3 Qualitative Response Models (II): Multiple Choices
      4.4 Tobit Models (I): Two-Step Procedure
      4.5 Tobit Models (II): MLE
      4.6 Regime Switching and Sample Selection
      4.7 Simultaneous Equation Systems Involving LDVs

V. Duration Models (Greene: Chapter 22)
      5.1 An Example of Search Unemployment
      5.2 Non-parametric Treatments
      5.3 Semi-parametric Estimation of Proportional Hazard Models
      5.4 Parametric Estimation: MLE

Duke University

G

Professor Mark Y. An
206 Social Science Building
Telephone: 660-1808
man@ping.econ.duke.edu

Fall 1994   Economics 347

Econometrics II

Course Description: This course presents the econometric methods for finite dimensional nonlinear parametric models. The treatment is organized around the unified asymptotic theory of estimation and inference under correct specification. There is substantial emphasis on the theory of estimation, though we will also see how those results could be applied.

The main text for the course is *Estimation and Inference in Econometrics* by Davidson and MacKinnon. *Advanced Econometrics* by T. Amemiya has a few nicely written chapters and plenty of instructive problem sets. *Nonlinear Statistical Models* A.R. Gallant is a superb reference for the area of interest. Those who want more thorough and more rigorous treatment of the probability foundations, might want to invest on Dhrymes' *Topics in Advanced Econometrics: Probability Foundations*.

The course grades will be based on a midterm (30%), a comprehensive final exam (50%), home assignments (20%). Both exams are in-class, closed book exams, though the students are allowed to bring to the midterm one sheet of notes and formulas (both sides) and to the final two sheets.

The lectures are between 8:45 to 10:00 am on Mondays and Fridays. Please note the typo in the ACES Book regarding this.

Topics:

I. Review of Probability Foundation
      1.1 Probability Space
      1.2 Random Variables
      1.3 Expectation and Different Inequalities
      1.4 Conditioning and Independence
      1.5 Stochastic Convergence
      1.6 LLN and CLT

II. Review of Linear Models
      2.1 Geometry of OLS
      2.2 Testing of Linear Constraints
      2.3 Asymptotics of OLS

III. Maximum Likelihood Estimation
      3.1 Likelihood and MLE
      3.2 Asymptotics
      3.3 C-R Bounds
      3.4 Tests Based on the MLE: Wald/LM/LR Tests
      3.5 Linear Models Revisited

IV. General Properties of Extremum Estimators
      3.1 Definition and Examples
      3.2 Consistency
      3.3 Asymptotic Normality
      3.4 Instrumental Variables
      3.5 Nonlinear Least Square Estimator
      3.6 Generalized Method of Moment Estimator
      3.7 Numerical Nonlinear Optimization

V. Application I: Non-spherical Errors
      5.1 Heteroskedasticity
      5.2 Autocorrelation
      5.3 Panel Data Models
      5.4 Hausman's Test

VI. Application II: Limited Dependent Variables
      6.1 Qualitative Response Models
      6.2 Censored and Truncated Regression
      6.3 Regime Switching and Sample Selection

Duke University

G

Mark Y. An
206 Social Science Building
Telephone: 660-1808
man@ping.econ.duke.edu

Spring 1995   Economics 348

Advanced Topics in Econometrics

Course Description:

This course covers selected topics in microeconometrics with an emphasis on "less" parametric setting. Students's active participation is expected. Students are encouraged to work in small groups for homework and readings. The final grade will be based on home assignments (25%), class presentations (25%), and a take-home final exam (50%). For the class presentations, each student chooses a paper from the reading list. Make arrangement to see me ASAP for your choice of papers. Each presentation lasts 35 minutes.

Two textbooks have been ordered for the course. Both are excellent.

Gibbons, J.D and S. Chakraborti (1992): *Nonparametric Statistical Inference*, Marcel Dekker.

Silverman, B.W. (1986): *Density Estimation for Statistics and Data Analysis*, London: Chapman and Hall.

Topics and Reading List:

Materials with an (*) denote required readings. I will pass a complete set of materials to Mr. Yaping Wang. You can make copies. Federal law prohibits my distributing published articles.

I. Non-parametric Methods: An Introduction

1.1 Order and Rank Statistics: Theory and Applications

(*) Gibbons, J.D and S. Chakraborti (1992): Chapters 1, 2, 3, 4, 5, 7.

1.2 Kernel Estimation of Density:

(*) Silverman, B.W. (1986): Chapters 1, 2, 3, 4.

1.3 Nonparametric Regression Analysis

(*) Bierens, H.J. (1987):"Kernel Estimators of Regression Function," in T.F. Bewley (ed), *Advances in Econometrics*, Cambridge: Cambridge University Press.

1.4 Applications

(*) Chamberlain, G. (1991):"Quantile Regression, Censoring and the Structure of Wages," Discussion Paper #1558, Harvard University.

An, M.Y. and J.Y. Lin (1995):"Institution and Production Stability: Evidence from Chinese Agriculture," In progress, Duke University.

II. Semiparametric Limited Dependent Variable Models

2.1 Binary Choice Models

(*) Cosslett, S. (1983):"Distribution-Free Maximum Likelihood Estimation of the Binary Choice Model," *Econometrica*, **51**, 765-781.

(*) Han, A. (1987):"Non-parametric Analysis of Generalized Regression Model: The Maximum Rank Correlation Estimator", *Journal of econometrics* **35** 303-316.

Manski, C. (1988):" Identification of Binary Response Models," *JASA*, **83**, 729-738.

Matzkin, R. (1992):"Nonparametric and Distribution-Free Estimation of the Binary Shreshhold Crossing and the Binary Choice Models," *Econometrica*, **60**, 239-270.

2.2 Multiple Choice Models

(*) McFadden, D. (1989):"A Method of Simulated Moments for Estimation of Discrete Response Models without Numerical Integration," *Econometrica*, **57**, 995-1026.

McCulloch, R. and P. Rossi (1994):"An Exact Likelihood Analysis of the Multinomial Probit Models." Working paper.

2.3 Censored Models

(*) Powell, J.L. (1986):"Symmetrically Trimmed Least Squares Estimation for Tobit Models," *Econometrica*, **54**, 1435-1460.

Newey, W. (1991):"Efficient Estimation of Tobit Models under Conditional Symmetry," in W.A. Barnett, J. Powell and G.E. Tauchen (eds.), *Nonparametric and Semiparametric Methods in Econometrics and Statistics*, Cambridge: Cambridge University Press.

(*) Andrews, D.W.K. and M. M.A. Schafgans (1994):"Semiparametric Estimation of a Sample Selection Model," Manuscript, Yale University.

Heckman, J.J and B. Honore (1990):"The Empirical Content of the Roy Model," *Econometrica*, Vol. 58, 1121-1149.

2.4 Limited Dependent Variables in Panel Data Setting

(*) Heckman, J.J (1981):"Statistical Models for Discrete Panel Data", in (Manski, C. and D. Mcfadden eds) *Structural Analysis of Discrete Data*, MIT Press.

Hyslop, D. (1994):"State Dependence, Serial Correlation and Heterogeneity in Intertemporal Participation Behavior: Monte Carlo Evidence and Empirical Results for Married Women," Manuscript, Princeton University.

(*) Kyriazidou, E. (1994):"Estimation of a Panel Data Sample Selection Model," Manuscript, Northwestern University.

III Semi-Parametric Models of Duration and Count Data

3.1 Single Risk Duration Models

(*) Kiefer, N. M. (1988):"Hazard Functions and Economic Duration Data." *Journal of Economic Literature*, **26**:2, 646-679.

(*) Ridder, G. (1990) "The Non-Parametric identification of Generalized Accelerated Failure-Time Models," *Review of Economic Studies*, **57**, 167-182.

An, M.Y and Y. Hong (in progress): "Consistent Test of Proportional Hazard Models. "

3.2 Competing Risk Models

(*) Tsiatis, A. (1975):"A Nonidentifiability Aspect of the Problem of Competing Risks." *Proceedings of the National Academy of Science*, **Vol. 72**.1. pp.20-22.

(*) Heckman, J.J. and B Honore (1989):"The Identifiability of Competing Risks Model." *Biometrica*. **76**, 325-330.

An, M.Y. (1994):"Econometric Analysis of Sequential Discrete Choices," *CAE Working Paper, 92-03*. Revised version.

3.3 Count Data

(*) Winkelmann, R and K.F. Zimmermann (1994):"Recent Developments in Count Data Modelling: Theory and Application," forthcoming in *Journal of Economic Surveys*.

IV. Mis-Specified Models and Indirect Inference

4.1 Misspecified Model

(*) White, H. (1982):"Maximum Likelihood Estimation of Misspecified Models," *Econometrica*, **50**. 1-26.

4.2 Indirect Inference

Gallant, R. and G. Tauchen (1994):"Which Moments to Match," Working paper.

(*) Gourieroux, C., A. Monfort and E. Renault (1993):"Indirect Inference," *Journal of Applied Econometrics*, Vol. 8, S85-118.

An, M.Y. (1994):"Initial Conditions Problem in Event History Analysis: An Indirect Inference Procedure," (forthcoming) *Life Time Data Analysis*. (Jewell. N.P., A.C. Kimber and G.A. Whitmore, eds.) Kluwer Academic Publisher.

4.3 Misspecification Testing

(*) Hausman, J.(1978):"Specification Tests in Econometrics," *Econometrica*, **46**. 1252-12724.

Wooldridge, J. (1991):"Specification Testing and Quasi-Maximum-Likelihood Estimation." *Journal of Econometrics*, **48**, 29-55.

(*) Hong, Y. and H. White (1993):"Consistent Specification Testing via Nonparametric Series Regression, Working Paper, ACCEDE.

Econometrics: A Mathematical Approach
Professor Orley Ashenfelter
Preceptor: Lara Shore-Sheppard
Economics 303, Fall 1994

Prerequisites: Math 201 (Calculus and linear algebra or equivalent)

Texts: Beals, Ralph E. *Statistics for Economists* (Chicago: Rand McNally, 1972),
             available at Gnomon Copy, 6 Nassau Street.

             Pindyck, Robert S. and Rubinfeld, Daniel L. *Econometric Models and Economic
             Forecasts* (New York: McGraw Hill,   1991), available at U Store.

             Hamilton, Lawrence, *Statistics with STATA 3* (Duxbury Press: Belmont, CA,
             1993), available at U-store.

Supplementary Texts: (Available in Firestone Reserve Room)
             Some other texts that are useful to look at for an alternative exposition of the
             material are:
             A: Degroot, *Probability and Statistics*
             B: Greene, *Econometrics*
             C: Hogg, *Introduction to Mathematical Statistics*
             D: Intriligator, *Econometric Models, Techniques, & Forecasts*
             E: Kmenta, *Elements of Econometrics*
             F: Maddala, *Introduction to Econometrics*
             G: Schmidt, *Econometrics*
             H: Wonnacott and Wonnacott, *Econometrics*

Organization:
       This course teaches you to use econometric methods. The supplementary texts are
entirely optional and are included only for those students who want an alternative approach to
the same material covered in class and in the two main texts. The most important part of this
class is learning how to solve econometric problems. Six problem sets will be assigned; four will
involve the use of a computer. We will make use of STATA, which will be available on the PC
cluster in McCosh and through the Unix system. The book by Hamilton listed above will be of
some considerable help to you in learning to use STATA also. In addition there will be a tutorial
devoted to using STATA in class.
       Final grades will be weighted 0.25 for the problem sets, 0.25 for the midterm exam, and
0.50 for the final exam.

Problem Set No.	Date	Lecture	Topic/Reading	
	9/13	1	1:	Introduction & Basic Probability Concepts, Chapters 1 & 2, Beals
1 out	9/15	2	2:	Random Variables and Univariate Distributions, Chapter 3, Beals
	9/20	3	3:	Mathematics of Expectations, Chapter 4, Beals
1 in, 2 out	9/22	4	4:	Multivariate Distributions, Chapter 5, Beals
	9/27	5	5:	Sampling Distributions, Chapter 6, Beals
	9/29	6	6:	Interval Estimation and Hypothesis Testing, Chapter 8, Beals
	10/4	7	7:	Estimation, Chapter 7, Beals
2 in, 3 out	10/6	8	8:	Sample Design
	10/11	9	9:	Simple Regression I, Introduction, Chapters 1, 2, & 3, Pindyck & Rubinfeld (P&R)
	10/13	10		Statistics with Stata
3 in	10/18	11		Simple Regression II
	10/20	12		**Midterm Exam**
4 out	11/1	13	10:	Multiple Regression, Chapters 4 & 5, P&R
	11/3	14	11:	Specification Error & Multicollinearity, Chapters 4.4, 7.3-7.5, P&R
	11/8	15		Specification Error & Multicollinearity II
	11/10	16	12:	Heteroscedasticity and Serial Correlation, Chapter 6, P&R
4 in, 5 out	11/15	17	13:	Measurement Error, Chapter 7.2, P&R
	11/17	18	14:	Binary and Discrete Choice Models, Chapter 10, P&R
	11/22	19	15:	Dummy Variables, Chapter 5.2, P&R
	11/29	20	16:	Time Series I, Chapters 9.1, 9.2, 14, 15, & 16 P&R
5 in, 6 out	12/1	21		Time Series II
	12/6	22	17:	Simultaneous Equations I, Chapter 11 P&R
	12/8	23		Simultaneous Equations II
	12/12	24		Simultaneous Equations III

Problem Set 6 is due at 5 PM Wednesday January 4, 1995.

Supplementary Text References

Topic   Text

	A	B	C	D	E	F	G	H
1	1, 2		1, 2		3	2		3
2	3	3.2	1, 3	App C.2	3.5, 3.6	3.1-3.4		4
3	4	3.3	1.9	App C.3	3.7	3.5-3.7		
4	3	3.9-3.10				3.8		
5	7	4.2	4		1, 2, 4			6
6	8	4.6-4.7	6, 9		5	4.4-4.6		8, 9
7	6	4.3-4.5	7, 8		6	4.1-4.3		7
8								
9	10	5			7	7		11, 12
10		6, 7		4, 5	10	8	1	13-15
11		8.4, 9.2		6.8, 6.2	10.3, 10.4	9.5, 10.1, 10.2		
12		14, 15		6.3, 6.4	8.2, 8.3	12	2.3	
13		9.5		6.9	9.1	13	3.4	
14		20			11.1			
15		8.2				9.2		
16		18						
17		19		10-13	13	11	4, 5	25

UNIVERSITY OF ILLINOIS
Department of Economics

Course: Econ 470, Fall 1994   August 29, 1994

Instructor: Anil K. Bera, 487 Comm. West
Phone: 333-4596
Class Hours: Section 1: 1-2:30 MW; Section 2: 3-4:30 MW   G
Class Room: 130 Comm West
Office Hours: 12-1 M W

... Statistics is the new technology of the present century.
                                        --P.C. Mahalanobis
                                        Founder of the Indian Statistical Institute

---

This is an introductory course in mathematical statistics, and its purpose is to prepare you for our advanced econometrics courses, such as Econ 476 and 477. To carry out a good applied econometrics study, it is necessary to master the econometric theory. Econometric theory requires a good knowledge of statistical theory which in turn has its foundation on probability theory. Finally, one cannot study probability without set theory. Therefore, we will begin at the beginning. We will start with the set theory, and discuss probability and the basic structure for statistics. Then we will slowly move into different probability distributions, asymptotic theory, estimation and hypothesis testing.

As you have guessed the course materials will be highly theoretical. No statistical background will be assumed. However, I will take it granted that you already know differential and integral calculus and linear algebra. Good Luck!

Course Outline:

1. *Introduction*
    i)   Structure of the course

2. *Probability Theory*
    i)   Algebra of sets
    ii)   Random variable
    iii)   Distribution of a random variable
    iv)   Probability mass and density functions
    v)   Conditional probability distribution
    vi)   Bayes theorem and its applications
    vii)   More on conditional probability distribution
    viii)   Mathematical expectation
    ix)   Bivariate moments
    x)   Generating functions
    xi)   Distribution of a function of a random variable

3. *Univariate Discrete and Continuous Distributions*
    i)   The basic distribution--hypergeometric
    ii)   Binomial distribution (as a limit of hypergeometric)

iii)   Poisson distribution (as a limit of binomial)

iv)   Normal distribution

v)   Properties of normal distribution

vi)   Distributions derived from normal (χ^2, t and F)

vii)   Distributions of sample mean and variance

4. *Asymptotic Theory*

i)   Law of large numbers

ii)   Central limit theorems

5. *Estimation*

i)   Properties of an estimator

ii)   Cramér-Rao inequality

iii)   Sufficiency and minimal sufficiency

iv)   Minimum variance estimator and Rao-Blackwell theorem

v)   Maximum likelihood estimation

6. *Hypothesis Testing*

i)   Notion of statistical hypothesis testing

ii)   Type I and II errors

iii)   Uniformly most powerful test and Neyman-Pearson lemma

iv)   Likelihood ratio test

v)   Examples on hypothesis testing

Textbook:	*Introduction to Statistics and Econometrics*, by Takeshi Amemiya, 1st Edition, 1994, Harvard University Press.
Recommended:	*Advanced Calculus with Applications in Statistics*, by André Khuri, 1st Edition, 1993, John Wiley and Sons.
	However, I will not follow any particular book. For your convenience detailed notes (in two volumes) on the whole course will be available on the first day of the class from The Dup-it copy shop, 808 S. Sixth St., 337-7000.
Assessment:	There will be two closed book examinations. You will also receive four homework assignments. The grading of the course will be based on:

Homework	20%
First Exam	40%
Second Exam	40%

Notes: (1)   The items marked with two asterisks (**) are to be on reserve,
                       or in the noncirculating Reference Section, in the library.

                (2)   A much longer list of econometrics references is given in Christ
                       (1990), which is included in Part III of this reading list.

                (3)   Abbreviations:

                       Em: Econometrica
                       IER: International Economic Review
                       JASA: Journal of the American Statistical Association

Part I. ARTICLES

Almon, Shirley (1965), "The Distribution Lag Between Capital Appropriations
    and Expenditures," Em 33 (January, 1965), 178–96.

Box, G. E. P., and D. R. Cox (1964), "An Analysis of Transformations,"
    Journal of the Royal Statistical Society, Series B, 26 (1964), 211–52.

Bronfenbrenner, Jean (1953) (now Jean B. Crockett), "Sources and Size of
    Least–Squares Bias in a Two–Equation Model," Chapter IX in Hood and
    Koopmans (1953), 221–35.

Chow, Gregory C. (1960), "Tests of Equality Between Sets of Coefficients in
    Two Linear Regressions," Em 28 (July, 1960), 591–605.

**Christ, Carl F. (1975), "Judging the Performance of Econometric Models of
    the U.S. Economy," IER 16 (February, 1975), 54–74.

**Christ, Carl F. (1985), "Early Progress in Estimating Quantitative Economic
    Relationships in America," American Economic Review 75 (No. 6, December,
    1985), 39–52.

Durbin, James (1960), "Estimation of Parameters in Time–Series Regression
    Models," Journal of the Royal Statistical Society, Series B, 22 (January,
    1960), 139–53.

Durbin, James and G. S. Watson (1951), "Testing for Serial Correlation in
    Least Squares Regression, II," Biometrika 38 (June, 1951), 159–78.

Engle, R.F., David F. Hendry, and J.F. Richard (1983), "Exogeneity," Em 51 (March, 1983), 227–304.

Engle, R.F. (1984), "Wald, Likelihood Ratio, and Lagrange Multiplier Tests," Ch. 13 in Griliches and Intriligator Vol. II (1984).

Engle, R.F. and C.W.J. Granger (1987), "Co–Integration and Error Correction: Representation, Estimation and Testing," Em 55 (March, 1987), 251–276.

Fisher, Franklin M. (1970), "Tests of Equality Between Sets of Coefficients in Two Linear Regressions: An Expository Note," Em 38 (March, 1970), 361–66.

Gilbert, Christopher (1986), "Practioners' Corner: Professor Hendry's Econometric Methodology," Oxford Bulletin of Economics and Statistics 48 (3, 1976), 283–307.

Griliches, Zvi (1967), "Distributed Lags: A Survey," Em 35 (January, 1967), 16–49.

**Haavelmo, Trygve (1943), "The Statistical Implications of a System of Simultaneous Equations," Em 11 (January, 1943), 1–12.

Haavelmo, Trygve (1944), "The Probability Approach in Econometrics," Em 12 (Supplement, July, 1944), 118 pages.

Hausman, J.A. (1978), "Specification Tests in Econometrics," Em 46 (November, 1978), 1251–71.

Koopmans, Tjalling C. (1949), "Identification Problems in Economic Model Construction," Chapter II in Hood and Koopmans (1953), 27–48; also in Em 17 (April, 1949), 125–44.

Koopmans, Tjalling C., and William C. Hood (1953), "The Estimation of Simultaneous Linear Economic Relationships," Chapter VI in Hood and Koopmans (1953), 112–99, (especially 112–55, 162–4, 166–70, 171–7).

**Liviatan, Nissan (1963), "Consistent Estimation of Distributed Lags," IER 4 (January, 1963), 44–52.

Lovell, Michael (1983), "Data Mining," Rev. Econ. and Statistics 65 (February, 1983), 1–12.

**Lucas, Robert E., Jr. (1976), "Econometric Policy Evaluation: A Critique," in Karl Brunner and Allan H. Meltzer, editors, The Phillips Curve and Labor Markets, Vol. I of the Carnegie–Rochester Conference Series on Public Policy, 1976, 19–46, with a comment by Robert A. Gordon, 47–61.

Manski, Charles F. (1991), "Regression," Journal of Economic Literature 29 (March, 1991), 34–50.

21

Marschak, Jacob (1953), "Economic Measurements for Policy and Prediction," Chapter I in Hood and Koopmans (1953), 1–26.

**McElroy, F. W. (1978), "A Simple Method of Causal Ordering," IER 19 (February, 1978), 1–23.

Nerlove, Marc and Kenneth F. Wallis (1966), "Use of the Durbin–Watson Statistic in Inappropriate Situations," Em 34 (January, 1966), 235–38.

Pagan, Adrian R., and M.R. Wickens (1989), "A Survey of Some Recent Econometric Methods," Economic Journal 99 (December 1989), 962–1025.

**Salkever, David S., "The Use of Dummy Variables to Compute Predictions, Prediction Errors, and Confidence Intervals," J. Econometrics 4 (1976), 393–97.

Sims, Christopher (1980), "Macroeconomics and Reality," Em 48 (January, 1980), 1–48.

Strotz, Robert H., and Herman O. A. Wold (1960), "A Triptych on Causal Systems," Em 28 (April, 1960), 417–63.

Zaman, Asad (1981), "Estimators Without Moments: The Case of the Reciprocal of a Normal Mean," J. Econometrics 15 (1981) 289–298.

Zellner, Arnold (1962), "An Efficient Method of Estimating Seemingly Unrelated Regressions and Tests for Aggregation Bias," JASA 57 (June, 1962), 348–368.

Zellner, Arnold (1985), "Bayesian Econometrics," Em 53 (March, 1985), 253–71.

**Zellner, Arnold, and Franz Palm (1974), "Time Series and Simultaneous Equation Econometric Models," Journal of Econometrics 2 (May, 1974), 17–54.

Zellner, Arnold, and H. Theil (1962), "Three–Stage Least Squares: Simultaneous Estimation of Simultaneous Equations," Em 30 (January, 1962), 54–78.

Part II. BOOKS

Amemiya, Takeshi (1985), Advanced Econometrics, Cambridge, Harvard U. Press.

Begg, David K. H. (1982), The Rational Expectations Revolution in Macro–economics, Baltimore, Johns Hopkins.

Berndt, Ernst (1991), The Practice of Econometrics, Reading, Mass., Addison–Wesley.

**Christ, Carl F. (1966), Econometric Models and Methods, New York, Wiley.

Dowling, J. M., and F. R. Glahe (1970), <u>Readings in Econometric Theory</u>, Colorado Associated University Press.

Epstein, Roy J. (1987), <u>A History of Econometrics</u> (<u>Contributions to Economic Analysis</u> No. 165), Amsterdam, North–Holland Publishing Co.

Fisher, Franklin M. (1966), <u>The Identification Problem in Econometrics</u>, New York, McGraw–Hill.

Griliches, Zvi, and Michael D. Intriligator (1983–84–85), <u>Handbook of Econometrics</u> (3 vols.), Amsterdam, North–Holland, and New York, Elsevier.

Hill, R. Carter (1989), <u>Learning Econometrics Using Gauss: A Computer Handbook</u> (to accompany Judge et al (1988)), New York, Wiley.

Hood, William C. and Tjalling C. Koopmans (1953), (editors) <u>Studies in Econometric Method</u>, Cowles Commission Monograph 14, New York, Wiley. (Especially chapters I, II, IV, V, VI, IX).

Hooper, John, and Marc Nerlove (1970), <u>Selected Readings in Econometrics from Econometrica</u>, Cambridge, M.I.T. Press.

Intriligator, Michael D. (1978), <u>Econometric Models, Techniques, and Applications</u>, Englewood CLiffs, N.J., Prentice–Hall.

**Johnston, J. (1972 and 1984), <u>Econometric Methods</u>, New York, McGraw–Hill, 2nd and 3rd eds.

Judge, George G., <u>et al</u>. (1988), <u>The Theory and Practice of Econometrics</u>, 2nd ed., New York, Wiley.

**Kmenta, Jan (1971 and 1986), <u>Elements of Econometrics</u>, New York, MacMillan, 1st and 2nd eds.

Leamer, Edward E. (1978), <u>Specification Searches</u>, New York, Wiley.

Lucas, Robert E., Jr., and Thomas J. Sargent (eds.) (1981), <u>Rational Expectations and Econometric Practice</u> (2 vols.), Minneapolis, U. of Minnesota Press.

Maddala, G. S. (1977), <u>Econometrics</u>, New York, McGraw–Hill.

Malinvaud, Edmond (1980), <u>Statistical Methods in Econometrics</u>, third edition, Amsterdam, North–Holland, and Chicago, Rand McNally. (Second edition, 1970. First edition, 1966).

Minford, Patrick, and David Peel (1983), <u>Rational Expectations and the New Macroeconomics</u>, Oxford, Martin Robinson.

Mishkin, Frederic S. (1983), <u>A Rational Expectations Approach to Macroeconometrics</u>, Chicago, U. of Chicago Press for the National Bureau of Economic Research.

Pindyck, Robert S., and Daniel L. Rubinfeld (1981), <u>Econometric Models and Economic Forecasts</u>, second edition, New York, McGraw–Hill.

**Theil, Henri (1971), <u>Principles of Econometrics</u>, New York, Wiley.

Zarembka, Paul (1974), <u>Frontiers of Econometrics</u>, New York, Academic Press.

Zellner, Arnold (1968), <u>Readings in Economic Statistics and Econometrics</u>, Boston, Little Brown.

Zellner, Arnold (1971), <u>An Introduction to Bayesian Inference in Econometrics</u>, New York, Wiley.

Part III. DUPLICATED MATERIAL

**Christ, Carl F. (1989), "Econometrics Bibliography, Spring 1992."

Part IV. Dictionaries and Encyclopedias

**<u>International Encyclopedia of the Social Sciences</u>, (1978), New York, Free Press.

**<u>The New Palgrave: A Dictionary of Economics</u>, (1987), New York, Stockton Press.

Time Series Econometrics
Economics 722

Hashem Dezhbakhsh
Office: 1641 N. Decatur
Tel: 727-4679

Grading:

Exam I: 40%   Exam II: 40%   Paper and Presentation: 20%.

Topics for papers should be chosen no later than the end of the sixth week.

G

Textbooks:

Chatfield, C. (1989), *The Analysis of Time Series: An Introduction*, Chapman and Hall, London.

Lutkepohl, H. (1993), *Introduction to Multiple Time Series Analysis*, Springer Verlag, Berlin.

Harvey, A. (1993), *The Econometric Analysis of Time Series*, MIT Press, Cambridge, MA.

Engle, R.F. and C.W.J. Granger (1991), *Long Run Economic Relationships: Readings in Cointegration*, ed.. Oxford University Press. Oxford.

Other Relevant Books

Box. G.E.P., G.M. Jenkins, and G.C. Reinsel (1994), *Time Series Analysis: Forecasting and Control*, Third Edition. Prentice Hall, Englewood Cliffs, new Jersey.

Dhrymes, P. (1985), *Distributed Lags: Problems of Estimation and Formulation*, Revised Edition, North Holland, Amsterdam

Greene, W.H. (1993), *Econometric Analysis*, Second Edition, Macmillan: New York.

Hamilton, J.D. (1994), *Time series Analysis*, Princeton University Press, Princeton, New Jersey.

Judge, G.G., W.E. Griffiths, R.C. Hill, H. Lutkepohl and T.C. Lee (1985), *The Theory and Practice of Econometrics*. Second Edition, Wiley, New York.

Hall, P. and C.C. Heyde (1980), *Martingale Limit Theory and Its Application*, Academic Press, Boston.

Karlin, S. and H.M. Taylor (1975), *A First Course in Stochastic Processes*, Academic Press, New York.

Reading List:

1. Preview and Preliminaries

Harvey, Ch 1

Greene. Chs 1-4

Lutkepohl, Appendices B & C

Hall & Heyde Chs 1-3

Dhrymes. Chs 1 & 2

2. Univariate Time Series Analysis

a) Descriptive Techniques

Chatfield, Chs 1 & 2

b) Probability Models

Chatfield, Ch 3

Judge et al, Sec 7.1 & 7.2

Box and Jenkins Chs 2-4

c) Identification and Estimation of ARIMA Models

Chatfield, Ch 4

Judge et al, Secs 7.4 & 7.5

Box and Jenkins, Chs 6-8

*Hannan, E.J., and B.G. Quinn (1979), "The Determination of the Order of an Autoregression," *Journal of the Royal Statistical Society*, 41B, 190-195.

d) Forecasting with ARIMA Models

Chatfield, Ch 5

Judge et al, Sec 7.3

Box and Jenkins, Ch 5

3. Dynamic Models

a) Regression Models with Serially Correlated Errors
Greene, Secs 15.1-15.3, 15.5-15.5.2, and 15.6-15.7.2

b) Distributed Lag Models
Greene, Secs 18.1-18.5
*Dhrymes, Chs 3-7

c) Lagged Dependent Variable Models: Serial Correlation Tests and Correction
Harvey, Ch 7
Greene 15.4, 15.5.3, and 15.7.3
Durbin, J. (1970), "Testing for Serial Correlation in Least Squares Regression When Some of
  Regressors are Lagged Dependent Variables," *Econometrica*, 38, 410-421.
Engle, R. (1984), "Wald, Likelihood Ratio, and Lagrange Multiplier Tests In Econometrics," in Z.
  Griliches and M. Intriligator, eds., *Handbook of Econometrics*, Vol. 2, North Holland, Amsterdam.
Godfrey, L.G. (1978), "Testing Against General Autoregressive and Moving Average Error Models
  When the Regressors Include Lagged Dependent Variables," *Econometrica*, 46, 1293-1302.
Godfrey, L.G. (1978), "Testing for Higher Order Serial Correlation in Regression Equations When the
  Regressors Include Lagged Dependent Variables," *Econometrica*, 46, 1303-1310.
Dezhbakhsh, H. and J.G. Thursby (1994), "Testing for Autocorrelation in Presence of lagged
  Dependent Variables: A Specification Error Approach," *Journal of Econometrics*, 60, 251-272.

d) Common Factor Analysis
Judge et al, Sec 10.2.2c and Harvey, Sec 8.4.
Sargan, J.D. (1980), "Some Tests of Dynamic Specification for a Single Equation," *Econometrica*, 48,
  879-897.
Hendry, D.F. (1980), "Econometrics-Alchemy or Science," *Economica*, 47, 387-406.
Hoover, K.D. (1988), "On the Pitfalls of Untested Common factor Restrictions: The Case of Inverted
  Fisher Hypothesis," *Oxford Bulletin of Economics and Statistics*, 50, 125-137.
Mizon, G.E. and D.F. Hendry (1980), "An Empirical Application and Monte Carlo Analysis of Tests of
  Dynamic Specification," *Review of Economic Studies*, 57, 21-45.
Hendry, D.F. and J.F. Richard (1982), "On the Formulation of Empirical Models in Dynamic
  Econometrics," *Journal of Econometrics*, 20, 3-33.

e) ARCH and Generalized ARCH Disturbances
Greene 15.9 and 19.7, and Harvey 6.9
Hamilton. Ch 21.
Engle, R. (1982), "Autoregressive Conditional Heteroscedasticity with Estimates of the Variance of
  United Kingdom Inflation," *Econometrica*, 50, 987-1008.
Bollerslev, T., R.Y. Chou, and K.F. Kroner (1992), "ARCH Modeling in Finance, A Review of the
  Theory and Evidence." *Journal of Econometrics*, 52, 1-59 (including Editor's Introduction).

4. Multivariate Time Series Analysis

a) Introduction
Chatfield, Ch 8
Greene, Secs 19.1-19.3
Lutkepohl, Ch 1 & Appendix A

b) Vector Autoregressive Modeling: Estimation and Forecasting
Lutkepohl, Secs 2.1, 2.2, 3.1-3.5, 4.1-4.4, and 5.1-5.3
Hamilton Ch 11
Sims, C.A. (1980), "Macroeconomics and Reality," *Econometrica*, 48, 1-48.
Runkle, D.E. (1987), "Vector Autoregression and Reality," *Journal of Business and Economic Statistic*,
  5, 437-454.
*Fair, R.C. and R.J. Shiller (1990), "Comparing Information in Forecasts from Econometric Models,"
  American Economic Review, 80, 375-389.

c) **Causality and Related Tests**

Harvey, Secs 8.7 & 8.8

Lutkepohl, Secs 2.3.1 & 3.6

Aigner, D.J. and A. Zellner (1988), "Editors' Introduction, *Journal of Econometrics*, 39, 1-5.

Zellner, A. (1988), "Causality and Causal Laws in Economics," *Journal of Econometrics*, 39, 7-21.

Granger, C.W.J. (1988), "Some Recent Developments in the Concept of Causality," *Journal of Econometrics*, 39, 199-211.

*Granger, C.W.J. (1969), "Investigating Causal Relations by Econometric Models and Cross Spectral Methods," *Econometrica*, 37, 424-438.

*Sims, C.A. (1972), "Money, Income and Causality," *American Economic Review*, 62, 540-552.

d) **Systems of Dynamic Simultaneous Equations and Transfer Function Models**

Harvey, Ch 9

Lutkepohl, Ch 10

*Box and Jenkins, Chs 10 & 11

5. Unit Root and Cointegration

a) **Unit Roots and Trends in Economic Time Series**

Engle and Granger, Ch 1

Greene, Secs 19.4 & 19.5

Dickey, D. and W. Fuller (1979), "Distribution of the Estimators for Autoregressive Time Series with a Unit Root," *Journal of the American Statistical Association*, 74, 427-431.

Dickey, D. and W. Fuller (1981), "Likelihood Ratio Tests for Autoregressive Time Series with a Unit Root, *Econometrica*, 49, 1057-1072.

Nelson, C.R. and C.I. Plosser (1982), "Trends and Random Walks in Macroeconomic Time Series: Some Evidence and Implications," *Journal of Monetary Economics*, 10, 139-162.

Said, S.E. and D.A. Dickey (1984), Testing for Unit Root in Autoregressive-Moving Average Models of Unknown Order, *Biometrika*, 71, 599-607.

Phillips, P.C.B. and Pierre Perron (1988), "Testing for a Unit Root in Time Series Regression," *Biometrika*, 75, 335-346.

Perron, P. (1989), "The Great Crash, the Oil Price Shock, and the Unit Root Hypothesis," *Econometrica*, 57, 1361-1401.

Kwiatkowski, D., P.C.B. Phillips, P. Schmidt, and Y. Shin (1992), "Testing the Null Hypothesis of Stationarity against the Alternative of a Unit Root, How Sure are We that Economic Time Series have a Unit Root?," *Journal of Econometrics*, 54, 159-178.

Dezhbakhsh, H. and D. Levy, (1995), "A Crossing Rate Test for Unit Roots in Autoregressive Time Series," Manuscript, Emory University.

Campbell, J.Y. and P. Perron (1991), "Pitfalls and Opportunities: What Macroeconomists Should Know about Unit Roots," in O.J. Blanchard and S. Fisher, eds., *NBER Macroeconomics*, MIT Press, Cambridge, MA, 141-219 (including the discussions).

West, K.D. (1988), "Asymptotic Normality when Regressors have a Unit Root," *Econometrica*, 56, 1397-1417.

Phillips, P.C.B. (1987), "Time Series Regression with a Unit Root," *Econometrica*, 55, 277-301.

Granger, C.W.J. and P. Newbold (1974), "Spurious Regressions in Econometrics," *Journal of Econometrics*, 2, 111-120.

Nelson, C.R. and H. Kang (1984), "Pitfalls in the Use of Time as an Explanatory Variable in Regression," *Journal of Business and Economic Statistics*, 2, 73-82.

*Stock, J. and M. Watson, "Testing for Common Trends," in Engle and Granger, 153-178.

*Evans, G. and N. Savin (1981), "Testing for Unit Roots: I," *Econometrica*, 49, 753-779.

*Evans, G. and N. Savin (1984), "Testing for Unit Roots: II," *Econometrica*, 52, 1241-1269.

*DeJong, D.N., J.C. Nankervis, N.E. Savin, and C.H. Whiteman (1992), "Integration Versus Trend Stationarity in Time Series, *Econometrica*, 2, 423-433.

b) Cointegration and Error Correction
Harvey, Secs 8.1-8.5
Hamilton, Ch 19
Hendry, D., "Econometric Modeling with Cointegrated Variables: An Overview," in Engle and Granger, 51-64.
Granger, C.W.J., "Developments in the Study of Cointegrated Economic Variables, in Engle and Granger, 65-80.
Engle, R. and C.W.J. Granger, "Cointegration and Error Correction: Representation, Estimation and Testing," in Engle and Granger, 81-112.
Murray, M.P. (1994), "A Drunk and Her Dog: An Illustration of Cointegration and Error Correction," *American Statistician*, 48, 37-39.
MacKinnon, J., "Critical Values for Cointegration Tests," in Engle and Granger, 267-276.
Johansen, S. (1991), "Estimation and Hypothesis Testing of Cointegration Vectors in Gaussian Vector Autoregressive Models," *Econometrica*, 59, 1551-1580.
Phillips, P.C.B. and S. Ouliaris (1990), "Asymptotic Properties of the Residual Based Tests for Cointegration," *Econometrica*, 165-193.
Phillips, P.C.B. (1991), "Optimal Inference in Cointegrated Systems," *Econometrica*, 59, 283-306.
*Campbell, J. and R. J. Shiller, "Cointegration and Tests of Present Value Models," in Engle and Granger, 191-218.
*Diba, B.T. and H.I. Grossman (1988), "Explosive Rational Bubbles in Stock Prices?," *American Economic Review*, 78, 520-530.

6. Special Topics: Stochastic Processes--Markov Chains

a) Discrete and Continuous Time Markov Chains Models
Karlin and Taylor, Chs 1, 2, and 4 (Secs 1, 2, and 4)
Geweke, J.(1986), "Exact Inference for Continuous Time Markov Chain Models," *Review of Economic Studies*, 53, 653-669.

b) Statistically Segmented Trend Models and Other Applications of Markov Chains
Hamilton, Ch 22
Hamilton, J.D. (1989), "A New Approach to the Analysis of Nonstationary Time Series and the Business Cycle," *Econometrica*, 57, 357-384.
*Engel, C. and J. D.Hamilton (1990), "Long Swings in the Doller: Are They in the Data and Do Markets Know It?," *American Economic Review*, 80, 689-713.
*McQueen, G. and S. Thorley (1991), "Are Stock Returns Predictable? A Test Using Markov Chains, " *The Journal of Finance*, 46, 239-263.

*A * marks optional material.*

Note: This syllabus is designed for a one semester graduate course in time series econometrics. Students taking this course are expected to have completed at least one semester of mathematical statistic and one semester of basic econometrics at the graduate level.

Dr. Gallant   **Research in Econometrics**   Econ 371-1
Syllabus   Fall 1994

The course covers nonlinear and nonparametric methods useful in economics and other disciplines. At the extreme, they allow efficient estimation of the parameters of a nonlinear structural model that is so intractable that one can only simulate data from it. General equilibrium models and systems of differential equations often lead to this situation. The prerequisites are a good understanding of linear models and of either multivariate linear regression or three-stage least-squares, Economics 271 and 273 for example.

Meets M, W, F, 10:00 a.m. to 10:50 a.m., Room 308 Gardner Hall. If there are no conflicts we will move to M and W, 10:00 a.m. to 11:15 a.m.

Topic   Reading Assignment

1. Deterministic chaos   Nychka et al. (1990) "Statistics for Chaos"
                               Statistical Computing and Statistical Graphics
                               Newsletter 1.

2. Neural nets   Gallant and White (1992) "Learning the
                               Derivatives of an Unknown Mapping ..."
                               Neural Networks 5.

3. Density estimation   Silverman (1986) Density Estimation for
                               Statistics and Data Analysis
                               Chapter 1, Chapter 2, Chapter 3.

4. Nonparametric regression   Bierens (1987) "Kernel Estimators of Regression
                               Functions" in Bewley, Advances in Econometrics

                               Robinson (1983) "Nonparametric Estimators for
                               Time Series," J. of Time Series Analysis 4.

5. Univariate nonlinear   Gallant (1987) Nonlinear Statistical Models
   models   Chapter 1. Univariate Nonlinear Regression.

6. Univariate nonlinear   Gallant (1987) Nonlinear Statistical Models
   models: special   Chapter 2. Univariate Nonlinear Regression.
   situations   Special situations.

7. Introduction to   Berndt and Wood (1975) "Technology, Prices, and
   multivariate and   the Derived Demand for Energy," Review of
   simultaneous equations   Economics and Statistics 3.
   models.

8. Nonlinear seemingly   Gallant (1984) Nonlinear Statistical Models.
   unrelated regression   Chapter 5. Multivariate Nonlinear Regression
   (Multivariate non-   Read only pages 267-357.
   linear regression)

9. Nonlinear two- and   Gallant (1987) Nonlinear Statistical Models
    three-stage least   Chapter 6, Nonlinear Simultaneous Equations Models
    squares

10. Generalized method of   Gallant (1985) Nonlinear Statistical Models
    moments estimators   Chapter 6, Nonlinear Simultaneous Equations Models

11. Seminonparametric   Gallant and Tauchen (1990) "A Nonparametric
    methods, time series   Approach to Nonlinear Time Series Analysis." in
    applications   Brillinger et. al. New Directions in Time Series

12. Efficient estimation   Gallant and Tauchen (1990) "Which Moments to
    of the parameters of   Match?"
    intractable models.

13. Nonlinear latent   Davidian and Gallant (1993) "The Nonlinear Mixed
    variables models.   Effects Model with a Smooth Random Effects Density"
                                Biometrika.

Office hours are Monday, Wednesday, and Friday from about 9 a.m. to 4 p.m.; an
appointment is suggested. Satisfactory completion of all homework earns a
grade of P. This, plus a passing score on the final exam earns a grade of H.
The final is optional. It can be used to supplement homework to earn an H or
to supplement homework to earn a P when homework performance is unsatisfactory.

University of Chicago

Econ 311 Reading List

G

James J. Heckman
Room: HM103
Class Time
Tues.& Thurs.:11:30-12:50
Two Review Problem Sessions
Fri: 1-30-3:00/3:30-5:00

Office: SS405
Office Hours: By Appointment Only
TA's: Neil Hohmann
Ben Sacks
Alex Monge
Lance Lochner

This course is the second part of a three part sequence designed to acquaint students with basic tools for research in empirical economics. The focus in this course is on microeconomics and the evaluation of microeconomic social programs.

This course is organized around discussions of important problems in economic policy. Samples of topics to be discussed this year include: What are the effects of education and training programs on earnings? Are training subsidies justified? Is labor supply inelastic with respect to tax and transfer policies? What is the economic return to education? Do educational policies of communities explain wages? How does unemployment respond to unemployment insurance benefit structures? Does parental background explain ability? Does ability explain wages and wage differentials? Discussions will be partly organized around Herrnstein and Murray's book - The Bell Curve. Students are required to write a paper on a topic in the original empirical section of the book. This paper is due on Feb. 23, which is the last scheduled lecture. (Problem sessions will continue until the end of the quarter).

Students will be expected to master both the economics and the econometrics relevant to resolving these issues and gain familiarity with the quality of the data sources required to answer these questions in an honest and rigorous fashion. Toward this end, students are expected to work through three problem sets which will partly motivate the discussion in class. There will also be a final exam, and the afore-mentioned paper. As previously advertised, authors of the top two papers will be excused from the final and given an A for the course.

In terms of econometric content, students will be exposed to (a) models for discrete choice and self-selection (b) latent variable models for panel data and (c) models for duration data. A basic tool will be likelihood-based inference. There will be discussion of the merits of social experimentation and general discussions of the general evaluation problem.

Note that I hope to schedule the course so it meets for 1 hour and 40 minutes each lecture. This way, the course ends after 8 weeks. (Room will be announced later). Lecture notes will be available for sale at SS101.

I. The Policy Evaluation Problem: Constructing Counterfactuals

Ashenfelter, O., "Discrete Choice in Labor Supply: The Determinants of Participation in the Seattle-Denver Income Maintenance Experiment", Journal of The American Statistical Association, Vol. 78, 1983, pp. 517-525.

Heckman, J., "Randomization and Social Program Evaluation" in C. Manski and I. Garfinkle, Evaluating Welfare and Training Programs, Harvard University Press, 1982.

_____, "The Case For Simple Estimators: Experimental Evidence From The National JTPA Study", University of Chicago, August, 1993.

Heckman, J. and Robb, R., "Alternative Methods For Evaluating The Impact of Interventions", in J. Heckman and Burton Singer Longitudinal Analysis of Labor Market Data, Cambridge, 1985.

_____ and Smith, J., "Assessing The Case For Randomized Evaluation of Training Programs", forthcoming, Journal of Economic Perspectives, 1995.

II. Background Lectures on Self-selection, Discrete choice and Maximum Likelihood Estimation

Amemiya, T., Advanced Econometrics, Chapter 9, Harvard University Press, 1985.

Cox, D. R. and Hinkley, D. V., Theoretical Statistics, Chapter 9, "Asymptotic Theory", Chapman-Hall, 1982.

Domenich, T. and McFadden, D., Urban Travel Demand, North-Holland, 1975, Chapters 3,4,5.

Greenberg, E. and C. Webster, Chapter 1, Advanced Econometrics: A Bridge To The Literature, Krieger, 1991.

Greene, W., Econometric Analysis, Chapter 21, MacMillian, 1990.

Heckman, J. and Honore B., "Empirical Content of The Roy Model", Econometrica, September, 1990.

III. Labor Supply and Transfer Policy: Tobit Models, Instrumental Variables and Generalizations With A Discussion of Specification Tests

Amemiya, T., op.cit,, Chapter 10.

Berndt, E., The Practice of Econometrics, Chap. 11, Addison-Wesley, 1991.

Greene, W., op.cit, Chapter 21.

Heckman, J., "Sample Selection Bias As A Specification Error", in Smith, J., ed. Female Labor Supply: Theory and Estimation, Princeton University Press, pp. 206-248.

Heckman, J. and MaCurdy, T., "New Methods For Estimating Labor Supply Functions: A Survey", in R. Ehrenberg, ed., Research in Labor Economics, Vol. 4, 1981, pp. 65-102.

_____ and Sedlacek, G., "Heterogeneity, Aggregation and Market Wage Functions: An Empirical Model of Self-Selection in the Labor Market", Journal of Political Economy, 1985, Vol. 93, No. 6, pp. 1077-1125.

Mroz, T., "The Sensitivity of An Empirical Model of Married Women's Work To Economic and Statistical Assumptions", Econometrica, Vol. 55, 1987, pp. 765-799.

IV. Do Repeated Measurements Help? Panel Data Models and Repeated Cross Sections: Errors in Variables, Incidental Parameters and Fixed Effect Models

Ashenfelter, 0. and Krueger, A., "Estimates of the Economic Returns to Schooling from a New Sample of Twins", unpublished manuscript, Princeton, 1992.

Chamberlain, G., "Panel Data", Chapter 22, Handbook of Econometrics, Vol. II, 1985.

Heckman, J., "Statistical Models For Discrete Panel Data", Chapter 3 and 4, in C. Manski and D. McFadden (eds), Structural Analysis of Discrete Data With Econometric Applications. M.I.T. Press, 1986.

Heckman, J., B. Singer and G. Tsiang, Lecture Notes on Panel Data, University of Chicago, 1984.

Hsiao, C., Panel Data, Chapter 1,2,3, Cambridge, 1986.

Johnston, J., Chapter on Errors in Variables, Econometric Methods, First Edition, McGraw Hill, 1963.

Judge, G., Griffiths, W., Hill, R. and Lee, T., The Theory and Practice of Econometrics, Chapter 13, "Unobserved Variables", Wiley, 1980.

V. Review of Regression Methods: Does Schooling Quality Raise Earnings? The Earnings Function and Hedonic Models: Age-Period-Cohort Effects, Specification Testing; Dummy Variables, The Lindley Paradox; Bayesian Methods

Berndt, E., op. cit, Chapter 5.

Card, D. and Krueger, A., "Does Schooling Quality Matter?", JPE, February, 1992, pp. 1-40.

_____, "School Quality and Black-White Relative Earnings", Quarterly Journal of Economics, Feb 1992.

Heckman, J., and A. Layne-Farrar and P. Todd, "Does Measured School Quality Really Matter? Understanding The Empirical and Economic Foundations of the Evidence", unpublished manuscript, University of Chicago, 1994.

Heckman, J. and Robb, R., "Using Longitudinal Data to Estimate Age, Period and Cohort Effects in Earnings Equations, in Cohort Analysis in Social Research Beyond the Identification Problem, ed. by William M. Mason and Stephen E. Feinberg, Springer-Verlag New York Inc. 1985.

Leamer, E., Specification Searches, Chapters 3 & 4, Wiley, 1978.

Smith, J. and F. Welch, "Black Economic Progress After Myrdal", Journal of Economic Literature, June 1989, pp. 519-564.

VI. The Impact of Training on Earnings

Ashenfelter, 0, "Estimating The Effect of Training Programs on Earnings", Review of Economics and Statistics, 1978, pp. 47-57.

_____ and D. Card, "Using The Longitudinal Structure of Earnings To Estimate The Effects of Training Programs", Review of Economics and Statistics, 1985, pp. 648-660.

Heckman, J. and R. Roselius, "Evaluating The Impact of Training on Earnings and The Labor Force Status of Young Women: Better Data Help A Lot", unpublished manuscript, University of Chicago, 1994.

34

VII. Unemployment and Turnover Dynamics: Duration Models

Amemiya, T., op.cit, Chapter 11.

Flinn C. and Heckman, J., "Models For The Analysis of Labor Force Dynamics", pp. 65-69, Advances in Econometrics, Vol. 1, ed. by R. Bassman and G. Rhodes, JAI Press.

_____ "The Likelihood Function" in Advances in Econometrics, Vol. 3, ed. by R. Bassman and G. Rhodes.

_____ "New Methods For Analyzing Structural Models of Labor Force Dynamics", Journal of Econometrics, Vol. 18, 1982, pp. 115-168.

Heckman, J., and B. Singer, "Social Science Duration Analysis", in Heckman, J. and B. Singer, Longitudinal Analysis of Labor Market Data, Cambridge, 1985.

Heckman, J., B. Singer, and G. Tsiang, op.cit, Chapters on Duration Analysis.

Lancaster, T., The Econometric Analysis of Transition Data, Chapter 1-4, Cambridge University Press, 1991.

Meyer, B., "Unemployment Insurance and Unemployment Spells", Econometrica, 1990.

Claremont Graduate School

ECONOMETRICS I
CGS ECONOMICS 382
SPRING/95
SYLLABUS

G

PROF. CHERYL HOLSEY
HARPER HALL EAST 208
621-8784

OFFICE HOURS:
T & TH: 3:00-4:00
And by appointment

This course will focus on the linear regression model. It is the primary tool of empirical research in economics and political science. Part I covers the linear regression model under ideal, or "classical," conditions. Part II details the modifications and extensions necessary to accommodate the most frequent departures from the classical conditions encountered in social science research. The class will be conducted primarily in lecture format. Regardless, questions will always be entertained, will often be welcome, and will frequently be encouraged.

Prerequisites

A basic knowledge of statistics, matrix algebra, and calculus. Equivalent courses are Econ 207 and Math 208. An upper division level course in calculus-based probability is highly desirable, but not required. If you have not had such a course, and you want to concentrate in quantitative methods, you should consider taking it at one of the undergraduate colleges as an elective (it's called Math 151 at CMC, HMC And Pomona). Computer experience is not a prerequisite.

Textbooks

Judge, Hill, Griffiths, Luktepohl and Lee, <u>Introduction to the Theory and Practice of Econometrics</u>, John Wiley and Sons, New York, 1988, 2nd ed.

P. Kennedy, <u>A Guide to Econometrics</u>, MIT Press, Cambridge, MA., 1992, 3rd ed.

W. Greene, <u>Econometric Analysis</u>, Macmillan, 1993, 2nd ed; on reserve at the library.

Computer Documentation

<u>Beginner's Guide to the CGSVAX</u>; current version available at the Computing Center for a small charge.

<u>TSP User's Manual, Version 4.2</u>, TSP International; Available for check-out at the Computing Center and on reserve at the library.

<u>TSP Reference Manual, Version 4.2</u>, TSP International; Available for check-out at the Computing Center and on reserve at the library.

Grading

Course grades will be calculated using the following weights:
1. Midterm, (Wednesday) March 8 (30%)
2. Comprehensive Final (40%)
3. Quizzes (10%)
4. Class Assignments (20%)

Both exams are closed-book and will be completed in class. Please note: The final is comprehensive. Quizzes are also closed-book and will completed in the bi-weekly computer lab. Your lowest quiz score will be dropped.

There are no make-up quizzes. Make-up exams are discouraged; they create serious equity problems for everyone involved with this course. Make-ups will be available, nevertheless, if I am informed before the scheduled exam and if I consider the reason legitimate (this may require documentation).

Problem sets will contain a mixture of computer assignments and theoretical problems based on the empirical analysis. Late Class Assignments will always be penalized. Assignments are due at the beginning of each lab class. Late papers will be subject to a grade reduction for every 24 hours, or portion thereof, that they are late.

TOPICS AND READING ASSIGNMENTS

0. Background Material - Not Covered in Lecture
   A. Matrix Algebra
      Judge: Appendix A
      Greene: Chapter 2
   B. Statistics
      Judge: Chapters 2 and 3
      Greene: Chapter 3

I. The Classical Linear Regression Model

1. Introduction to Econometric Modeling
   Judge: Chapter 1
   Kennedy: Chapter 1
   Greene: Chapter 1

2. Properties of Estimators
   Judge: Section 3.3

3. The General Linear Model
   A. Non-Matrix Notation
      Greene: Chapter 5
      Gujarati: Chapters 7 and 8 (Xeroxes on reserve at Honnold)

B. Matrix Notation
Judge: Chapter 5
Kennedy: Chapter 3
Greene: Chapter 5 and 6

4. **The Normal General Linear Model and Maximum Likelihood Estimation**
Judge: Section 6.1
Greene: Section 10.5

5. **Properties of OLS and MLE estimators Under the Classical Assumptions**
Judge: Sections 5.6-5.7 and 6.6
Greene: Section 10.3

6. **Interval Estimation and Hypothesis Testing**
Judge: Sections 6.3-6.5
Kennedy: Chapter 4
Greene: Section 7.2

7. **Prior Information in the Linear Model**
Judge: Section 6.2
Kennedy: Sections 11.1-11.3

8. **Dummy/Qualitative Independent Variables**
Judge: Sections 10.1-10.3
Kennedy: Chapter 13
Greene: Section 7.3

II. **Violations of the Classical Assumptions and Other Difficulties**

9. **Nonspherical Disturbances**
   A. **Generalized Least Squares**
      Judge: Sections 8.1-9.2
      Kennedy: Sections 7.1-7.2
      Greene: Chapter 13
   B. **Heteroscedasticity**
      Judge: Sections 9.3-9.4
      Kennedy: Section 7.3
      Greene: Chapter 14
   C. **Auto/Serial Correlation**
      Judge: Sections 9.5-9.6
      Kennedy: Section 7.4
      Greene: Chapter 15

10. **Data Problems**
   A. **Stochastic Regressors and Measurement Error**
      Judge: Chapter 13
      Kennedy: Chapter 8
      Greene: Section 9.5
   B. **Missing Observations and Grouped Data**
      Greene: Sections 9.3-9.4

Claremont Graduate School

ECONOMETRICS II
CGS ECONOMICS 383
FALL/1992
SYLLABUS

G

PROF. CHERYL HOLSEY
Harper Hall East 208
X3358

OFFICE HOURS:
MW 2:30-3:30
And by appointment

This course will build upon the basic econometric skills presented in Econometrics I to provide the student with a thorough understanding of all standard econometric methods. The class will be conducted primarily in lecture format. Regardless, questions will always be entertained, will often be welcome, and will frequently be encouraged.

Prerequisites

It is expected that you have successfully completed Econ 382.

Textbooks

W. Greene, _Econometric Analysis_, Macmillan, 1990.
J. Johnston, _Econometric Methods_, McGraw-Hill, New York, 1984
(third edition). **On reserve at Honnold Library.**

P. Kennedy, _A Guide to Econometrics_, MIT Press, 1985 (second
or third edition).

Computer Documentation

Beginner's Guide to the CGS VAX, current version available at the
Computing Center for a small charge.
TSP User's Manual, Version 4.2, TSP International. Available for
check-out at the Computing Center, and on reserve at the
library.
TSP Reference Manual, Version 4.2, TSP International. Available
for check-out at the Computing Center and on reserve at the
library.

Although the textbooks listed above include discussions of almost all of the topics that are covered in this course, you should be aware that there are many other excellent econometrics textbooks available. Most of these textbooks cover the same topics but have different presentation styles. You may wish to experiment with different texts to find a presentation style that especially appeals to you. Such a text will not only be helpful in fully understanding the topics covered in this course, it may also provide you with a convenient reference manual for your future empirical research. Other texts (which should be available in the library) are:

M. Intrilligator, <u>Econometric Models, Techniques and Applications</u>, Prentice-Hall, Englewood Cliffs, N.J., 1978.
Judge, Hill, Griffiths, Lutkepohl and Lee, <u>Introduction to the Theory and Practice of Econometrics</u>, John Wiley and Sons, New York, 1988 (second edition).
Kelejian and Oates, <u>Introduction to Econometrics; Principles and Applications</u>, Harper and Row, New York, 1981 (second edition).
J. Kmenta, <u>Elements of Econometrics</u>, The Macmillan Publishing Co., New York, 1971.
G.S. Maddala, <u>Econometrics</u>, McGraw-Hill, New York 1977.
G.S. Maddala, <u>Introduction to Econometrics</u>, Macmillan, New York, 1988.
E. Malinvaud, <u>Principles of Econometrics</u>, North-Holland, Amsterdam, 1980 (third edition).
H. Theil, <u>Principles of Econometrics</u>, John Wiley & Sons, New York, 1971.
Wonnacott and Wonnacott, <u>Econometrics</u>, John Wiley & Sons, New York, 1979 (second edition).

GRADED REQUIREMENTS

1. Midterm exam (Wednesday, October 28th)
2. Final exam (during finals week)
3. Problem Sets (to be announced in class)

Both exams will be completed in class. They will be closed-book exams. There will be a comprehensive final.

GRADING

Course grades will be calculated using the following weights:

1. Midterm exam (30%)
3. Final exam (50%)
4. Problem Sets (20%)

Make-up exams are discouraged; they create serious equity problems for everyone involved with this course. Make-ups will be available, nevertheless, if, within reason, I am informed before the scheduled exam and if I consider the reason legitimate (this may require documentation).

There will be 5 to 6 problems sets assigned approximately one every 2 weeks. The problem sets will contain a mixture of theoretical problems and computer assignments. The computer assignments will be geared toward using the TSP (Time Series Processor) econometric package on the CGS VAX mainframe computer. It is permissible to use a personal computer, other packages, or other languages to complete assignments.

Late problem sets will always be penalized. Problem sets will be due at the beginning of the class period. Late papers will be subject to a 1/3 of a grade reduction for every 24 hours, or portion thereof, that they are late.

TOPICS AND READING ASSIGNMENTS

Scheduled readings are listed below. Please note, however, that this schedule may be extended to include additional readings. In this event, these readings will be placed on reserve in Honnold Library.

1. Review of the General Linear Model and Discussion of Large Sample Theory
   Greene: Chapters 5 and 6, Sections 4.1 - 4.5 and 10.1 - 10.3
   Kennedy: Chapters 2 and 3
   Johnston: Chapter 5

2. Data Problems
   A. Missing Observations and Grouped Data
      Greene: Sections 9.3 and 9.4
   B. Measurement Error and Proxy Variables
      Greene: Section 9.5

3. Generalized Least Squares
   A. Nonspherical Disturbances
      Greene: Chapter 13
      Kennedy: Sections 7.1 and 7.2
      Johnston: Sections 8.1 - 8.3

   B. Heteroscedasticity
      Greene: Chapter 14
      Kennedy: Section 7.3
      Johnston: Section 8.4

   C. Autocorrelation
      Greene: Chapter 15
      Kennedy: Section 7.4
      Johnston: Section 8.5

4. Pooling Cross-Sectional and Time Series Data

A. Common Intercept and Slope Models
    Greene: Sections 16.1 - 16.3.3
    Johnston: p. 396 - 398

B. Fixed Effects Model
    Greene: Sections 16.4.1 and 16.4.2
    Johnston: p. 398-399

C. Random Effects/Error Components Model
    Greene: Sections 16.4.3 and 16.4.4
    Johnston: p. 398 - 405

D. Seemingly Unrelated Regressions
    Greene: Sections 17.1 and 17.2
    Johnston: Section 8.6

E. Random Coefficients Model
    Greene: Section 16.3.4
    Johnston: p. 410 - 415

5. Binary and Multinomial Choice Models
    Greene: Chapter 20
    Kennedy: Sections 14.1 and 14.2
    Johnston: Section 10.5

6. Limited Dependent Variable Models
    Greene: Chapter 21
    Kennedy: Section 14.3
    Johnston: Section 10.5

7. Nonlinear Regression Models
    Greene: Chapter 11

8. Econometrics in Practice: Problems and Perspectives
    Johnston, Chapter 12
    E.E. Leamer, "Let's Take the Con Out of Econometrics",
        American Economic Review, March, 1983
    E.E. Leamer, "Sensitivity Analyses Would Help", American
        Economic Review, June, 1985
    McAleer, Pagan and Volker, "What Will Take the Con Out of
        Econometrics?", American Economic Review, June, 1985

This course is designed to teach you how to build and test econometric models. It will cover a wide variety of estimation methods that are frequently used in applied econometrics, graphical techniques for diagnosing a model's adequacy, and formal specification tests. The emphasis will be on learning when and how to use the methods that are covered. There will be little theory. You will acquire experience in empirical econometrics through computer-based demonstrations and exercises carried out in class, computer-based homework assignments, and an original research paper.

All required computing will be done on microcomputers using GAUSS and STATA. You are expected to teach yourselves to use GAUSS and STATA, both of which are on the computer network in the College of Business Administration. The course meets one of the computerized classrooms of the Business College. You may use your own microcomputer or those in the College's computer laboratory to carry out homework assignments.

You are expected to have taken an introductory econometrics course at the level of 6E:221. I will assume that you are familiar with the standard linear regression model, including least-squares estimation and hypothesis testing.

The assigned text for the course is

E.R. Berndt, *The Practice of Econometrics: Classic and Contemporary*, Addison-Wesley, 1991.

Most of the homework assignments will be taken from this book, and you should buy it. It is available at the Iowa Book and Supply Company. In addition, the following book will be the main reference on econometric theory:

W.H. Greene, *Econometric Analysis*, 2nd edition, Macmillan, 1993.

This book also is available at the Iowa Book and Supply Company. I recommend but do not require that you buy it. I will cite Greene frequently as a source of information on econometric theory, but you may rely on other theory books if you prefer to do so. I will also make use of the journal articles that are listed in the reference section of this outline. These articles are on reserve in the Business Library along with several other textbooks on econometric theory.

There will be no examinations in the course. Homework will be assigned at intervals of 1-2 weeks. In addition, you must complete a research paper that has original empirical content. It is intended that this paper will make use of the techniques taught in class or more advanced techniques. Examples of acceptable papers are ones that:

a. Elaborate, extend or test an empirical result in the literature

b. Apply a relatively new estimation technique to an interesting empirical problem

c. Carry out an empirical test of a prediction of economic theory.

Papers whose only "empirical" content is a Monte Carlo simulation are not acceptable. Monte Carlo methods may be useful, however, for investigating the finite-sample performance of an estimator before applying it to real data.

Organizing a data set can take a long time. Moreover, many important econometric techniques will be covered in the second half of this course. Therefore, it is likely that the work involved in preparing a good paper will extend beyond the end of the semester. Accordingly, the paper will be due on August 1, 1995. You may submit the paper earlier if you like.

To insure that the paper deals with an acceptable topic, you must prepare a research proposal that will be submitted to me by March 28, 1995. The contents of the proposal will be described in a separate handout. I will review the proposals and indicate any revisions that are needed. Revised proposals are due on April 25, 1992.

The following is a tentative list of the topics that will be covered in the course. This is an ambitious list; if we run out of time, I will drop some topics. Reference numbers in the outline refer to the bibliography at the outline's end. The references are on reserve in the Business Library. Other references will be announced in class.

I.   The Linear Model

   A.   Review of theory   (1, Ch. 1; 7, Ch. 5-7)
   B.   Specification errors and multicollinearity -- theory and consequences
        (7, Ch. 8-9, Sec. 13.2)
   C.   Graphical diagnostics

        1.   Residuals plots
        2.   Graphical test of distributional assumptions

   D.   Specification tests

        1.   Testing the mean function (20)
        2.   Comparing non-nested mean functions (7, Sec. 7.7; 6; 16)
        3.   Heteroskedasticity (7, Sec. 14.3; 5; 15)
        4.   Non-normality (12)

II. Extensions of the Linear Model

   A.   Models with heteroskedasticity (7, Sec. 14.4-14.5; 20)
   B.   Nonparametric estimation (8; 19; notes that will be available from
        the copy center)

        1.   Nonparametric density estimation
        2.   Nonparametric regression
        3.   Dimension reduction

   C.   Models for time-series data (7, Ch. 15; 17)
   D.   Simultaneous-Equations models (7, Ch. 20; 9)

III. Nonlinear Models

   A.   Maximum likelihood estimation
   B.   Hypothesis tests based on maximum likelihood estimation (3, 18)
   C.   Models for duration data (1, Ch. 11; 10; 11)
   D.   Models with discrete dependent variables (7, Ch. 21; 18)
   E.   Models with censored or truncated dependent variables (7, Ch. 22; 10)

IV. The Bootstrap (Notes that will be available in the copy center)

Readings:

1. Amemiya, T. (1985). Advanced Econometrics, Harvard University Press.

2. Amemiya, T. and Powell, J.L. (1981). A comparison of the Box-Cox maximum likelihood estimator and the non-linear two-stage least squares estimator, Journal of Econometrics, 17, 351-381.

3. Andrews, D.W.K. (1988). Chi-square diagnostic tests for econometric models: theory, Econometrica, 56, 1419-1453.

4. Berndt, E.R. (1990). The Practice of Econometrics: Classic and Contemporary, Addison Wesley.

5. Breusch, T.S. and Pagan, A.R. (1979). A simple test for heteroscedasticity and random coefficient variation, Econometrica, 47, 1287-1294.

6. Davidson, R. and MacKinnon, J.G. (1981). Several tests for model specification in the presence of alternative hypotheses, Econometrica, 49, 781-793.

7. Greene, W.H. (1993). Econometric Analysis, 2nd edition, Macmillan.

8. Härdle, W. (1990). Applied Nonparametric Regression, Cambridge University Press.

9. Hausman, J.J. (1978). Specification tests in econometrics, Econometrica, 46, 1251-1272.

10. Horowitz, J.L. and Neumann, G.R. (1989). Specification testing in censored regression models: parametric and semiparametric methods, Journal of Applied Econometrics, 4, S61-S86.

11. Horowitz, J.L. and Neumann, G.R. (1992). A generalized moments specification test of the proportional hazards model," Journal of the American Statistical Association, 87, 234-240, 1992

12. Jarque, C.M. and Bera, A.K. (1987). A test for normality of observations and regression residuals, International Statistical Review, 55, 163-172.

13. Johnston, J. (1984). Econometric Methods, 3rd edition, McGraw-Hill.

14. Judge, G. et al. (1985). The Theory and Practice of Econometrics, 2nd edition, Wiley.

15. Koenker, R. (1981). A note on studentizing a test for heteroskedasticity, Journal of Econometrics, 17, 107-112.

16. MacKinnon, J.G., White, H. and Davidson, R. (1983). Tests for model specification in the presence of alternative hypotheses: some further results, Journal of Econometrics, 21, 53-70.

17. Newey, W.K. and West, K. (1987). A simple, positive-semidefinite heteroskedasticity and autocorrelation consistent covariance matrix. Econometrica, 55, 703-798.

18. Pagan, A. and Vella, F. (1989). Diagnostic tests for models based on individual data: a survey. Journal of Applied Econometrics, 4, S29-S59.

estimation of index coefficients, Econometrica, 57, 1403-1430.

20. Thursby, J.G. and Schmidt, P. (1977). Some properties of tests for specification error in a linear regression model, Journal of the American Statistical Association, 72, 635-641.

21. White, H. (1980). Heteroskedasticity-consistent covariance matrix estimator and a direct test for heteroskedasticity, Econometrica, 48, 817-838.

University of Iowa
DISCRETE-CHOICE ANALYSIS
G

INSTRUCTOR: Joel Horowitz, W384 PBAB, 335-0844, Hours: MW 11-12, TTh 2:30-3:30

TEXTBOOK (available at Iowa Book and Supply): Ben-Akiva, M.E. and Lerman, S.R., *Discrete Choice Analysis: Theory and Application to Travel Demand*, MIT Press.

COURSE DESCRIPTON: The course is about how to develop econometric models of an individual's choice among discrete alternatives (e.g., brands of a product, mode of travel to work). The following is a list of topics that we will discuss. The number in the reference column indicates the reference on the attached bibliography. The reference material is on reserve in the Business Library.

COURSE OUTLINE (APPROXIMATE)

Topic	Reference
Choice theory and random utility models	2 (Ch. 3)
The binary and multinomial logit models	1 (Ch. 9), 2 (Ch. 4-5), 14 (Ch. 4)
Generalized extreme value models	1(Ch. 9), 2 (Ch. 10), 12 (Ch. 5)
Binary and multinomial probit models	1 (Ch. 9)
Estimation of random utility models	1 (Ch. 9), 2 (Ch. 4,5), 14 (Ch. 4)
Simulation methods for probit computations	3, 10 (Ch. 19, 20)
Specification tests	2 (Ch. 7), 6, 7, 8
Illustrative applications	2 (Ch. 7), 4, 12 (Ch. 6)
Estimation from a subset of the choice set	2 (Ch. 9, sec. 3)
Estimation from choice-based samples	1 (Ch. 9), 2 (Ch. 8), 12 (Ch. 1,2)
Relation to discriminant analysis	Lecture notes
Analysis of panel data	1 (Ch. 9), 5, 12 (Ch. 3,4)
Semiparametric estimation	6, 9, 10 (Ch. 2), 11, 13

There will be several problem sets assigned during the course, and you must carry out an empirical project. There will be no examinations. The project must involve estimating a discrete-choice model using data of your own choosing. By March 9, you should submit a 1-page project proposal describing the problem you will address and the data. A paper about your work is due on the last day of class. The paper should motivate your research, describe the data and analytic methods, and present the results.

1. Amemiya, T. <u>Advanced Econometrics</u>

2. Ben-Akiva, M.E. and Lerman, S.R., <u>Discrete Choice Analysis: Theory and Application to Travel Demand</u>

3. Börsch-Supan, A. and Hajivassiliou, V.A., Smooth unbiased multivariate probability simulators for maximum likelihood estimation of limited dependent variable models, <u>Journal of Econometrics</u>, 58, 347-368, 1993.

4. Gönül, F. and Srinivasan, K., Modeling multiple sources of heterogeneity in multinomial logit models: methodological and managerial issues, <u>Marketing Science</u>, 12, 213-229, 1993.

5. Heckman, J.J. and Willis, R.J., A beta-logistic model for the analysis of sequential labor force participation by women, <u>Journal of Political Economy</u>, 85, 27-58, 1977.

6. Horowitz, J.L., Semiparametric estimation of a work-trip mode choice model, <u>Journal of Econometrics</u>, 58, 49-70, 1993.

7. Horowitz, J.L., Testing probabilistic discrete choice models of travel demand by comparing predicted and observed aggregate choice shares," <u>Transportation Research</u>, 19B, 17-38, 1985.

8. Horowitz, J.L. and Louviere, J.J., Testing predicted choices against observations in probabilistic discrete-choice models, <u>Marketing Science</u>, 12, 270-279, 1993

9. Klein, R.W. and Spady, R.H., An efficient semiparametric estimator for binary response models, <u>Econometrica</u>, 61, 387-421, 1993

10. Maddala, G.S., Rao, C.R., and Vinod, H.D., <u>Handbook of Statistics</u>, Vol. 11, Econometrics, North-Holland Publishing Company, 1993.

11. Manski, C.F., Semiparametric analysis of discrete response: asymptotic properties of the maximum score estimator, <u>Journal of Econometrics</u>, 27, 313-334, 1985.

12. Manski, C.F. and McFadden, D., <u>Structural Analysis of Discrete Data with Econometric Applications</u>

13. Powell, J.J., Stock, J.H., and Stoker, T.M., Semiparametric estimation of index coefficients, <u>Econometrica</u>, 57, 474-523, 1989.

14. Zarembka, P., <u>Frontiers in Econometrics</u>

Econometric Theory I

FINAL EXAMINATION

Problem 1

Let b_n be the OLS estimator of β in the regression model

$$Y = X\beta + U,$$

where the dimensions are $Y = n\times1$, $X = n\times K$, $\beta = K\times1$, $U = n\times1$, and realizations of U are independent but may be heteroskedastic. Define

$$S_n = n^{-1} \sum_{i=1}^{n} e_i^2 x_i x_i',$$

where x_i is the i'th row of X and e_i is the i'th element of the column vector of residuals $Y - Xb_n$. Suppose you estimate the covariance matrix of the asymptotic distribution of $n^{1/2}(b_n - \beta)$ by

$$\Omega_n = n^2 (X'X)^{-1} S_n (X'X)^{-1}.$$

Is this a consistent estimator? If so, prove it. If not, give a counterexample.

Problem 2

Let Y be a random variable, and let $\{Y_i: i = 1,\ldots,n\}$ be a random sample of Y. Let $1(A) = 1$ if the event A occurs and 0 otherwise. Consider the estimator $b_{n\alpha}$ that is the solution to

$$\text{minimize:} \quad n^{-1} \sum_{i=1}^{n} \{(1 - \alpha)\cdot 1(Y_i \le b) + \alpha\cdot 1(Y_i > b)\}|Y_i - b|,$$

where $0 < \alpha < 1$.

    a.   What feature of the distribution of Y, if any, does $b_{n\alpha}$ estimate consistently?

    b.   Explain how you can use the estimator to construct a test for symmetry of the distribution of Y. You need not prove all mathematical details, but you must provide enough information to make it clear how the estimator will be constructed and what must be proved.

Problem 3

Suppose that $Y = \mu + U$, where μ is an unknown constant and U is independently and identically distributed with mean 0. Let $\{Y_n: n = 1,\ldots,n\}$ be a random sample of size n. Consider the estimator

$$m_n = \arg\min_{m} \sum_{i=1}^{n} |Y_i - m|^P,$$

where $p > 1$ is an integer.

50   a.   Under what conditions is m_n a consistent estimator of μ?

b. Are there distributions of U for which m_n is consistent but asymptotically less efficient than the sample mean? If yes, give an example of such a distribution. If no, prove it.

Problem 4

Let $Y = X\beta + U$, where $U \sim N[0, f(Z\alpha)]$, Z is a vector of explanatory variables (possibly but not necessarily the same as X), and f is a positive function that has as many derivatives as you like but is otherwise unknown. There is no constant term in Z. Observe that U is homoskedastic if $\alpha = 0$ and heteroskedastic otherwise. Derive a Lagrangian multiplier statistic for testing the hypothesis $\alpha = 0$ (i.e., testing for homoskedasticity of U). You should obtain a result that does not require knowledge of f.

Problem 5

Consider the kernel nonparametric density estimator

$$p_n(x) = (nh_n)^{-1} \sum_{i=1}^{n} K\left[\frac{X_i - x}{h_n}\right],$$

where $\{X_i: i = 1, \ldots, n\}$ is a random sample of the variable X whose true but unknown probability density function is $p(\cdot)$, $\{h_n\}$ is a sequence of bandwidths that converges to 0 as $n \to \infty$, and K is a bounded, symmetrical about 0, and with support $[-1,1]$. K is called a "4th order kernel" if

$$\int_{-1}^{1} z^j K(z) dz = \begin{array}{l} 1 \text{ if } j = 0 \\ 0 \text{ if } j = 1, 2, \text{ or } 3 \\ A > 0 \text{ if } j = 4 \end{array}$$

Because its "variance" is zero, a 4th order kernel cannot be a probability density function. Here is an example of a 4th order kernel:

$$K(z) = (105/64)(1 - 5z^2 + 7z^4 - 3z^6)1(|z| \leq 1). \tag{1}$$

In what follows, assume that K is 4th order though not necessarily of the form (1). Also assume that $h_n \to 0$ and $nh_n \to \infty$ as $n \to \infty$.

a. Prove that $\text{plim}_{n \to \infty} p_n(x) = p(x)$.

b. Assume that p is 4 times continuously differentiable, and let $p^{(4)}(\cdot)$ denote the 4th derivative of p. Prove that

$$E[p_n(x)] = (1/4!)Ah_n^4 p^{(4)}(x) + o(h_n^4)$$

and

$$\text{Var}[p_n(x)] = (nh_n)^{-1}Bp(x) + o[(nh_n)^{-1}],$$

where

$$B = \int_{-1}^{1} K(z)^2 dz.$$

c. The asymptotic mean square error (AMSE) of p_n is

$$\text{AMSE}(x) = [(1/4!)Ah_n^4 p^{(4)}(x)]^2 + (nh_n)^{-1}Bp(x).$$

Find the value of h_n that minimizes AMSE.

d. If h_n converges to 0 at the rate found in part c, what is the rate of convergence in probability of $p_n(x)$ to $p(x)$?

e. If the rate of convergence found in part d is n^{-r}, what is the asymptotic distribution of $n^r[p_n(x) - p(x)]$?

1. Suppose that the random variable X has the probability density function $f(X - \theta)$, where θ is a constant parameter. Let $\{X_i: i = 1, \ldots, n\}$ be a random sample of X, and let c be a positive constant. Let $1(A)$ be the indicator of the event A. That is, $1(A) = 1$ if A occurs and 0 otherwise. Let t_n be the estimator of θ that is obtained as the solution to

    $$\text{minimize:} \quad n^{-1} \sum_{i=1}^{n} [1(|X_i - t| \leq c)(X_i - t)^2/2$$

    $$+ 1(|X_i - t| > c)(c|X_i - t| - c^2/2)].$$

    Let m_n denote the sample mean of X.

    a. Show that if $f(\cdot)$ is symmetrical about 0 (that is, $f(z) = f(-z)$ for any z), t_n is a consistent estimator of θ. Is t_n consistent if f is not symmetrical? You may assume that θ is contained in a known, compact set.

    b. Under what conditions is m_n a consistent estimator of θ?

    c. Can you think of a density function f such that t_n is consistent for θ but m_n is not?

    d. Suppose there are functions $\Omega_t(x,c)$ and $\Omega_m(x)$ such that

    $$n^{1/2}(t_n - \theta) = n^{-1/2} \sum_{i=1}^{n} \Omega_t(X_i,c) + o_p(1)$$

    and

    $$n^{1/2}(m_n - \theta) = n^{-1/2} \sum_{i=1}^{n} \Omega_m(X_i) + o_p(1)$$

    whenever f is symmetrical about 0 and m_n is consistent for θ. For example, $\Omega_m(x) = x - \theta$. Construct a test of the hypothesis that f is symmetrical. Give the test statistic in terms of t_n, m_n and the Ω's, and find its asymptotic distribution. State any assumptions other than those already given here that are needed to make your result correct.

2. Consider the model

    $$g(Y_i, \theta) = X_i\beta + \epsilon_i, \quad i = 1, \ldots, n$$

    where g is a known function, θ and β are parameters whose values must be estimated from data, X is random and $E(\epsilon|X) = 0$. You do not know the distribution of ϵ but may assume that it has as many moments as you like. Assume that $g(y,\theta)$ is a monotone increasing function of y for each θ.

    a. The non-linear least squares estimator of (θ,β) is obtained by minimizing

    $$\sum_{i=1}^{n} [g(Y_i, \theta) - X_i\beta]^2$$

    52 Is this estimator consistent for (θ,β)?

b.   Derive the asymptotic distribution of your estimator. (Note: Whether this is an easy or complicated matter depends a great deal on the notation you adopt. Try to find notation that enables you to avoid lots of messy but straightforward algebra.)

3.   Consider a regression model where the conditional mean of one random variable depends linearly on the conditional variance of a second variable (e.g., options price on stock price). Suppose that the conditional mean of the second variable is linear. That is

$$Y_i = \beta \text{Var}(W_i | X_i) + \epsilon_i, \qquad E(\epsilon | X) = 0 \tag{1}$$

$$W_i = X_i'\pi + \eta_i, \qquad E(\eta | X) = 0. \tag{2}$$

a.   Let $\{\hat{\eta}_i\}$ denote the residuals from OLS estimation of π in (2). Suppose you carry out OLS estimation of b in

$$Y_i = b\hat{\eta}_i^2 + \nu_i.$$

Is the estimator of b consistent for β?

b.   What is the asymptotic distribution of this estimator?

4.   Suppose you want to test the hypothesis that a certain random variable X has the exponential distribution with density $f(x) = \alpha \exp(-\alpha x)$, $x \geq 0$, for some unknown $\alpha > 0$. According to the theory of maximum likelihood estimation, $E[\partial^2 \log f(X, \alpha)/\partial \alpha^2] = -E[\partial \log f(X, \alpha)/\partial \alpha]^2$ if the hypothesis is true.

a.   Derive a statistic for testing H_0: $E[\partial^2 \log f(X, \alpha)/\partial \alpha^2] = -E[\partial \log f(X, \alpha)/\partial \alpha]^2$

b.   Find the asymptotic distribution of your statistic under H_0.

c.   Can you think of an alternative hypothesis (that is, a non-exponential distribution of X) under which the asymptotic distribution of your test statistic is the same as it is under H_0?

1. Suppose that you are trying to decide which of two models best explains a certain phenomenon. The models are:

   Model A: $Y = X\beta + u, \quad u \sim N(0, \sigma_A^2)$ (1)

   and

   Model B: $Y = Z\gamma + v, \quad v \sim N(0, \sigma_B^2),$ (2)

   where X and Z are random and $(X'X/n)$ and $(Z'Z/n)$ have nonsingular probability limits. Assume that models A and B are non-nested. That is, $P(X\beta = Z\gamma) < 1$ for all permissible values of β and γ. In less formal terms, there are no permissible values of β and γ such that $X\beta = Z\gamma$ for all X and Z. Let $\hat{\gamma}$ denote the ordinary least squares estimate of γ in (2).

   The J test of the hypothesis that model A is correct against the alternative that model B is correct consists of testing the hypothesis H_0: $\alpha = 0$ in the regression

   $Y = X\beta + \alpha(Z\hat{\gamma}) + \nu.$ (3)

   Derive the asymptotic distribution of the OLS t statistic for testing the hypothesis $\alpha = 0$ in (3).

2. Consider the model

   $Y_i = \beta_0 + \beta_1 X_i + u_i, \quad i = 1, \ldots, n$

   where the X's are random scalars, $\beta_1 > 0$, and u is iid $N(0, \sigma^2)$. Let k be any known, non-zero constant. Let $\hat{\beta}_1$ denote the OLS estimator of β_1, and let $\hat{V}$ denote the estimated variance of the asymptotic distribution of $n^{1/2}(\hat{\beta}_1 - \beta_1)$.

   a. Derive the Wald statistic for testing the hypothesis H_0: $\beta_1^k = 1$.

   b. Observe that since $\beta_1 > 0$, H_0 is the same hypothesis regardless of the value of k. Show that if H_0 is true, the Wald statistics for all non-zero values of k are asymptotically equivalent. That is, they differ by terms of size $o_p(1)$.

   c. Suppose that $\hat{\beta}_1 \neq 0$. Show that for any fixed sample size n, it is always possible to choose k so that H_0 is rejected, regardless of whether it is true.

3. Consider the model

   $g(Y_i, \theta) = X_i\beta + \epsilon_i, \quad i = 1, \ldots, n$

   where g is a known function, θ and β are parameters whose values must be estimated from data, X is random and $E(\epsilon | X) = 0$. You do not know the distribution of ϵ but may assume that it has as many moments as you like. Assume that $g(y, \theta)$ is a monotone increasing function of y for each θ.

   a. Show that the non-linear least squares estimator obtained by minimizing

54

$$\sum_{i-1}^{n} [g(Y_i, \theta) - X_i \beta]^2$$

is not consistent except, possibly, in special cases.

b.   Find a consistent extremum estimator of (θ, β) that does not require knowing the distribution of u. (Hint: Use the fact that $E[g(Y,\theta) - X\beta | X] = 0$.)

c.   Derive the asymptotic distribution of your estimator. (Note: Whether this is an easy or complicated matter depends a great deal on the notation you adopt. Try to find notation that enables you to avoid lots of messy but straightforward algebra.)

4.   Suppose you know that the scalar random variables Y and X are related by

$$Y - f(X) + u,$$

where $E(u|X) - 0$. In other words, you know that $E(Y|X) - f(X)$. You do not know the functional form of f or the distribution of u, and X has an unknown probability density $p(x)$. You want to estimate $f(x)$ for some x. One way to do this nonparametrically is as follows. Let $\{(Y_i, X_i): i - 1, \ldots, n\}$ be a random sample of (Y, X). Let ϕ denote the standard normal density function. Let $\{h_n: n - 1, 2, \ldots\}$ be a sequence of positive constants such that $h_n \to 0$ as $n \to \infty$. Estimate $f(x)$ by

$$f_n(x) - g_n(x)/p_n(x),$$

where

$$g_n(x) - (nh_n)^{-1} \sum_{i-1}^{n} Y_i \phi\left(\frac{X_i - x}{h_n}\right)$$

and

$$p_n(x) - (nh_n)^{-1} \sum_{i-1}^{n} \phi\left(\frac{X_i - x}{h_n}\right).$$

Intuitively, f_n is a weighted average of the Y_i's. Y_i's corresponding to X_i's close to x have higher weights than do Y_i's corresponding to X_i's that are far from x. Since $h_n \to 0$, asymptotically only Y_i's for which X_i is arbitrarily close to x receive any weight.

a.   Prove that if $nh_n \to \infty$ as $n \to \infty$, then $\text{plim}_{n \to \infty} f_n(x) - f(x)$.

Define $A_n(x)$ by

$$A_n(x) - [nh_n p(x)]^{-1} \sum_{i-1}^{n} [Y_i - f(x)] \phi\left(\frac{X_i - x}{h_n}\right). \tag{4}$$

b.   Prove that if f is twice continuously differentiable at x and p is once continuously differentiable, then

$$E[A_n(x)] - 0.5h_n^2 \left[f''(x) - \frac{2f'(x)p'(x)}{p(x)}\right] + o(h_n^2).$$

c.   Assume that $\sigma^2(z) - E\{[Y - f(X)]^2 | X-z\} - \text{Var}(Y|X-z)$ is a bounded, continuous function of z. Prove that

$$Var[A_n(x)] \; = \; \frac{\sigma^2(x)}{nh_np(x)} \int_{-\infty}^{\infty} \phi(u)^2 du + o[(nh_n)^{-1}].$$

d. Suppose that $h_n \propto n^{-1/5}$. Prove that

$$f_n(x) - f(x) \; = \; A_n(x) + o_p(n^{-2/5})$$

and, therefore, that $n^{2/5}[f_n(x) - f(x)] = O_p(1)$. [Hint: To solve this problem, you must first show that $p_n(x) - p(x) = o_p(1)$.]

e. Prove that $n^{2/5}A_n(x)$ and, therefore, $n^{2/5}[f_n(x) - f(x)]$, are asymptotically normal. [Note: You cannot invoke any of the central limit theorems discussed in class because the summand in A_n depends on n through h_n. But you can easily modify the proof of the Lindeberg-Levy theorem to deal with this problem.)

Indiana University

E770
Instructor: Thomas J. Kniesner
Seminar in Econometrics
Office: Ballantine Hall 816
Second Semester 1994-1995
Telephones: 855-7256 (O); 333-2582 (H)
Times: M 2:30-3:45 in BH006 & either
Office Hours: W 1-5, confirm by e-mail
    F 2:30-4:00 in BH137
E-mail address: Kniesne
  or F 4-5:30 in BH005 depending on the week

E770 has multiple goals: (1) to solidify your knowledge of how empirical economic research feeds into a dissertation, (2) to help you to locate a dissertation topic, (3) to help you locate the relevant background literature to read as part of your dissertation writing process, (4) to help you find a dissertation committee, (5) to teach you the fine points of expressing the results of economic research for an audience of professional economists, and (6) to get you started on writing your dissertation, and (7) to expose you to presentations of empirical economic research in its formative stages so that you may learn by the example of what others are doing.

Please note that attendance at all class meetings is mandatory and I expect you to inform me in advance of any special circumstance that you believe will make you miss any class.

Grades

Your course grade will be based on the following four tasks with the weights noted

1. presentation to the class of one of the readings: 10%
2. outline of a writing assignment that is part of your dissertation proposal: 15% (**due 2/20**)
3. first draft of the writing assignment: 25% (**due 3/27**)
4. second draft of the writing assignment: 50% (**due 4/28**)

Because of the diversity of the class we will individualize the writing assignments so that you will decide with me the most fruitful writing task to aid in producing your dissertation proposal.

Required Readings

You need to buy the following books

1. Donald N. McCloskey, *The Writing of Economics*, Macmillan Publishing Company, 1987.
2. Edward R. Tufte, *The Visual Display of Quantitative Information*, Graphics Press, 1983.
3. Richard J. Light & David B. Pillemer, *Summing Up, The Science of Reviewing Research*, Harvard University Press, 1984.
4. Kjell Erik Rudestam & Rae R. Newton, *Surviving Your Dissertation*, Sage Publications, 1992.

Recommended Readings

The following two items that are used regularly in writing dissertations and research papers

1. *Webster's New World Dictionary of American English*, Third College Edition, Prentice Hall, 1994.
2. *The Chicago Manual of Style*, Fourteenth Edition, The University of Chicago Press, 1993.

Scheduling Flexibility

Because we are also functioning as the Econometrics Workshop there will be visiting speakers whose schedules will be formalized only at the last minute, and who may also be scheduled to

speak on Tuesdays at 4-5:30. When there is an outside speaker the seminar will replace our Friday class. Get used to having to change what we will be doing any particular day on short notice. Already planned speakers are 2–6 job candidates in econometrics, Anil Bera, Sandy Darity, John Garen, Maureen Pirog-Good, David Good, Ben Gutierrez, Scott Long, Anthony Lo Sasso, David Neumark, Chuck Manski, and Steve Ziliak.

Readings to Be Presented in E770

Listed below are the readings in order of their presentation to the class by one of its members. We will have a lottery to determine the order in which you may choose the item you will present.

1. Donald N. McCloskey, *The Writing of Economics*, entire book.
2. Edward R. Tufte, *The Visual Display of Quantitative Information*, Chapters 1 & 9.
3. Edward R. Tufte, *The Visual Display of Quantitative Information*, Chapter 2 & 3.
4. Richard J. Light & David B. Pillemer, *Summing Up, The Science of Reviewing Research*, Chapter 2.
5. Richard J. Light & David B. Pillemer, *Summing Up, The Science of Reviewing Research*, Chapter 3.
6. Dana Goldman, dissertation proposal, "The Economics of Health Insurance Plan Choice."
7. Daniel Zabinski, dissertation proposal, "Taxes, Equity, and Efficiency in Health Insurance."

E770: Outline of Required Reading

Reading: _____ Your Name: _____

In the space allocated below describe the following features of the reading

(1) Author's Purpose

(2) Three Things You Learned That Will Improve Your Economic Research/Writing Skills

(3) What is the One Thing You Wish the Author Had Explained Better or More Completely?

E770: Presentation Rating Form

Your Student ID Number: _____ Presenter: _____

(1) Choice of Material: How well did the presenter budget the time available? Was the important material emphasized and the other material de-emphasized or ignored?

(2) Clarity of Presentation: How well did the presenter clarify the material for you? Be sure to comment on verbal pacing and use of visual aids, including the chalkboard or overheads.

(3) Originality of Presentation: Evaluate the quantity and quality of the fresh (original) insights the presenter provided. How much did you learn over and above what you learned by reading the material yourself?

(4) Other Comments: What can you tell the presenter concerning how to improve future presentations of economic material?

(5) Grade: How would you grade the presentation? (circle one)   A   A–   B+   B   B–   C   F

E770 Course Calendar
Second Semester 1994-1995

JANUARY

M, 1/9   Organizing Meeting

F, 1/13   Individual Student Conferences with TJJK in his Office,

----

M, 1/16   Student Presentation: Anthony T. Lo Sasso, *The Writing of* Economics. Outline of reading due in TJJK's mailbox by noon. Presentation Rating form due in TJJK's mailbox by noon on Thursday, 1/19.

F, 1/20   Dissertation Proposal Defense: Anthony T. Lo Sasso, "Two Essays on Medicaid and Its Incentives for the Prime-Aged And Aged Populations to Use Medical Care."

M, 1/23   Student Presentation: Christopher A. Richardson, *The Visual Display of Quantitative Information*, Chapters 1 & 9. Outline of the reading is due in TJJK's mailbox by noon. Presentation Rating Form due in TJJK's mailbox by noon on Thursday, 1/26.

F, 1/27   Maureen Pirog-Good, SPEA faculty, research presentation on child poverty. **Class will be held at 2:30–4pm in Ballantine 137.**

M, 1/30   Student Presentation: Kevin Condit, *The Visual Display of Quantitative Information*, Chapters 2 & 3. Outline of the reading is due in TJJK's mailbox by noon. Presentation Rating Form due in TJJK's mailbox by noon on Thursday, 2/2.

T, 1/31   Seminar by job candidate in econometrics, Yannis Bilias, of the University of Illinois: "A Sequential Hazard/Duration Model with an Application to the Pennsylvania Re-employment Bonus Experiment," **4:00–5:30pm in Ballantine 331.**

FEBRUARY

M, 2/6   Student Presentation: Wonjoo Park, *Summing Up*, Chapter 2. Outline of the reading is due in TJJK's mailbox by noon. Presentation Rating Form due in TJJK's mailbox by noon on Thursday, 2/9. Discussion also of what we learned from the talks by Pirog-Good and Bilias

T, 2/7   Seminar by job candidate in econometrics, Marcia Schafgans of Yale University: "Semiparametric Estimation of a Sample Selection Model," **4–5:30pm in Ballantine Hall 146.**

→F, 2/10← Seminar by job candidate in econometrics, Professor Choon-Geol Moon of Rutgers University, **4–5:30pm in Ballantine Hall 005.**

M, 2/13   Student Presentation: Kevin Stroupe, *Summing Up*, Chapter 3. Outline of the reading is due in TJJK's mailbox by noon. Presentation Rating Form due in TJJK's mailbox by noon on Thursday, 2/16. Discussion also of what we learned from the talks by Schafgans and Moon. **No other class meeting will be held T 2/14 to F 2/17 because we had three events the previous week.**

Double Header Monday
M, 2/20   Regular Class @ 2:30: Presentation by Brenda Drake of SPEA and the Bowen Research Center of the IU Medical School describing her hands-on experience in doing a large meta-analysis of the efficacy of medical procedures. ****Memo outlining your writing assignment is due today.**

M, 2/20   Extra class @ 4-5:30 in BH 005: Presentation by Deborah Garlow of the Dana Goldman dissertation proposal, "The Economics of Health Insurance Plan Choice." Outline of the reading is due in TJJK's mailbox by noon. Presentation Rating Form due in TJJK's mailbox by noon on Thursday, 2/23. Discussion also of what we learned about the technical details of doing a meta-studies from Brenda Drake's talk.

Double Header Monday
M, 2/27   Regular Class @ 2:30, we will discuss and provide helpful comments on the memos outlining each class member's writing assignment plans.

M, 2/27   Extra class @ 4-5:30 in **BH 245**: Presentation by Mousumi Duttaray of the Daniel Zabinski, dissertation proposal, "Taxes, Equity, and Efficiency in Health Insurance." Outline of the reading is due in TJJK's mailbox by noon. Presentation Rating Form due in TJJK's mailbox by noon on Thursday, 3/2.

MARCH

M, 3/6   Progress reports on your writing assignments one-on-one with TJJK in his office.

R, 3/9   Research Presentation by Professor Charles Manski of the University of Wisconsin, "Identification Problems in the Social Sciences," **4–5:30pm in the University Club, Main Lounge, Indiana Memorial Union.**

M, 3/20   Regular Class @ 2:30. Ray Smith and Lisa Kurz of the Campuswide Writing Program, "Good versus Bad Writing in the Social Sciences."

F, 3/24   Research Presentation by Stephen Ziliak of University of Iowa, "The Standard Error of Regressions," **2:30–4:00pm in Ballantine Hall 137.**

Double Header Monday
M, 3/27   Regular Class @ 2:30. We will discuss what we learned from the presentations by Manski, Smith & Kurz, and Ziliak.

M, 3/27 Research Presentation by Professor David Neumark of Michigan State University, "The Effects of the Minimum Wage on Teenage School Enrollment and Work," **4–5:30pm in Ballantine Hall 005. **First draft of your writing assignment is due in class.**

APRIL

M, 4/3 Discussion of what we learned from the talk by Neumark followed by in-class progress reports on everyone's writing assignments.

F, 4/7 Research Presentation by Professor John Garen of University of Kentucky, "The Difficulty of Observing Output and the Decision to Become Self Employed," **2:30–4:00pm in Ballantine Hall 137.**

T, 4/11 Research Presentation by Professor William A. Darity Jr. of University of North Carolina, "Disaggregate Estimates of the Effects of Ethnicity on Labor Market Success," **3:30–5:00pm in the University Club, Faculty Lounge, Indiana Memorial Union.**

F, 4/14 Research Presentation by Professor Anil Bera of University of Illinois, "Simple Diagnostic Tests for Spatial Dependence," **2:30–4:00pm in Ballantine Hall 137.**

M, 4/17 Discussion of what we learned from the talks by Darity and Bera followed by in-class progress reports on everyone's writing assignments.

M, 4/24 Free time to work put the finishing touches on your writing assignments. TJJK in his office for last minute walk-in help/advice.

***F, 4/28 Final Draft of your writing assignment is due in TJJK's mailbox.

Note: There are two sections of 742. This is the theoretical section meant for students going to take the econometrics sequence and the field exam in econometrics. The other is the applied section for those who are not choosing econometrics as their field.

Texts:
1. G. S. Maddala, *Introduction to Econometrics* (2nd edition), Macmillan.
2. A. C. Harvey, *The econometric Analysis of Economic Time Series*, MIT Press.
   I will be supplementing these books with my own notes.

Econ 742 Introduction to Econometrics
Practice Questions for Midterm Exam
Dr. Maddala
Fall 1992

1. Define Plim, LimE, AE. Give examples where they are equal and where they are not.

2. Consider the regression model with k regressors

$$y = X\beta + u.$$

We have four samples with sizes n_1, n_2, n_3 and n_4. Explain how you will test the hypothesis $\beta_1 = \beta_2 = \beta_3 = \beta_4$ if

   (i) $n_1 > k, n_2 < k, n_3 < k, n_4 < k$;
   (ii) $n_1 > k, n_2 < k, n_3 = k, n_4 > k$.

State the assumptions under which the tests are valid. What will you do if those assumptions are violated.

3. Define

   (i) least squares residuals
   (ii) predicted residuals
   (iii) studentized residuals
   (iv) recursive residuals

   (a) Explain the relationships among them.
   (b) What are the problems with each of these and what are their uses?
   (c) Explain how you would compute them?
   (d) Show that the sum of squares of the recursive residuals is equal to sum of squares of OLS residuals. (see Harvey p. 55)

4. Explain the basis for the min $\hat{\sigma}^2$ rule for choosing between different linear models. What are the problems with this rule?

5. Consider the regression model

$$y = X\beta + u,$$

$$E(uu') = V.$$

(a) What is the best linear unbiased estimator of β?
(b) Given that the model has been estimated with T observations, what is the best linear unbiased predictor for y_{T+1}?
(c) If you estimate this model by OLS assuming $E(uu') = I\sigma^2$, derive the covariance matrix of $\hat{\beta}_{OLS}$.

6. Consider the regression model

$$y = X_1\beta_1 + X_2\beta_2 + u$$

X_1 is $n \times k_1$, X_2 is $n \times k_2$, $k_1 + k_2 = k$. Let $\hat{\beta}_1, \hat{\beta}_2$ be the estimates of β_1 and β_2 from this model. Instead suppose you estimate the model

$$y = X_1\beta_1 + v.$$

Let $\tilde{\beta}_1$ be the estimate of β_1 from this misspecified model. Derive the expression for:
(i) $E(\hat{\beta}_1) - E(\tilde{\beta}_1)$
(ii) $V(\hat{\beta}_1) - V(\tilde{\beta}_1)$

7. Consider the regression model

$$y = X\beta + u,$$

$$E(uu') = V.$$

The regressors in X are correlated with the errors u. Let Z be the set of instrumental variables. X is $n \times k$, Z is $n \times m$. What is the best instrumental variable estimator of β if
(i) $m > k$
(ii) $m = k$

(iii) $m < k$

8. An AR(2) model is fitted to a series by regressing y_t on y_{t-2}. Find an expression for the covariance matrix of the estimators of ϕ_1 and ϕ_2, if the observations are actually generated by an AR(1) process. Compare the variance of the estimator of ϕ_1 with the variance of the estimator of the AR coefficient obtained by fitting an AR(1) model.

9. Examine whether the following statements are True (T), False (F) or Uncertain (U). Give a brief explanation.

(i) An unbiased estimator is consistent.

(ii) An unbiased estimator is asymptotically unbiased.

(iii) If we are estimating a regression model with k regressors, based on two samples of sizes n_1 and n_2 with $n_1 > k$, $n_2 < k$, we should use the predictive test for stability. This will tell whether the model is stable between the two periods.

(iv) In the regression equation

$$\hat{y} = \hat{\alpha} + \hat{\beta}_1 x_1 + \hat{\beta}_2 x_2$$

$\hat{\beta}_1$ measures the effect of x_1 on y. If it is not significantly different from zero, it means x_1 has no effect on y.

(v) Between the equations $y = \beta x + u$ and $y = \beta x + \gamma z + v$, we should always choose the one that maximizes $\overline{R}^2$ or minimizes $\hat{\sigma}^2$.

(vi) In the estimation of an autoregressive model, we can use the usual expressions for the multiple regression model for standard errors and tests of significance.

(vii) Each equation of a VAR model can be estimated by OLS. This gives efficient estimates, even with the errors across equations correlated.

(viii) The statement in (vii) is true even if there are constraints across equations provided the errors across equations are independent.

(ix) To overcome the multicollinearity problem in the estimation of a VAR model, you have to use a Bayesian VAR model.

(x) Omitting relevant variables in a multiple regression is not always a problem.

(xi) The sum of squares of predicted residuals is always smaller than the sum of squares of OLS residuals.

(xii) In the estimation of the autoregressive model

$$y_t = \alpha y_{t-1} + u_t,$$

there are no problems if $\alpha = 0.999$. Problems arise only if $\alpha = 1.000$.

(xiii) In the regression model

$$y = \beta_1 x_1 + \beta_2 x_2 + \beta_3 x_3 + u.$$

If x_3 is omitted, we can still get unbiased estimates of β_1, provided x_3 and x_1 are uncorrelated.

(xiv) In the regression model

$$y = \beta_1 x_1 + \beta_2 x_2 + \beta_3 x_3 + u,$$

if an irrelevant variable x_4 is included, the estimator $\widehat{\beta}_1$ is still unbiased and its standard error is also correct. Thus superfluous explanatory variables cause no problems.

(xv) Including a trend in a regression equation gives us estimates of regression parameters among detrended variables. Thus we get short-run elasticities if we include a trend term as a regressor.

(xvi) Ridge regression is entirely different from the Theil-Goldberger mixed estimation.

(xvii) Ridge regression is related to Bayesian estimation with prior information.

(xviii) The reason why Bayesian VAR models give good forecasts is that they are related to Ridge regression.

1. Define the following:

   (i) Score vector

   (ii) Information matrix

   (iii) Cramer-Rao lower bound

   (iv) Score test

   (v) Wald test

   (vi) Likelihood ratio test

   (vii) Information matrix test

   (viii) Hausman test

   (ix) Hypothesis test and specification test

   (x) Cox test and J-test

   (xi) GMM estimators

   (xii) AIC and BIC

   (xiii) Residual based model selection criteria

   (xiv) Cointegration

   (xv) Stationary time series

   (xvi) Dickey-Fuller test

   (xvii) Stochastic trend

2. State and prove the Cramer-Rao inequality.

3. Derive the score vector and information matrix for the parameters $\theta = (\beta_1, \beta_2, \sigma^2)$ in the model:

$$
\begin{aligned}
y &= X_1\beta_1 + X_2\beta_2 + u, \\
u &\sim N(0, I\sigma^2).
\end{aligned}
$$

Hence derive the LR, Wald and Score tests for the hypothesis $\beta_2 = 0$. Explain the connection between these tests and the usual F-test.

4. Derive the score vector and information matrix for the parameters $\theta = (\alpha, \beta, \rho, \sigma^2)$ in the model

$$
\begin{array}{lll}
y_t = \alpha y_{t-1} + \beta x_t + u_t & |\alpha| < 1 & \\
u_t = \rho u_{t-1} + e_t & |\rho| < 1 & e_t \sim IN(0, \sigma^2).
\end{array}
$$

Hence derive the LR, Wald and Score tests for the hypothesis $\rho = 0$. Explain how the score test reduces to a test for a parameter in an artificial linear regression.

5. Explain the Hausman test and derive the Hausman test for the hypothesis $\beta_2 = 0$ in the model $y = X_1\beta_1 + X_2\beta_2 + u$. Explain its connection to the usual F-test.

6. Derive the BHHH algorithm for solving the likelihood equations in the theory of ML estimation.

7. Consider the models:

$$
\begin{array}{lll}
H_0 &: y = X\beta + u & u \sim N(0, I\sigma_0^2), \\
H_1 &: y = Z\gamma + v & v \sim N(0, I\sigma_1^2).
\end{array}
$$

Define the pseudo-ML estimates of $\theta_0 = (\beta, \sigma_0^2)$ and $\theta_1 = (\gamma, \sigma_1^2)$. Explain the tests of the non-nested hypotheses H_0 versus H_1 in terms of the pseudo-ML estimates.

8. What are the advantages of GMM estimators relative to ML estimators?

9. Consider the regression of y on x. In each of the following cases, examine whether the regression equation makes sense or not. Give a brief explanation.

(i) y = dividends, x = earnings
(ii) y = detrended consumer expenditures, x = detrended disposable income
(iii) y = seasonally adjusted sales, x = advertising expenditures
(iv) y = seasonally adjusted expenditures on durables, x = disposable income

10. Explain the difference between deterministic trend (DT) and stochastic trend (ST). Consider the regression of y on x. In each of the following cases examine whether the regression makes sense or not. Give a brief explanation.
   (i) x has DT, y has DT;
   (ii) x has DT, y has no trend;
   (iii) x has DT, y has ST;
   (iv) x has ST, y has ST;
   (v) x has no trend, y has ST;
   (vi) x has DT, y has DT;
   (vi) x has ST, y has DT.

11. Define "recursive residuals". Explain how you can use the dummy variable method to calculate "recursive residuals" using this derive the recurrence relation:

$$RSS_t = RSS_{t-1} + \nu_t^2$$

where RSS_t is residual sum of squares with t observations and ν_t is t-th recursive residual. (Note that Harvey just states this recursive relation. He does not derive it.) Hence show that $\sum \nu_t^2 = \sum \widehat{u}_t^2$ where $\widehat{u}_t$ are the least squares residuals.

12. Explain the problems with using the Durbin-Watson statistic for testing for serial correlation in dynamic linear regression (DLR) models.

13. What are the special problems with model choice dealing with time series models?

1. Define the terms:
(i) Order condition for identification
(ii) Rank condition for identification
(iii) Indirect least squares
(iv) Simultaneity bias

2. Examine whether the following statements are True (T), False (F) or Uncertain (U). Give a brief explanation.

(i) Any variable can be endogenous in one equation and exogenous in another.

(ii) Some simultaneous equations system can be estimated by OLS.

(iii) The R^2 for an equation estimated by OLS is always higher than the R^2 from the equation estimated by 2SLS. Hence OLS is always better than 2SLS.

(iv) In exactly identified equations, the choice of which variable to normalize does not matter.

3. In the 2SLS methods what happens if we replace all endogenous variables (both on the left hand side and right hand side of the equation) by their fitted values from the reduced form?

4. Consider the model

$$y_1 = \alpha y_2 + \delta x + u_1$$

$$y_2 = \beta y_1 + u_2$$

α is exogenous, y_1 and y_2 are endogenous.
(i) Which of the parameters are estimable?

(ii) Suggest a method of estimating them.
(iii) What is the asymptotic covariance matrix of your estimator?
(iv) How will you conduct tests of significance in practice?
(v) How do you calculate R^2 for the equation you are estimating?

5. The structure of a model with 4 endogenous and 3 exogenous variables is as follows:
(1 denotes presence and 0 denotes absence of the variable in the equation).

$$
\begin{array}{ccccccc}
1 & 0 & 1 & 1 & 1 & 0 & 0 \\
1 & 1 & 1 & 0 & 0 & 1 & 1 \\
0 & 0 & 1 & 0 & 1 & 0 & 0 \\
1 & 0 & 1 & 1 & 0 & 1 & 0 \\
\end{array}
$$

Which of the four equations are identified?

6. Show that the 2SLS is the 'best' instrumental variable method.

7. What is meant by the phrase "Invariant to normalization"? If an estimator is not invariant to normalization, what problems will arise? Which of the following methods give estimators invariant to normalization?
(i) Indirect Least Squares
(ii) 2SLS
(iii) IV method
(iv) LIML
(v) GMM

Econ 840 Introduction to Time Series Analysis
Dr. Maddala
Fall 1994

G

This course will cover new developments in Time Series Analysis. Particularly, non-stationary time series. The emphasis will be to give students a broad perspective of the area. Detailed proofs will be omitted - references will be given that students can consult. Students are expected to work through some of these proofs by themselves. Going through the proofs will get us bogged down in detail and it would not be possible to cover all the material needed to give the students a comprehensive view of the area. In addition to non-stationary time series, Kalman filtering and time-varying parameter models will also be covered.

Texts:
1. Chapters 13 and 14 of G. S. Maddala *Introduction to Econometrics,* 2nd edition, (Macmillan).
2. A. C. Harvey *Econometric Analysis of Economic Time Series* (MIT Press).
3. A. Banerjee, J. Dolado, J. Galbraith and D. Hendry *Co-integration, Error-correction, and the Econometric Analysis of Non-stationary Data* (Oxford University Press - paperback).

Econ 840 Introduction to Time Series
Fall 1994
Dr. Maddala

1. Explain the Box-Jenkins approach to time-series.

2. Define the following terms:
i) Stationary time series
ii) Non-stationary time series
iii) Random walk
iv) Random walk with drift
v) ARMA process
vi) Correlogram
vii) Stability condition of an AR process
viii) Invertibility condition of a MA process

3. i) Show that the following AR(2) process is stable and find its correlogram:

$$x_t = 0.9x_{t-1} - 0.2x_{t-2} + e_t$$

ii) Show that the following MA(2) process is invertible and find its correlogram:

$$x_t = e_t - 0.9e_{t-1} + 0.2e_{t-2}$$

4. Define the terms:
i) Deterministic and stochastic trends
ii) Deterministic and stochastic seasonals
iii) TSP and DSP
iv) ARFIMA models

5. Explain what the Beveridge-Nelson decomposition is and illustrate it with reference to the ARIMA(0,1,1) model. What are the limitations of this decomposition?

6. Derive an expression for $\sum_1^T t^4$. Hence derive the asymptotic distribution of the least squares estimators of (a, b, c) in the model

$$
\begin{aligned}
y_t &= a + bt + ct^2 + u_t \\
u_t &\sim IID(0, 1).
\end{aligned}
$$

Why do you need to normalize the coefficients with different normalization factors?

7. Explain the differences between the Dickey-Fuller and Bhargava approaches to unit root testing.

8. Consider the two equations Engle-Granger model in the notes.
i) Which parameters are estimable?
ii) What procedures would you use to estimate them?
iii) What are short-run parameters?
iv) What procedures would you use to estimate the LR parameter?
v) Under what conditions would there be no cointegrating relationship? What would you do in this case?

9. Explain the following:
(i) UCARIMA model. How is it related to the ARIMA model?
(ii) ECM model. How is it related to the partial adjustment model?
(iii) DLR model. How is it related to ECM?

10. How do you estimate the SR and LR response of an endogenous variable to changes in the exogenous variable in the :
(i) partial equilibrium model
(ii) the ECM model
(iii) the DLR model

1. In the regression equation

$$y = \beta' x + \gamma' z + u$$

where y and x are $I(1)$ and z and u are $I(0)$.

(i) Show that the asymptotic distributions of β and γ are independent. What are these distributions?

(ii) Suppose that the variables x are subject to one cointegration restriction, then what happens? (e.g. consider $y = \beta_1 x_1 + \beta_2 x_2 + \gamma z + u$ and x_1 and x_2 are cointegrated.)

(iii) Explain how result (i) is useful in deriving the distribution of the ADF test statistic.

2. If

$$\begin{pmatrix} y_1 \\ y_2 \end{pmatrix} \sim \left(\begin{pmatrix} \mu_1 \\ \mu_2 \end{pmatrix}, \begin{pmatrix} \Sigma_{11} & \Sigma_{12} \\ \Sigma_{21} & \Sigma_{22} \end{pmatrix} \right).$$

Write down the marginal distribution of y_1 and the conditional distribution of y_2 given y_1. Explain the usefulness of this result in the derivation of the Kalman filter.

3. Consider the local trend model

$$y_t = \mu_t + \varepsilon_t,$$
$$\varepsilon_t \sim N(0, \sigma_\varepsilon^2),$$
$$\mu_t = \mu_{t-1} + \eta_t,$$
$$\eta_t \sim N(0, \sigma_\eta^2),$$

ε's and η's are mutually independent.

(i) Under what conditions will we get a deterministic trend model in the case of the local trend model?

74

(ii) How can we use to test whether the trend is deterministic or stochastic?

(iii) Write down the model in the state-space form.

(iv) Write down the recursive estimation equations for the model.

4. y and x are two $I(1)$ variables that are cointegrated. Consider the cointegration regression

$$y = \beta x + u$$

where u is $I(0)$. Let $\widehat{\beta}$ be the OLS estimator of β.

Answer the following:

(i) What are the endogeneity and serial correlation problems?

(ii) Explain how the following methods address these problems:

a. Phillips-Hansen's FMOLS method

b. Phillips-Loretan's method

c. Johansen method

5. Consider the DLR model with one explanatory variable and two lags each.

(i) What is the equilibrium response?

(ii) What is the short-run response?

(iii) How do you estimate the equilibriun response and its standard error?

6. Define the following terms:

(i) VAR model

(ii) VARMA model

(iii) VARMAX model

7. Consider a VAR model with two endogenous variables y_1 and y_2 and one exogenous variable x (one lag each).

(i) How do you estimate the SR response of each of y_1 and y_2 to a unit change in x.

(ii) How do you estimate the LR response?

1. Show that

$$\left| \begin{array}{cc} A & B \\ B' & C \end{array} \right| = |A| \cdot \left| C - B'A^{-1}B \right| = |C| \cdot \left| A - BC^{-1}B' \right|$$

2. In the multiple regression equation $y = X\beta + u$, let RSS denote residual sum of squares. Show that if

$$\left[\begin{array}{cc} y'y & y'X \\ X'y & X'X \end{array} \right]^{-1} = \left[\begin{array}{cc} a & c' \\ c' & D \end{array} \right]$$

then $a = 1/RSS$.

3. If

$$\left[\begin{array}{cc} Y'Y & Y'X \\ X'Y & X'X \end{array} \right] = \left[\begin{array}{cc} A & B \\ B' & C \end{array} \right]$$

then show that

$$A = [Y'Y - Y'X(X'X)^{-1}X'Y]^{-1}.$$

(This is a generalization of (2).) What is the statistical interpretation of this result?

4. In the multiple regression

$$y = X_1\beta_1 + X_2\beta_2 + u$$

show that $\hat{\beta}_2$ is the same as the estimate of the regression coefficient in a regression of Ny on NX_2 where $N = I - X_1(X_1'X_1)^{-1}X_1'$.

5. Show that

$$\underset{x}{Max} \; \frac{x'Ax}{x'Bx}$$

is given by the largest characteristic root of $|A - \lambda B| = 0$.

6. (i) State the Cauthy-Schwartz (CS) inequality and prove the generalized CS inequality

$$(x'y) \leq (x'Ax)(y'A^{-1}y)$$

where A is a symmetric non-singular matrix.

(ii) Hence show that in a multiple regression of y on $x_1, x_2, \ldots, x_k$

$$R^2 = \underset{\beta}{Max} \frac{(\beta'X'y)^2}{(\beta'X'X\beta)(y'y)}$$

the maximum being attained at $\hat{\beta} = (X'X)^{-1}X'y$.

(iii) Show that the canonical correlations between $Y' = (y_1, \ldots, y_m)$ and $X' = (x_1, \ldots, x_k)$ with $m < k$ are given by the m characteristic roots of the matrix $(Y'Y)^{-1}Y'X(X'X)^{-1}X'Y$.

7. consider $y = X\beta + u$, $u \sim N(0, \sigma^2 I)$. Let $RSS = y'y(1 - R^2)$. Show that

$$^*(L_{max})^{-2/T} = RSS = (y'y)(1 - R^2)$$

where T is the total number of observations.

* In the multivariate case, $y'y$ is replaced by the generalized variance $|Y'Y|$ and $(1 - R^2)$ is replaced by $\prod_i(1 - \lambda_i)$ where λ_i are the canonical correlations. That is why in the Johansen test we get

$$(L_{max})^{-2/T} = |S_{oo}| \cdot \prod_{i=1}^{r}(1 - \lambda_i).$$

1. Statistical (Multivariate Regression)

1. In the multiple regression of y on $x_1, x_2, \ldots, x_k$ based on n observations we know that

(i) $\hat{\beta} = (X'X)^{-1}X'y$

(ii) $Res.S.S. = y'y - y'X(X'X)^{-1}X'y = (1 - R^2)S_{yy}$

(iii) $R^2 = y'X(X'X)^{-1}X'y/y'y$

where y is an $n \times 1$ vector and X is an $n \times k$ matrix.

Define the corresponding terms in the case of the multivariate regression of $(y_1, y_2, \ldots, y_m)$ on $(x_1, x_2, \ldots, x_k)$. Define the orders of the matrices you use.

2. In the case of the normal multivariate regression model we know that

$$MaxL = \text{const (a fn. of } n) * (RSS)^{-n/2}$$

where n is the sample size. State the corresponding result for the multivariate regression.

3. Show that if λ_i are the characteristic roots of A, the characteristic roots of $(I - A)$ are $(1 - \lambda_i)$. Hence show that, in the multivariate normal regression of $(y_1, y_2, \ldots, y_m)$ on $(x_1, x_2, \ldots, x_k)$, with $m < k$,

$$MaxL. = \text{const } |Y'Y| \prod_{i=1}^{m}(1 - \lambda_i)$$

where λ_i are the (squared) cannonical correlations and Y is the $m \times m$ matrix of sums of squares and sums of products of the variables $(y_1, y_2, \ldots, y_m)$.

4. If

$$\begin{pmatrix} y_1 \\ y_2 \end{pmatrix} \sim N\left(\begin{pmatrix} \mu_1 \\ \mu_2 \end{pmatrix}, \begin{pmatrix} \Sigma_{11} & \Sigma_{12} \\ \Sigma_{21} & \Sigma_{22} \end{pmatrix} \right).$$

Write down the marginal distribution of y_1 and the conditional distribution of y_2 given y_1. Explain the usefulness of this result in the derivation of the Kalman filter.

2. Bayesian Inference

1. Define the terms: Posterior distribution and predictive distribution. What are the main differences between the classical and Bayesian approaches to inference.

2. What are the main problems in the application of Bayesian methods to the problem of testing for unit roots?

3. Describe the following methods of model selection.
(i) Posterior Odds
(ii) Predictive Odds
(iii) Sequential Predictive Odds

3. Cointegration

y and x are two $I(1)$ variables that are cointegrated. Consider the cointegrating regression $y = \beta x + u$, where u is $I(0)$. Let $\widehat{\beta}$ be the OLS estimator of β.

Answer the following:
1. What are the endogeneity and serial correlation problems?

2. Show that $\widehat{\beta}$ is superconsistent even in the presence of these problems and that there is no simultaneity bias in the OLS estimation of cointegrated systems.

3. Derive the asymptotic distribution of $\widehat{\beta}$ and show that it depends on these two problems.

4. Explain how the following methods address these problems:
a. Engle-Granger methods
b. Phillips-Hansen's FMOLS method
c. Phillips-Loretan's method
d. Johansen method

Reference: P.C.B. Phillips and M. Loretan (1991), "Estimating LR Economic Equilibria". *Review of Economic Studies*, 58, 403-436.

5. Show that in the case of this two variable cointegrated model β is unique. If this is the case what are the advantage of the Johansen type system method compared to the single equation methods a - d in question 4?

6. Which of all these results change if we have more than two variables in the system?

4. Estimation of Models with I(1) and I(0) Variables

1. In the regression equation

$$y = \beta' x + \gamma' z + u$$

where y and x are $I(1)$ and z and u are $I(0)$, show that the asymptotic distributions of β and γ are independent. What are those distributions?

2. Suppose that the variables x are subject to one cointegration restriction, then what happens? (e.g. consider $y = \beta_1 x_1 + \beta_2 x_2 + \gamma z + u$ and x_1 and x_2 are cointegrated.)

3. Explain how result 1 is useful in deriving the distribution of the ADF test statistic.

5. Granger Representation Theorem

1. State the Granger representation theorem.

2. Illustrate its usefulness with respect to a 2-equation model.

6. Kalman Filtering

Consider the following models:
(A) Local level model

$$y_t \;=\; \mu_t + \epsilon_t,$$

$$\epsilon_t \sim N(0, \sigma_\epsilon^2),$$
$$\mu_t = \mu_{t-1} + \eta_t,$$
$$\eta_t \sim N(0, \sigma_\eta^2),$$

ϵ's and η's are mutually independent.

(B) The local trend model

$$y_t = \mu_t + e_t$$
$$\mu_t = \mu_{t-1} + \beta_{t-1} + u_t$$
$$\beta_t = \beta_{t-1} + v_t$$

where

$$e_t \sim IN(0, \sigma_e^2),$$
$$u_t \sim IN(0, \sigma_u^2),$$
$$v_t \sim IN(0, \sigma_v^2),$$

and e_t, u_t, v_t are mutually independent. μ_t is the trend and β_t is the slope of the trend. The stochastic terms u_t and v_t allow the level and slope to change slowly over time.

Questions:

1. Write down these two models in the state-space form.

2. Under what conditions will we get a deterministic trend model in the case of the local trend model?

3. How can we use this to test whether the trend is deterministic or stochastic?

4. State the Beveridge-Nelson decomposition theorem. What are the main differences between the Beveridge-Nelson decomposition and the unobserved components decomposition in Model (B)?

5. Write down the recursive estimation equations for Models (A) and (B).

6. Explain how you will estimate the parameters in Models (A) and (B).

7. Explain how you will use these models for prediction.

8. If y_t is $I(0)$ then Δy_2 has a MA unit root. Hence the hypothesis

$$H_0 \;:\; y_t \text{ is stationary}$$
$$\text{vs. } H_1 \;:\; y_t \text{ has a unit root}$$

is often tested by testing the hypothesis:

$$H_0 \;:\; \Delta y_t \text{ has a MA unit root}$$
$$\text{vs. } H_1 \;:\; \Delta y_t \text{ does not have a MA unit root.}$$

Explain how the model (B) can be used to test the null of nonstationarity vs. the null of non-stationarity.

Econometrics Qualifying Exam
The Ohio State University   G
September 1994

Answer all questions.

1. (60 points)
Consider the two equation system

$$y_t + \beta x_t = u_{1t} \qquad u_{1t} = u_{1,t-1} + e_{1t}$$
$$y_t + \alpha x_t = u_{2t} \qquad u_{2t} = \rho u_{2,t-1} + e_{2t} \qquad |\rho| < 1$$

e_{1t} and e_{2t} are $iid(0, \sigma_1^2)$ and $(0, \sigma_2^2)$, respectively.

(a) Show that both x_t and y_t are $I(1)$.

(b) Which is the cointegrating regression?

(c) Explain why the equation system is identified even though both the equations "look alike".

(d) Explain how you would estimate α, β, ρ.

(e) Derive the corresponding ECM and the corresponding VAR.

(f) What are all the different methods you could use to estimate the parameters? What are the relative merits of the different procedures?

(g) What special problems arise if this model is extended to k variables?

2. (20 points)
Given a set of data on consumer expenditures c_{it} and disposable income y_{it} for a set of N families $(i = 1, 2, ..., N)$ over a time period $T(t = 1, 2, ..., T)$, explain the different models you would estimate and why you would consider them.

3. (30 points)
A random variable x $(0 < x < 1)$ has probability density

$$f(x) = ax^{a-1}$$

where $a > 0$ is an unknown parameter. A sample of n independent observations $x_i(i = 1, ..., n)$ is available. We want to test the hypothesis $H_0 : a = 1$ against the alternative $H_1 : a \neq 1$. Find expressions for (i) the Wald test statistic, (ii) the likelihood ratio test statistic, and (iii) the Lagrange multiplier test statistic for this hypothesis test.

4. (40 points)
Consider the model

$$
\begin{aligned}
y_i &= \alpha + \beta x_i + u_i \quad \text{if } \alpha + \beta x_i + u_i > 0 \\
&= 0 \qquad\qquad\quad \text{otherwise}
\end{aligned}
$$

where the error terms u_i are independently normally distributed with mean zero and variance σ^2, and the explanatory variables x_i are exogenous.

(a) Give an example of an application of this model.
(b) Consider the following methods of estimating the parameter β.
(i) Estimate by ordinary least squares, using all observations.
(ii) Estimate by ordinary least squares, using only those observations with $y_i > c\sqrt{n}$ where c is a given positive constant.
(iii) Estimate by ordinary least squares, using only those observations with $y_i > 0$, with the additional regressor $z = \phi(\tilde{\alpha} + \tilde{\beta} x_i)/\Phi(\tilde{\alpha} + \tilde{\beta} x_i)$, where ϕ is the standard normal density function, Φ is the standard normal cumulative distribution function, and $\tilde{\alpha}$ and $\tilde{\beta}$ are initial consistent estimators of α and β.
(iv) Estimate by maximum likelihood.
Which of these estimators are consistent? Explain your answers. (Formal proofs are not required.)
(c) Suggest a suitable initial consistent estimator for (b) (iii).
(d) Considering only the consistent estimators in part (b), what are their relative advantages and disadvantages?

5. (20 points)
In the linear regression equation

$$
y = X\beta + \varepsilon
$$

the regressors are exogenous and the error terms are i.i.d. normal mean zero and variance σ^2. The data consists of a random sample of size n with observations on x and y. Consider the following estimation method (an exercise, not a practical estimator).

(i) Generate n independent standard normal random variables u_i.

(ii) For given parameter values $\tilde{\beta}$ and $\tilde{\sigma}^2$, construct the simulated endogenous variables as $\tilde{y} = X\tilde{\beta} + \tilde{\sigma}u$ (with the same values for the exogenous variables X as in the real data).

(iii) Find the values of $\tilde{\beta}$ and $\tilde{\sigma}^2$ that equate the observed and simulated moments, $X'y = X'\tilde{y}$ and $y'y = \tilde{y}'\tilde{y}$.

(a) Show that this leads to the equations

$$\tilde{\beta} = (X'X)^{-1}X'(y - \tilde{\sigma}u)$$
$$\tilde{\sigma}^2 = \frac{\varepsilon' M \varepsilon}{u' M u}$$

where

$$M = I - X(X'X)^{-1}X'.$$

(b) Show that this estimator of β is consistent, and that its large-sample variance is twice that of the OLS estimator.

6. (20 points)
Explain the differences between a random effects model and a fixed effects model. Discuss the model specifications that would make each appropriate. Explain how the Hausman specification test is used to guide the choice of the appropriate model.

7. (25 points)
Suppose an investigator has data drawn on individuals from a clustered sample, that is, groups of n observations are drawn from k geographic areas yielding a total sample size of $N = nk$. In a clustered sample observations from the same geographic area exhibit a correlation in their error terms because of common, unmeasured ecological factors. Standard errors computed for cross sectional data typically assume a simple random sample, that is, there is no intra-cluster correlation. Set up a stochastic specification that represents this sampling scheme and explain how you would compute the correct standard errors for an OLS regression based upon a clustered sample.

8. (8 points)
Consider a regression equation with the error term having a finite variance and following a first-order autoregressive process. If one of the regressors is a time trend term, the least squares estimate of the time trend coefficient will have

a small-sample bias. However, if the other regressors are all exogenous no other coefficient will be biased in small samples. True, false or uncertain? Why?

9. (7 points)
If the error terms of a regression are normally, independently and identically distributed, then if the sample size is n and there are k regressors, each regression coefficient will follow a t-distribution with $n - k - 2$ degrees of freedom. True, false or uncertain? Why?

10. (10 points)
Explain the difference between a cost function and a production function. Is there any relation between the two? Why might an econometrician choose to estimate the cost function rather than the production function?

Answer all 8 questions.
Please note that in question 4 you should choose five of the sections (a) -(h).

1. (30 points)
Consider the following system of simultaneous equations:

$$y_{1,t} = a_1 + b_1 x_{1,t} + e_{1,t}$$
$$y_{2,t} = a_2 + c_1 y_{1,t} + c_2 x_{2,t} + c_3 x_{3,t} + e_{2,t}$$

(a) Is this system just-, over-, or exactly identified?
(b) How many sets of parameters will the method of indirect least squares generate?
(c) What can be said in general about the relative efficiency in this problem of using indirect least squares versus full information maximum likelihood to estimate the a's, b's and c's?

2. (15 points)
Suppose one wishes to estimate a demand system conditioning upon the amount of one commodity purchased. Would one use as regressors the quantity, price, or both, for the commodity being conditioned upon?

3. (35 points)
Let $\overline{Y}_n$ be the sample mean drawn with a simple random sample from a random variable Y, where the sample size is n, with the distribution of $\overline{Y}_n$ being $F_n(\overline{Y})$. Provide a definition of the limiting distribution of $\overline{Y}_n$. Prove that if Y is normally distributed the limiting distribution of the sample mean is the distribution of the scalar equal to the true mean.

4. (40 points)
Consider

$$y_t = \beta x_t + u_t$$

$$\Delta x_t = v_t$$

$$u_t \text{ and } v_t \text{ are } I(0)$$

$$u_t \sim IID(0, \sigma_u^2), \, v_t \sim IID(0, \sigma_v^2)$$

and

$$cov(u_t, v_t) = \delta_{ts} \delta_{uv}$$

where δ_{ts} is a Kronecker delta. Answer any 5 of the following sections (a) – (h). Identify your choices.

(a) Show that the OLS estimator $\hat{\beta}$ of β from a regression of y_t on x_t is 'superconsistent'.

(b) Obtain the distribution of $T(\hat{\beta} - \beta)$.

(c) Describe the residual based tests for cointegration.

(d) If u_t and v_t are serially correlated, what residual based tests would you use?

(e) Describe the ECM based test for cointegration in this model.

(f) Describe the Johansen test in this model.

(g) In the case u_t and v_t are serially correlated, describe instrumental variable tests for cointegration in this model.

(h) Explain why these different tests would give different results.

5. (25 points)
Consider the random coefficient model

$$\begin{aligned} y_t &= \beta_i x_{it} + u_{it} \\ u_{it} &\sim IN(0, \sigma_u^2) \\ \beta_i &\sim IN(\overline{\beta}, \sigma_v^2) \end{aligned}$$

i.e.

$$\beta_i = \overline{\beta} + v_i$$

with

$$v_i \sim IN(0, \sigma_v^2).$$

Obtain an efficient estimator for $\overline{\beta}$. How will you estimate σ_u^2 and σ_v^2?

6. (15 points)
Explain the conditions under which you would consider using:
(a) a fixed effect model

(b) a random effects model

(c) a random coefficient model

7. (40 points)

Consider the nonlinear simultaneous equations system

$$y_{1i} = f(y_{2i}, x_i, \theta) + \varepsilon_{1i}$$
$$y_{2i} = g(y_{1i}, x_i, \theta) + \varepsilon_{2i}$$

where f and g are specified functions, x is a vector of exogenous variables, θ is a vector of parameters to be estimated, and the error terms $(\varepsilon_{1i}, \varepsilon_{2i})$ are serially uncorrelated with mean zero and unknown variance matrix Σ. A large random sample of observations on y_1, y_2, and x is available.

(a) Three of the methods available for estimating the parameters of this model are: nonlinear two-stage least squares (2SLS), nonlinear three-stage least squares (3SLS), and maximum likelihood (ML). Each of these estimators involves maximization or minimization (with respect to θ) of some function. For each of the estimators, specify the function to be maximized or minimized.

(b) What are the relative advantages and disadvantages of each of the three estimators proposed in part (a)?

(c) Suppose that the model had instead been specified in the "implicit" form

$$f(y_{1i}, y_{2i}, x_i, \theta) = \varepsilon_{1i},$$
$$g(y_{1i}, y_{2i}, x_i, \theta) = \varepsilon_{2i}.$$

Discuss briefly the special problems that may arise in this case.

8. (30 points)

In an econometric model, two latent variables u_t and v_t are jointly normally distributed, with each mean 0 and variance 1. They also satisfy the relationship

$$u_t = \beta v_t + \varepsilon_t$$

where $cov(v_t, \varepsilon_t) = 0$. The observed variables are

$$y_t = 1(u_t > c_1)$$
$$x_t = 1(v_t > c_2)$$

where c_1 and c_2 are constants, and $1(\cdot)$ denotes an indicator function. A large random sample of observations on x and y is available.

Assume that you have a computer package which can maximize or minimize a given function, and which can evaluate the functions that you need.

Explain carefully, step by step, how you would obtain an estimate $\widehat{\beta}$ of β, and an estimate of its standard deviation, $SE(\widehat{\beta})$.

Answer all Questions.

1. Suppose we have a noisy indicator y of an underlying variable η. So that $y = \eta + e$. Suppose that the measurement error e is $N(0, \theta^2)$ and η is $N(m, \sigma^2)$, with e uncorrelated with η. Show that the optimal estimate of η is given by

$$E(\eta \mid y) = m + \frac{\sigma^2}{\theta^2 + \sigma^2}(y - m)$$

with associated MSE

$$E[\eta - E(\eta \mid y)]^2 = \frac{\sigma^2 \theta^2}{\theta^2 + \sigma^2}.$$

Discuss the meaning of this result as $\theta^2 \to \infty$ and $\theta^2 \to 0$.

2. Consider the following bivariate VAR

$$\begin{aligned}
y_{1t} &= 0.4 y_{1,t-1} + 0.8 y_{2,t-1} + e_{1t} \\
y_{2t} &= 0.6 y_{1,t-1} + 0.4 y_{2,t-1} + e_{2t}
\end{aligned}$$

$$\begin{aligned}
E(e_{1t}, e_{1s}) &= 2 \text{ for } t = s \\
&= 0 \text{ otherwise}
\end{aligned}$$

$$\begin{aligned}
E(e_{2t}, e_{2s}) &= 1 \text{ for } t = s \\
&= 0 \text{ otherwise.}
\end{aligned}$$

Calculate the fraction of MSE of the two period ahead forecast error for y_1

$$E[y_{1,t+2} - \widehat{E}(y_{1,t+2} \mid y_t, y_{t-1}, \ldots)]^2$$

that is due to $e_{1,t+1}$ and $e_{1,t+2}$.

3. Suppose the binary variable y is given by the probit model:

$$y_i^* = x_i'\beta + u_i$$
$$y_i = 1\{y_i^* > 0\}$$

where

y_i is the observed dependent variable

y_i^* is not observable

x_i is a k-dimensional vector of observed exogenous variables

β is an unknown k-dimensional parameter vector

the error terms u_i are $IN(0, \sigma^2)$

$1\{A\}$ denotes the indicator function for the event A.

The data consists of a random sample of n observations ($i = 1, \ldots, n$).

(a) Explain why some parameter(s) of this model cannot be identified. What is the usual way of handling this problem?

(b) Write down the log likelihood function for this sample.

(c) Find an expression for the asymptotic variance of the maximum likelihood estimator of β.

(d) Show that the data is also represented by the nonlinear regression equation

$$y_i = f(x_i'\beta) + \epsilon_i$$

where $f(x'\beta) = E[y \mid x]$ and $E[\epsilon \mid x] = 0$. What is the function f in this case?

(e) Find the asymptotic variance of the nonlinear least-squares estimator of β from the regression in part (d). Is this asymptotic variance always greater than the asymptotic variance of the maximum likelihood estimator that you found in part (c)?

(f) Would there be any reason to use the nonlinear least-squares estimator rather than the maximum likelihood estimator to estimate β in this model?

4. The structural equations of a two-equation system are

$$y_{1i} = \alpha_1 + \beta_1 y_{2i} + \gamma_1 x_{1i} + u_{1i}$$
$$\log y_{2i} = \alpha_2 + \beta_2 \log y_{1i} + \gamma_2 \log x_{2i} + u_{2i}$$

where y_1 and y_2 are endogenous variables, and x_1 and x_2 are exogenous variables. Observations are also available on x_3, another exogenous variable. The error terms u_{1i} and u_{2i} satisfy

$$E[u_{ki}] = 0$$

$$E[u_{ki}u_{li}] = \sigma_{kl}$$

$$E[u_{ki}u_{lj}] = 0 \qquad (i \neq j)$$

(a) Explain why this is considered to be a nonlinear system, even though each equation is a linear regression equation.

(b) Discuss the relative merits of the following estimation methods:

(i) estimate each equation separately by ordinary least squares;

(ii) estimate each equation separately by (nonlinear) two-stage least squares;

(iii) estimate both equations jointly by (nonlinear) three-stage least squares;

(iv) estimate both equations jointly by maximum likelihood.

(c) Describe carefully, step by step, how the three-stage least squares estimator can be computed for this system. (Details of numerical optimization methods are not required.)

5. Part I. The true generating process (DGP) is known as

(i) $y_t = \alpha x_t + e_t, \quad (t = 1, 2, ..., T)$,

where y_t, x_t are $I(1)$ and e_t is $I(0)$. But we observed $y_t^* = y_t + v_t$, where v_t is $I(0)$ and v_t is independent of e_s at all t and s, and obtained the OLS estimate of α given as $\hat{\alpha} = \sum_{t=1}^{T} x_t y_t^* / (\sum_{t=1}^{T} x_t^2)$. Discuss the validity of the following statements regarding the asymptotic properties of $\hat{\alpha}$.

(1) $\hat{\alpha}$ is consistent for the coefficient α.

(2) $\hat{\alpha}$ is subject to higher sampling variability than $\bar{\alpha} = \sum_{t=1}^{T} x_t y_t / (\sum_{t=1}^{T} x_t^2)$ in the limit.

(3) When x_t is independent of e_s for all t and s, the t-ratio based on $\hat{\alpha}$ converges in distribution to a standard normal variable.

Part II. We assume equation (i) in Part I represents the true DGP. Assume that we observe $x_t^* = x_t + w_t$, where w_t is $I(0)$ and w_t is independent of e_s at all t and s. The OLS estimate of α using x_t^* and y_t is given as $\tilde{\alpha} = \sum_{t=1}^{T} x_t^* y_t / (\sum_{t=1}^{T} x_t^{*2})$. Discuss the validity of the following statements.

(1) $\tilde{\alpha}$ is consistent for the coefficient α.

(2) $\tilde{\alpha}$ is subject to higher sampling variability than $\bar{\alpha} = \sum_{t=1}^{T} x_t y_t / (\sum_{t=1}^{T} x_t^2)$ in the limit.

(3) When x_t is independent of $\{e_s, w_s\}$ foe all t and s, the t-ratio based on $\tilde{\alpha}$ converges in distribution to a standard normal variable.

6. Consider the AR(1) process

$$y_t = \alpha y_{t-1} + e_t, \quad (t = 1, 2, ..., T)$$

where y_0 is a constant and $e_t \sim iidN(0, \sigma^2)$.

(1) Devise the LM test for the null hypothesis $H_0 : \alpha = \alpha^0$. Specify carefully how the information matrix is estimated.

(2) Derive the limiting distributions of the LM test for the cases (i) $|\alpha^0| < 1$ and (ii) $\alpha^0 = 1$.

Econometrics Qualifying Exam
The Ohio State University
June 1993

Answer all questions.

1. (40 points)

Discuss the validity of the following statements. Each may be true, false, or uncertain.

(a) The characteristic function of a random variable always exists.

(b) Most statistical tests in applied econometric work are unreliable because the assumption of normally distributed errors is almost never checked.

(c) The fact that the Durbin-Watson statistic is significant does not necessarily mean there is serial correlation in the errors. One has to apply some other tests to reach that conclusion.

(d) In the 2SLS method we should replace the endogenous variables on the right hand side by their fitted values. We should not replace the endogenous variable on the left hand side by its fitted value.

(e) Unit root tests (whether for the AR unit root or the MA unit root) are all biased toward acceptance of the unit root null hypothesis.

(f) Suppose x_t and y_t both have unit roots. When we estimate a VAR model for these two variables, the coefficients of x_{t-1} in the equation for x_t and the coefficient of y_{t-1} in the equation for y_t will both be close to 1.

(g) If x_t and y_t are both $I(1)$, it really does not matter whether we regress y_t on x_t, or x_t on y_t to get an estimate of the cointegration vector and to perform tests for cointegration.

(h) An overdifferenced time series has zero spectral density at zero frequency.

2. (25 points)
Consider the standard regression model

$$y_t = x_t'\beta + u_t, \qquad (t = 1, 2, ..., T)$$

where $\{x_t\}$ is a sequence of constant vectors and $u_t \sim iidN(0, \sigma^2)$. We are interested in testing the null hypothesis $H_0 : \beta = 0$. Assuming that σ^2 is known, formulate the likelihood ratio test for this hypothesis, and derive its exact distribution.

3. (30 points)
Consider the cointegrating regression
(i) $y_t = \alpha'x_t + u_t, \qquad (t = 1, 2, ..., T)$,
where x_t, y_t are $I(1)$ and it is known that

$$u_t = \rho u_{t-1} + e_t$$

$$|\rho| < 1$$

$$e_t \sim iid(0, \sigma^2).$$

We are interested in testing the null $H_0 : \rho = 0$ by using the statistic $t(\hat{\rho}) = T^{1/2}\hat{\rho}$ where $\hat{\rho} = (\sum_{t=2}^{T} \hat{u}_{t-1}^2)^{-1} \sum_{t=2}^{T} \hat{u}_t \hat{u}_{t-1}$ and $\hat{u}_t$ is the OLS residual from the regression equation (i).
(a) Show that $t(\hat{\rho}) \to N(0, 1)$ under the null.
(b) Show that the test $t(\hat{\rho})$ is consistent.

4. (20 points)
An economist ran the multiple regression

$$y = x_1\hat{\alpha}_1 + x_2\hat{\alpha}_2 + \hat{u}.$$

Another economist instead ran the OLS regression

$$y^* = x_2^*\hat{\beta} + \hat{v},$$

where

$$y = x_1\widehat{\gamma}_{OLS} + y^*,$$
$$x_2 = x_1\widehat{\delta}_{OLS} + x_2^*.$$

Determine whether $\widehat{u}$ is equal to $\widehat{v}$ numerically.

5. (20 points)
Consider the linear regression model

$$y_i = \beta x_i + u_i$$

where x is a positive variable and the error terms u_i are i.i.d with zero mean. (There is no intercept term.) Data (x_i, y_i) is available from a large random sample.

(a) What does it mean to say that x is *exogenous*?

(b) Describe carefully, step by step, a method for testing whether x is exogenous in this model. State clearly any additional assumptions that you make.

6. (30 points)
(a) Explain carefully what it means to say that a parameter is *identified* in an econometric model.

(b) Consider the model

$$y_t = \alpha x_t + u_t$$
$$y_t = \beta x_t + v_t$$

where x and y are endogenous (there are no exogenous variables). Suppose it is known that $var(u_t) = var(v_t)$, $cov(u_t, v_t) = 0$ and $\alpha > \beta$. Determine whether α and β are identified.

(c) Discuss briefly whether *identification* of a parameter vector θ is equivalent to the following (considered separately):

(i) The existence of a consistent estimator of θ.

(ii) Nonsingularity of the information matrix for θ.

7. (35 points)
Consider the state-space model

$$y_t = \beta_t x_t + u_t \qquad u_t \sim IN(0, \sigma_u^2),$$

$$\beta_t = \beta_{t-1} + v_t \qquad v_t \sim IN(0, \sigma_v^2).$$

(a) Write down the Kalman filter (KF) equations for the successive estimates of β_t.

(b) Write down the likelihood function. Explain how you would get the ML estimates and how you would handle the initial conditions.

(c) How are the KF equations changed

(i) if the transition equation is changed to

$$\beta_t = \beta_{t-1} + \gamma z_t + v_t.$$

(ii) if the specification of the errors u_t and v_t is changed to

$$u_t = \rho u_{t-1} + e_t$$

$$e_t \sim IN(0, \sigma_e^2)$$

$$|\rho| < 1$$

and

$$v_t = \alpha v_{t-1} + w_t$$

$$w_t \sim IN(0, \sigma_w^2)$$

$$|\alpha| < 1.$$

Also write down the likelihood function for this model.

Econometrics Qualifying Exam
The Ohio State University
September 1992

Answer all questions.

1. (70 points)
Discuss the validity of the following statements.

(a) If an estimator has infinite variance in finite samples, then any inferences based on its asymptotic variance are necessarily unreliable.

(b) Breusch and Pagan's test for heteroskedasticity requires specifying a functional form of heteroskedasticity.

(c) Suppose that the true model is

$$y_t = x'_t\beta + u_t$$

where $y_t, x_t = I(1)$, $u_t \sim iid(0, \sigma^2)$, and x_t is independent of u_t. Considering the nonstationary nature of y_t and x_t, we regressed Δy_t on Δx_t in order to obtain the OLS estimate for the coefficient vector β. Because $\Delta y_t, \Delta x_t$ are $I(0)$, the standard Wald test for the coefficient vector β from this regression has a χ^2 distribution in the limit.

(d) When we estimate the MA(1) model

$$u_t = e_t + \theta e_{t-1}$$

by using the autocorrelation function, we need to restrict the parameter space to $\{\theta \mid |\theta| \le 1\}$ in order to avoid the identification problem. Assume that the process is known to be MA(1).

(e) Aggregating AR processes results in ARMA processes.

96

(f) When the linear regression model

$$y_i = \alpha + x_t'\beta + u_i$$

is estimated by ordinary least squares, the residuals $\hat{u}$ are necessarily orthogonal to the regressors x. It is therefore impossible to tests the classical assumption that x and u are uncorrelated.

(g) Suppose that

$$y_t = \alpha + \beta y_{t-1} + u_t$$

where $u_t \sim iid(0, \sigma^2)$. Although the regressor y_{t-1} is stochastic, the ordinary least squares estimator of β is still unbiased because u_t and y_{t-1} are independent.

2. (30 points)
Consider the two-equation linear model

$$
\begin{aligned}
y_{1,t} &= x_{1,t}'\beta_1 + u_{1,t} \\
y_{2,t} &= x_{2,t}'\beta_2 + u_{2,t}
\end{aligned}
$$

where $x_{1,t}$ and $x_{2,t}$ are k-dimensional vectors of exogenous variables; β_1 and β_2 are k-dimensional vectors of unknown parameters; and the error terms $u_{1,t}$ and $u_{2,t}$ are serially uncorrelated with mean zero and unknown finite second moments $E[u_{i,t}u_{j,t}] = \sigma_{ij}$.

(a) Explain carefully, step by step, how you test the hypothesis $H_0 : \beta_1 = \beta_2$ against the alternative $H_1 : \beta_1 \neq \beta_2$. (You need not give details of standard techniques such as ordinary least squares.)

(b) Suppose that $\beta_1 = \beta_2 \equiv \beta$. Explain carefully, step by step, how you would estimate β in this case.

(c) A commonly used estimation strategy is to first carry out the test in part (a); if H_0 is rejected, estimates of β_1 and β_2 are presented; if H_0 is not rejected, then the model is reestimated with $\beta_1 = \beta_2 = \beta$ and an estimate of β is presented. Discuss any problems that may arise as a result of this two-step approach. (Assume that the set of regressors and the covariance structure of the error terms are correctly specified.)

3. (40 points)

Consider the cointegrating regression

$$y_t = x_t'\beta + u_t, \qquad (t = 1, 2, ..., T),$$

where $x = x_{t-1} + v_t$ and

$$\begin{pmatrix} u_t \\ v_t \end{pmatrix} \sim iidN \left(0, \begin{bmatrix} \sigma_u^2 & 0 \\ 0 & \sigma_v^2 I_m \end{bmatrix} \right).$$

We are interested in testing the null hypothesis $H_0 : \beta = \beta^0$ by using the Wald test.

(a) Show that the limiting distribution of the Wald test is chi-square.

(b) Formulate the local alternatives for the null hypothesis. Is the limiting distribution of the Wald test still chi-square under the local alternatives? Specify what parameters the asymptotic local power of the Wald test depends on.

(c) Discuss the usefulness and limitations of the asymptotic local power in evaluating the finite sample power.

4. (40 points)

Consider the nonlinear regression model

$$y_t = (\alpha_1 + \alpha_2 t)^2 + e_t, \qquad (t = 1, 2, ..., T)$$

where $\{e_t\}$ is a martingale difference sequence with a constant variance σ^2 and satisfies the moment conditions for a martingale central limit theorem.

(a) Derive the limiting distribution of the nonlinear least squares estimators $(\widehat{\alpha}_{1NL}, \widehat{\alpha}_{2NL})$.

(b) Test the null $H_0 : \alpha_2 = 0$ against $H_1 : \alpha_2 \neq 0$ by using the results in part (a).

(c) Alternatively, we may consider the linear regression

$$\begin{aligned} y_t &= \widehat{\gamma}_1 + \widehat{\gamma}_2 t + \widehat{\gamma}_3 t^2 + \widehat{e}_t, \\ \gamma_1 &= \alpha_1^2, \ \gamma_2 = 2\alpha_1\alpha_2, \ \gamma_3 = \alpha_2^2. \end{aligned}$$

Find the limiting distribution of the estimator of α_2 by using this regression, and compare it to that of $\widehat{\alpha}_{2NL}$.

5. (40 points)

Consider the following model for the rate at which used automobiles are scrapped:

(i) The price p of automobiles in working order is assumed to be exponentially distributed with mean γ, i.e., the cumulative distribution function of p is

$$F_p(p) = 1 - e^{-p/\gamma}.$$

(ii) Assume that, in a given period, the probability that an automobile will break down is α.

(iii) If a breakdown occurs, the repair cost c is assumed to be exponentially distributed with mean β, i.e.,

$$F_c(c) = 1 - e^{-c/\beta}.$$

If no breakdown occurs, then $c = 0$.

(iv) The variables p and c are assumed to be statistically independent.

(v) The automobile is scrapped in the current period if and only if $c < p$.

A random sample of size N is drawn from all automobiles that were scrapped during a given period.

(a) What is the log likelihood for this sample, if both c and p are observed?

(b) What is the log likelihood if p is observed but not c?

(c) Explain carefully what it means to say that a parameter (say, θ) in an econometric model is *identified*.

(d) Discuss the identification of the parameters α, β and γ in case (a) and in case (b).

(e) What additional assumptions, if any, are needed for consistency and asymptotic normality of the maximum likelihood estimators of the identified parameters in case (a)?

(f) Suggest some additional data that would allow all parameters of the model to be identified.

Econometrics Qualifying Exam
The Ohio State University
August 1992

Do two questions from Section A and the question in Section B. Each question
is worth equal points. Please show all working so that you can (at least) receive
partial credit. The time limit is 3 hours - no longer. Good Luck!

Section A: 2 hours

1. Consider the following structural equations of a simultaneous equation
system,

$$
\begin{aligned}
y_1 &= \beta_{12}y_2 + u_1 \\
y_2 &= \beta_{21}y_1 + \gamma_{21}x_1 + u_2
\end{aligned}
$$

where y_1 and y_2 are endogenous variables, x_1 is an exogenous variable, u_1 and
u_2 are disturbances that have constant variances σ_1^2 and σ_2^2 and covariance σ_{12}.
Assume n independent observations.

(a) Derive the reduced form for this model.

(b) Use your result from (a) to show that β_{12} is identified but that β_{21} and γ_{21}
are not identified.

(c) Does the OLS estimator of the first equation yield a consistent estimate of
β_{12}?

(d) Does the ILS estimator of the first equation yield a consistent estimate of
β_{12}?

(e) Assuming that u_1 and u_2 are normally distributed, write out the likelihood
function for a sample of n observations. Are the MLE's equivalent to OLS on
both equations when $\sigma_{12} = 0$?

2. Consider the simple linear model, based on N observations,

$$
y_i = \alpha + \beta x_i + u_i
$$

where u_i are i.i.d. $(0, \sigma^2)$.

An econometrician suggests that the following estimator for β will work:

$$\tilde{\beta} = \frac{1}{N-1} \sum_{i=2}^{N} \frac{y_i - y_1}{x_i - x_1}.$$

In what sense is the econometrician correct and in what sense is his suggestion not so good?

3. Suppose that y_i, $i = 1, \ldots, N$ is distributed Poisson with parameter $\lambda_i = \exp(x_i\beta)$ where x_i is some covariate. (Remember that a random variable z is said to be Poisson with parameter λ if it has a (discrete) probability density function

$$f(k) = \Pr(z = k) = \frac{\lambda^k \exp(-\lambda)}{k!}$$

for $k = 0, 1, 2, \ldots$).

(a) Find the log-likelihood for a sample of N observations $\{y_i, x_i\}$ and show that it is globally concave in β.

(b) Find the first order conditions for the MLE of β.

(c) Using (a) and (b) or otherwise sketch a proof that the MLE is consistent.

(d) It is known in general that the MLE is asymptotically normally distributed. Find an expression for the asymptotic variance covariance matrix and a consistent estimator for it.

(e) Find the LM test statistic for testing the hypothesis that $\beta = 0$ using the following information,

$$\sum_{i=1}^{N} x_i = 5$$

$$\sum_{i=1}^{N} x_i^2 = 2.5$$

$$\sum_{i=1}^{N} x_i y_i = 10.$$

(Hint: Use the Hessian form of the variance covariance matrix estimator).

Section B: 1 hour

4. (a) Consider the error correction model,

$$\Delta y_t = \alpha \Delta y_{t-1} + \beta \Delta x_t + \gamma (y - \delta x)_{t-1} + u_t$$

α, β, γ are supposed to measure short-run dynamics and δ the long-run relationship. Explain the Engle-Granger 2-step procedure for the estimation of this model. Give the Bewley representation and explain how all the parameters $(\alpha, \beta, \gamma, \delta)$ are estimated simultaneously.

(b) What are the important lessons for the formulation and estimation of VAR models you learn from the cointegration literature?

Econometrics Qualifying Exam
The Ohio State University
June 1992

Answer all questions.

1. (20 points)
Regarding the augmented Dickey-Fuller test for the null of a unit root with drift, explain
(a) the model and underlying assumptions
(b) how it is derived
(c) why it is a consistent test against the alternative of trend-stationarity.

2. (30 points)
Consider the regression model

$$y_t = \beta t + \alpha x_t + e_t, \qquad (t = 1, ..., T)$$

where $x_t = \mu t + \alpha x_{t-1} + v_t$, $|\alpha| < 1$; and $\{v_t\}$ and $\{e_t\}$ are independent martingale difference sequences with finite variances σ_v^2 and σ_e^2, respectively.
(a) Show that the OLS estimate of α, $\hat{\alpha}_{OLS}$, is invariant to μ in finite samples.
(b) Derive the asymptotic distribution of $\hat{\alpha}_{OLS} - \alpha$.

3. (70 points)
Discuss the validity of each of the following statements.

(a) When a linear regression equation has endogenous explanatory variables, the two stage least squares estimator is preferred to the limited-information maximum likelihood estimator because we cannot be sure that the error terms are normally distributed.

(b) When we are estimating a system of linear equations with exogenous regressors but with contemporaneous correlation among the error terms, we should use Zellner's SUR estimator instead of ordinary least squares in order to get consistent errors of the estimated coefficients.

(c) H. Theil has estimated a model of consumer expenditures (on various categories of goods) using aggregate data from each of a number of different countries, with per capita income as an explanatory variable. Per capita income is subject to measurement errors in this data, so the distance of the country from the equator was used as an instrumental variable, on the grounds that this instrument is exogenous but is correlated with per capita income. However, it is implausible that this instrument would appear as an explanatory variable in any econometric system of structural equations. This is therefore a counter-example to the rule that only the exogenous explanatory variables of the system should be used as instruments in two-stage least squares estimation.

(d) In the regression model

$$y_i = f(x_i) + \varepsilon_i,$$

(where x is a vector of exogenous explanatory variables), nonparametric regression techniques can be used to obtain a consistent estimator of $E[y \mid x]$. But, by definition of the regression function, $f(x) \equiv E[y \mid x]$. Therefore, the problem of specification error does not arise in nonparametric regression.

(e) In the linear regression model with stochastic (but still exogenous) regressors, the variance of the ordinary least squares estimator is $var[\hat{\beta}] = \sigma^2 E[(X'X)^{-1}]$, where X is the matrix of regressors and σ^2 is the error variance. However, the usual estimate of the variance is $s^2(X'X)^{-1}$, which is an unbiased estimator of the *conditional* variance $var[\hat{\beta} \mid X]$. Here are three points of view on this:

(i) The usual estimate is incorrect: it is not an unbiased estimator of the actual variance of $\hat{\beta}$.

(ii) Since we only have sample data on x, the expression $(X'X)^{-1}$ is our best estimate of the true value of $E[(X'X)]^{-1}$.

(iii) The distribution of the exogenous variables is irrelevant to estimation of a regression function, and therefore the conditional variance $var[\hat{\beta} \mid X]$, not $var[\hat{\beta}]$, should be used as a measure of the precision of our estimates.

(f) In the linear regression model

$$y = X\beta + e,$$

where $e \equiv N(0, kI)$ and k is a random variable which is positive a.s., the F-test for the null $H_0 : \beta = \beta^0$ has an F-distribution in finite samples.

(g) We will always reject the null hypothesis in the classical approach to inference, when sample size is large.

4. (40 points)

(a) Explain carefully what it means to say that a parameter (say, β) in an econometric model is *identified*.

(b) Consider the following system of linear simultaneous equations:

$$y_{1,i} = \alpha_1 + \beta_1 x_i + \gamma_1 y_{2,i} + \varepsilon_{1,i}$$
$$y_{2,i} = \alpha_2 + \gamma_2 y_{1,i} + \varepsilon_{2,i}$$

where y_1 and y_2 are endogenous variables, and x is an exogenous variable. The error terms ε_1 and ε_2 have zero means, constant variances σ_{11} and σ_{22} and covariance σ_{12}, and no serial correlation. Determine which of the parameters of this model are identified.

(c) Suppose that, in the model of part (b) of this question, it is known that $\gamma_1 = \gamma_2$. Determine which of the parameters of the model are identified in this case.

(d) Going back to the original model of part (b), with no additional restrictions on the regression parameters, suppose it is known that $\sigma_{12} = 0$. Determine which of the parameters of the model are identified in this new case.

5. (40 points)

Consider the regression equation

(A) $y_1 = Y_2\beta + x_1\delta + u$,

which constitutes a single equation in a simultaneous equations system. The reduced form for this system is written as

$$[y_1 : Y_2] = [x_1 : x_2] \begin{bmatrix} \pi_{11} & \pi_{12} \\ \pi_{21} & \Pi_{22} \end{bmatrix} + [v_1 : V_2].$$

(1) Derive the identifiability relation for equation (A) and state a necessary and sufficient condition for identifying equation (A).

(2) Assume that $T^{-1}x'x$ is nonsingular in the limit, and that $T^{-1}x'V_2 = 0$ as $T \to \infty$. Show that the 2SLS estimate of (β', δ') is consistent if and only if equation (A) is identified.

(Hint: use the augmented reduced form
$[y_1 \, Y_2 \, X_1] = X \begin{bmatrix} \pi_{11} & \pi_{12} & I \\ \pi_{21} & \pi_{22} & 0 \end{bmatrix} + [v_1 \, V_2 : 0])$

ROBERTO S. MARIANO
Fall 1994

COURSE OUTLINE   G

BILITY, STATISTICS, AND REGRESSION ANALYSIS

TALS OF PROBABILITY THEORY - REVIEW

ity Theory
Analysis
bles
Multivariate Probability Distributions
Expectations and Moments

ROBABILITY DISTRIBUTIONS

omial, Multinomial
ic

egative Binomial

mal
t, F-distributions

DISTRIBUTIONS OF FUNCTIONS OF RANDOM VARIABLES

ent-Generating Functions
ariable Technique
Simulations

THEORY AND SAMPLING DISTRIBUTIONS

pling
of sample mean and variance from a normal distribution
of sample mean from a non-normal distribution - analytical,
e Carlo
nvergence and limiting distributions
e numbers
theorems

AL ESTIMATION

finding point estimators - method of moments, generalized method of
ents, maximum likelihood, least squares, Bayesian
point estimators - small samples: bias, precision, sufficiency, completeness.

ECON 6   ROBERTO S. MARIANO
INTRODUCTION TO ECONOMETRICS   SPRING 1995
                                         U

COURSE DESCRIPTION

This course is designed to introduce the student to econometric techniques and their applications in economic and business analysis. The main objective of the course is to train the student in understanding

1. what these econometric techniques are,
2. why they work,
3. how they are implemented through the computer, and
4. how they are applied in practice in economics and business.

The course covers regression analysis, complications in the linear statistical model, simultaneous-equations econometric models, time-series and dynamic economic models, and applications in forecasting and policy analysis.

Microtsp will be used for computer-based calculations.

COURSE TEXT:

Griffiths, Hill and Judge (1993). **Learning and Practicing Econometrics**. J. Wiley.

Quantitative Micro Software (1994). EVIEWS (Microtsp For Windows and the Macintosh) User's Guide and Software Package.

COURSE OUTLINE

I.   THE SIMPLE LINEAR STATISTICAL MODEL (2 weeks; Required Readings: Chapters 5, 6, 7, 8 of Course Text)

Basic concepts and model
Least squares and maximum likelihood estimation
Sampling characteristics and properties of estimators
Interval estimation, hypothesis testing, prediction
R^2, coefficient of determination
Choice of functional forms
Computer implementation and reporting regression results
Numerical examples and practical applications

II. **THE GENERAL LINEAR STATISTICAL MODEL** (2 weeks; Required
Readings: Chapters 9, 10, 11 of Course Text)

Multiple linear regression model
Review of basic matrix algebra
Least squares estimators and their sampling properties
Using Microtsp
Confidence intervals
Testing hypotheses -- for a single coefficient and for some
  coefficients
ANOVA tests for linear restrictions
Testing a linear versus a log-linear model
Forecasting
Examples and applications in economics and business

III. **COMPLICATIONS IN THE GENERAL LINEAR MODEL** (2 weeks;
Required Readings: Chapters 12, 13, 14 of Course Text)

Dummy variables and varying coefficient models
Multicollinearity
Models with random regressors
Large-sample behavior of least squares
Instrumental variable estimation
Applications

IV. **LINEAR MODELS WITH A GENERAL ERROR STRUCTURE** (2 weeks;
Required Readings: Chapters 15, 16 of Course Text)

Properties of least squares in this general case
Generalized least-squares procedures
Heteroskedastic errors -- detection, estimation, computer implementation
Autocorrelated errors -- detection, estimation, computer implementation
Forecasting
Practical applications

V. **SIMULTANEOUS-EQUATIONS ECONOMETRIC MODELS** (3 weeks;
Required Readings: Chapters 17, 18, 19 of Course Text)

Seemingly unrelated regressions
Examples of simultaneous-equations models
Structural and reduced-form equations
Identification
Estimation by two-stage least-squares and instrumental-variable methods
Validation and applications through model simulations
Computer implementation and practical examples through TSP

VI. **TIME-SERIES AND DYNAMIC EC**
Readings: Chapters 20, 21 of Cour

Univariate time-series analysis and fo
Distributed lag models
Vector autoregressive processes
Computer implementation and examp

COURSE REQUIR

The final grade for the course will be based on the fol

1. Mid-term exam 1, covering Topics I-
   of final grade);

2. Mid-term exam 2, covering Topics II
   of final grade);

3. A final exam, covering Topics IV-VI
   University calendar for final exams (4

All mid-term and final exams are closed books and

Homework exercises will be assigned throughout th
be teaching rather than grading devices. Students ar
to discuss homework problems and submit homework
be submitted on specified due dates; late submission:
of homework exercises will be considered in determ

OFFICE HO

Roberto S. Mariano   Tuesday & Thursday;

ECON 705
Econometrics

PR

I. **FUNDA**

Basic Pr
Combina
Random
Univaria
Mathema

II. **SPECIA**

Bernoulli
Hyperge
Poisson
Geometri
Gamma
Gaussian
Chi-squa

III. **DERIVI**

Use of M
Change-o
Monte Ca

IV. **SAMPLI**

Random s
Distributi
Distributi
  M
Stochastic
Laws of l
Central li

V. **STATIST**

Methods f
  mo
Properties

efficiency

Properties of point estimators - large samples: consistency, limiting distribution, asymptotic efficiency

Interval estimation

VI. HYPOTHESIS TESTING

Elements of a statistical test, critical region, size of a test, power of a test

Unbiased, consistent, similar tests

Likelihood ratio, Wald, and Lagrange multiplier tests: definitions, geometric interpretation

Asymptotic tests

Tests based on comparisons of alternative estimators

Tests based on conditional moment restrictions

Finite-sample properties of tests - equivalence of LR, W, LM tests in quadratic likelihood functions, optimality of certain tests in terms of highest power within a class of tests

Large-sample properties of tests

Examples and economic applications

VII. BAYESIAN INFERENCE

Basic notions: prior and posterior distributions

Bayesian inference for the mean of a normal distribution with known variance

Bayesian point estimators

Bayesian inference for the mean and variance of a normal distribution

VIII. GENERAL LINEAR STATISTICAL MODEL

Basic assumptions and the data generating process

Simple linear regression

Multiple linear regression

Components of the model and classical assumptions

Least squares estimation

Statistical properties of least squares estimators under normal and non-normal cases; Gauss-Markov theorem

Restricted least squares

Least squares and maximum likelihood estimation

Applications in economic analysis

Interval estimation

Prediction and prediction intervals

Tests of hypotheses about regression coefficients

Measuring goodness of fit of estimated regression line

Exact probability distributions of least squares estimators: analytical derivation and Monte Carlo simulation

Large-sample asymptotic distribution of least squares estimators

Functional forms in regression

LECTURE HOURS: TUESDAYS & THURSDAYS
10:30 - 12:00, 395 McNeil

TEXT: Richard Larsen and Morris Marx. **Introduction to Mathematical Statistics and Its Applications, Second Edition.** Prentice Hall, 1986.

ADDITIONAL REFERENCES

Bickel, Peter J. and Kjell A. Doksum. **Mathematical Statistics: Basic Ideas and Selected Topics.** Holden Day, 1977.

Cox, David R. and D.V. Hinkley. **Theoretical Statistics.** Chapman and Hall, 1979.

Freund, John E. and Ronald E. Walpole **Mathematical Statistics, Fifth Edition.** Prentice-Hall, 1992.

Goldberger, Arthur S. **A Course in Econometrics.** Harvard University Press, 1991.

Greene, William H. **Econometric Analysis, Second Edition.** Macmillan, 1993.

Hoel, Paul G. **Introduction to Mathematical Statistics, Fifth Edition.** J. Wiley, 1984.

Hoel, P.G., S.C. Port, and C.J. Stone. **Introduction to Probability Theory.** Houghton Mifflin, 1972.

Hoel, P.G., S.C. Port, and C.J. Stone. **Introduction to Statistical Theory.** Houghton Mifflin, 1972.

*Hogg, Robert V. and Allen T. Craig. **Introduction to Mathematical Statistics, Fourth Edition.** Macmillan, 1978.

Judge, George et.al. **Introduction to the Theory and Practice of Econometrics, Second Edition.** J. Wiley 1988.

Kelejian, Harry H. and Wallace E. Oates. **Introduction to Econometrics - Principles and Applications, Third Edition.** Harper & Row, 1989.

Lehman, Erich L. **Theory of Point Estimation.** J. Wiley, 1983.

Lehman, Erich L. **Testing Statistical Hypotheses, Second Edition.** J. Wiley, 1986.

Mood, Alexander J., Franklin A. Graybill, and Duane C. Boes. **Introduction to the Theory of Statistics, Third Edition.** McGraw-Hill, 1974.

COURSE REQUIREMENTS

The final grade for the course will be based on two mid-term exams, a final exam, and submission of solutions to homework exercises.

Homework exercises will be assigned throughout the course. Students are required to solve these exercises and submit solutions on time. These exercises are intended to be teaching rather than grading devices -- so students are encouraged to form study groups (of two or three) to discuss the homework problems and submit solutions as a team. Submitted solutions will not be graded but timeliness of submissions will be duly recorded.

Mid-term and final exams are <u>closed-book</u> and <u>closed-notes</u>, with the following schedule.

	% of Final Grade	Date	Coverage
Mid-term Exam 1	30%	Oct. 11	Topics II-IV
Mid-term Exam 2	30%	Nov. 10	Topics IV-VI
Final Exam	40%	Dec. 15-23	Topics V-VII

The mid-term exams will be given in class. The final exam will be given during the Final Examination period as scheduled by the University Registrar.

Economics D80-3   Bruce Meyer
Spring 1993

Northwestern University G
GRADUATE ECONOMETRICS III

ADMINISTRATIVE DETAILS:

1. Your grade will be based on your performance on approximately 8 problem sets (15%), the
    midterm exam (35%), and the final exam (50%). The midterm is on Monday, May 10
    during class and the final is on Monday, June 7, from 9-11.

2. The T.A. for this course is Katherine Czukas. She will meet with you on Friday from 9-11 in
    AAH G-192.

3. My office hours are Tuesday 1-3, and my office is AAH G-242.

PREREQUISITES: Economics D80-1,2.

COURSE DESCRIPTION: This course covers a wide variety of econometric tools needed for writing
and understanding empirical work in economics.

TEXTS:

Required:

J. Johnston, Econometric Methods, McGraw Hill, 1984. (Cited as "Johnston" below.)

William H. Greene, Econometric Analysis, Second Edition, Macmillan, 1993. (Cited as "Greene"
below.)

Takeshi Amemiya, Advanced Econometrics, Harvard University Press, 1985.   (Cited
as "Amemiya" below.)

Other Helpful Texts:

Zvi Griliches and Michael D. Intriligator, Handbook of Econometrics, North-Holland, 1983.
(Especially volumes I and II.)

George G. Judge, et al., The Theory and Practice of Econometrics, Second Edition, John Wiley &
Sons, 1985.

G. S. Maddala, Limited-Dependent and Qualitative Variables in Econometrics, Cambridge University
Press, 1983.

COURSE OUTLINE:

(1) Panel Data (3 lectures): error components models, random effects, fixed effects, within versus
between, quasi-differences, effects of relative size of variance components, asymptotics, efficiency,
testing, specification testing, Hausman-Taylor estimation.

>   Johnston, 10.3.
>   Greene, Chapter 16.
>   Amemiya, 6.6.
>   Jerry Hausman and William Taylor (1981): "Panel Data and Unobservable Individual
>   Effects," Econometrica 49, pp. 1377-1398.

(2) Data Problems (1 lecture): measurement error bias in the univariate case, multivariate case and
panel data, missing data and proxy variables, solutions to measurement error problem using prior
information, ML.

Johnston, 10.6.
Greene, 9.3-9.5.
Zvi Griliches and Jerry Hausman (1986): "Measurement Error in Panel Data," Journal of Econometrics, pp. 93-118.

(3) Introduction to Instrumental Variables (1 lecture): IV as a solution to the measurement error problem, simple cases such as repeated observations, requirements on instruments.

(4) Simultaneous Equations, System Estimation and IV (4 lectures): SUR, the general form of the simultaneous equations problem, two equation examples using supply and demand, ILS, uses of other information, identification, just identification versus overidentification, estimation of simultaneous equations, general exposition of IV, 2SLS, 3SLS, FIML, testing.

Johnston, Chapter 11.
Jerry Hausman, Chapter 7 in Handbook of Econometrics.
Greene, Chapters 17 and 20.
Amemiya, Chapter 7.

(5) Nonlinear Models (4 lectures): consistency and asymptotic normality of nonlinear least squares, similarity to least squares with derivatives, nonlinear optimization approaches, one-step estimates, maximum likelihood, testing in nonlinear models, nonlinear simultaneous equations, generalized method of moments.

Amemiya, Chapters 4 and 8.
Takeshi Amemiya, Chapter 6 in Handbook of Econometrics.
Greene, Chapters 11 and 12
Lars Hansen (1982): "Large Sample Properties of Generalized Method of Moments Estimators," Econometrica, pp. 1029-1054.

(6) Discrete Choice Models (2 lectures): difficulties with OLS, probit, logit, NLLS versus ML, multinomial models, ordered models.

Amemiya, Chapter 9.
Greene, Chapter 21.

(7) Limited Dependent Variable and Duration Models (2 lectures): bias of OLS, tobit models, censoring or truncation, selection models, duration models.

Amemiya, Chapters 10 and 11.
Greene, Chapter 22.

Problem Set 1
Economics D80-3
3/31/93

1. You have a sample of data for which you want to estimate the model

$y_{it} = x'_{it}\beta + \lambda_t + \epsilon_{it}$, where $i = 1, 2, \ldots, N_t$, and $t = 1, 2, \ldots, T$. Note that the number of

observations per time period is not identical. This type of situation is sometimes called the

"unbalanced" data case.

(i)   Derive formulae for unbiased estimates of the variance components, σ_λ^2 and σ_ϵ^2.

(ii)   Derive the form of the quasi-differenced model that can be easily used to obtain GLS estimates.

2.

(i)   For the regression model $y = X\beta + u$, X a $T \times k$ matrix, $Euu' = \Omega \neq \sigma^2 I$, show that GLS and OLS are equally efficient if and only if $\Omega X = X\Gamma$, where Γ is a $k \times k$ matrix of full rank.

(ii)   Show that OLS estimates on deviations from time means for the model of problem 1 are as efficient as GLS estimates on the deviations from time means. Note that the covariance matrix of the errors is singular so that you will need to use a generalized inverse.

Problem Set 2
Economics D80-3
4/07/93

1.   Consider writing the 2 error components model (2ECM) as

$y_{it} = (x_{it} - x_{i.})'\beta + x_{i.}'\delta + \mu_i + \epsilon_{it}$, where $i = 1, 2, \ldots, N$, and $t = 1, 2, \ldots, T$. Construct a Wald test of the hypothesis $H_o: \beta = \delta$. Show that this test is the same as the Specification Test which compares Fixed Effects and GLS estimates of β from the usual way of writing the 2ECM.

2.   Consider the 3 error components model from class:

$y_{it} = x_{it}'\beta + u_{it}$
$u_{it} = \mu_i + \lambda_t + e_{it}, \quad or$
$y_{it} = x_{it}'\beta + \mu_i + \lambda_t + e_{it}$
$i = 1, 2, \ldots, N$
$t = 1, 2, \ldots, T$,

where the stochastic assumptions on error components are: $\{\mu_i\}$, $\{\lambda_t\}$, $\{\epsilon_{it}\}$ iid, mean zero, mutually independent with

$E\mu_i^2 = \sigma_\mu^2$, $E\lambda_t^2 = \sigma_\lambda^2$, $Ee_{it}^2 = \sigma_e^2$.

114

For simplicity, also assume x_{it} is nonstochastic and $\sum_i \sum_t x_{it} = 0$.

(a)   Show that the difference between the Fixed Effects and GLS covariance matrices for β is a positive semi-definite matrix.

(b)   Now assume that N and T both go to infinity in such a way that $N = aT$, for some positive constant a. Compare the efficiency of Fixed Effects and GLS in this case (hint: Fixed Effects and GLS are equally efficient). You may need to make plausible assumptions about X'X. Will estimates of μ_i and λ_t be consistent?

(c)   How would your answer to (b) change if N were fixed and T went to infinity? You may need to make additional assumptions about X'AX, and X'BX where $A = I_N \otimes J_T$ and $B = J_N \otimes I_T$.

Problem Set 3
Economics D80-3
4/14/93

1.   Derive equations (14) and (15) in Griliches and Hausman (1986).

2.   Suppose you estimate a wage equation for males born in the 1910's and 1920's and you think that being a veteran affects wages so you include a dummy variable for veteran status on the right-hand side. For example, you estimate $w_i = v_i \beta + x_i' \delta + \epsilon_i$, where w_i is the wage in 1970 for person i, $v_i = 1$ if person i is a veteran, and 0 otherwise, x_i is a set of additional variables affecting wages for person i, and $i = 1, \ldots, N$. You also believe that veteran status is correlated with the unobservable fitness of individuals because of the armed services selection procedure and you believe that fitness affects wages. In addition, you know each person's year and calendar quarter of birth.

(i)   Men were drafted in WWII not by lottery number, but by date of birth. Men born January 1 were considered first, then those born January 2 and so on. In most years, most people born in the later months were not even considered for induction in the armed forces. Describe how you might consistently estimate the wage equation, and why it works.

115

4

(ii)   Suppose you think that years of education affects wages and that being a veteran increases the years of education completed because the government provides eductional subsidies to veterans that are not available to other individuals. Explain whether or not you still can consistently estimate the coefficient on veteran status in the wage equation.

---

3.   Consider the permanent income model of consumption, $C_{it} = \beta Y_i^* + \epsilon_{it}$, where $Y_{it} = Y_i^* + \nu_{it}$, $i = 1, 2, \ldots, N$, $t = 1, 2, \ldots, T$, C_{it} and Y_{it} are measured consumption and measured income for household i in period t and Y_i^* is unmeasured "permanent" income. Some possible estimators of β are (1) OLS regression of C_{it} on Y_{it} for $i = 1, 2, \ldots, N$, and $t = 1$, $2, \ldots T$, (2) OLS regression of $C_{i.}$ on $Y_{i.}$ for $i = 1, 2, \ldots, N$, where $C_{i.}$ and $Y_{i.}$ are the mean over all t of C_{it} and Y_{it}, and (3) IV estimation of $C_{it} = \beta Y_{it} + \epsilon_{it}$ using $\tilde{Y}_{it} = \frac{\sum_{s \neq t} Y_{is}}{T-1}$ as the instrument. Derive the properties (the plim and, when the estimator is consistent, the asymptotic distribution) of estimators (1) through (3) as N goes to infinity assuming $E(\nu_{it}) = 0$ and $E(\nu_{it} \nu_{ir}) = 0$.

---

4.   Suppose you have the model $y_t = x_t' \beta + \epsilon_t$, $t = 1, 2, \ldots, T$ where $E\epsilon\epsilon' = \sigma^2 I$, x_t' is a k dimensional vector and $\text{plim}(x'\epsilon/T) = 0$ and $\text{plim}(x'z/T)$ has column rank k.

(i)   Show that $\hat{\beta}_{IV} = (x' P_z x)^{-1} x' P_z y$ is consistent but inefficient here relative to OLS. $P_z = z(z'z)^{-1}z'$.

(ii)   Now suppose that we are uncertain that $\text{plim}(x'\epsilon/T)$ is in fact 0, but we are confident that $\text{plim}(z'\epsilon/T) = 0$ and $\text{plim}(x'z/T)$ exists and has column rank k. Suggest a test for the null hypothesis that $\text{plim}(x'\epsilon/T) = 0$.

116

Problem Set 4
Economics D80-3
4/21/93

1. Consider the consumption function $C_t = a_1 + a_2 Y_t + \epsilon_t$. Consider Haavelmo's approach to the problem. He treated income as endogenous, being determined through the identity $Y_t = C_t + Z_t$ where $Z_t = I_t + G_t$ was treated as an exogenous variable. I_t is investment and G_t is government spending. Assume homoskedasticity and no serial correlation for ϵ_t.

(i) Subtract off means from all the variables to make things simpler, and then compute plim a_2 from OLS. What is the direction of the bias, and what is the intuition for this result?

(ii) Calculate the two reduced from equations (for C_t and Y_t) and find a_2 by indirect least squares (ILS). Can one estimate a_2 using Z_t or its components as instruments? Does I_t seem like a good instrument to use? Hint: Think of the accelerator model of investment.

(iii) Given the reduced form estimates calculate the asymptotic variance of the ILS or IV estimate of a_2. Be sure to note the relationship between the reduced form errors.

(iv) Is ILS or IV unbiased here in finite samples?

2. Consider the system of equations:

$$\beta_{11} y_1 + \beta_{12} y_2 + \gamma_{11} x_1 + \gamma_{12} x_2 = u_1$$
$$\beta_{21} y_1 + \beta_{22} y_2 + \gamma_{21} x_1 + \gamma_{22} x_2 = u_2$$

where y_i, x_i, and u_i, $i = 1,2$ are $T \times 1$ vectors and the x's and u's are uncorrelated.

(i) Suppose a priori restrictions are $\gamma_{12} = 0$, $\gamma_{21} = 0$. In general, is the first equation identified? What happens if $\gamma_{22} = 0$? Discuss both the rank and order conditions in both situations. Then if γ_{22} does not equal zero, explicitly compute the parameters of the structural first equation from the parameters of the reduced form.

(ii) Now consider a priori restrictions $\gamma_{11} = 0$, $\gamma_{12} = 0$ and discuss identification of both equations. Choosing the normalization $\beta_{11} = 1$, calculate β_{12} in terms of the reduced form coefficients. If one were to estimate the reduced form coefficients and then use them to solve for a unique β_{12} what restriction might one want to impose when estimating the reduced form equations? Could we have used a subset of the restrictions to identify the structural parameters of the first equation?

117

1. Suppose you have the simultaneous equations model

   (I) $\quad y_t = \beta_{11}P_t + \epsilon_{1t}$

   (II) $\quad P_t = \beta_{21}y_t + \gamma_{21}z_{1t} + \gamma_{22}z_{2t} + \epsilon_{2t}$

   where $t = 1, 2, \ldots, T$, and z_{1t} and z_{2t} are uncorrelated with ϵ_{1t} and ϵ_{2t}.

   (i) Derive the reduced form equations for y_t and P_t.

   (ii) What is the bias of the estimator for β_{11} obtained from OLS applied to (I).

   (iii) Write out the indirect least squares estimators for β_{11} and derive their asymptotic properties.

   (iv) Write out the 2SLS estimator for β_{11} and compare its asymptotic variance to that of an optimal weighted average of the indirect least squares estimators from (iii).

2. Consider the Hausman and Taylor (1981) model:

   $y_{it} = x_{it}'\beta + z_i'\gamma + \mu_i + \epsilon_{it},\ i = 1, 2, \ldots, N,\ t = 1, 2, \ldots, T,\qquad x_{it}' = (x_{1it}'\ x_{2it}')$ and $z_i' = (z_{1i}'\ z_{2i}')$ where the dimensions of the vectors x_{1it}, x_{2it}, z_{1i} and z_{2i} are k_1, k_2, g_1, and g_2 respectively, x_{1it} and z_{1i} are uncorrelated with μ_i but x_{2it} and z_{2i} are correlated with μ_i. Give conditions under which γ can be consistently estimated and describe how to do it.

118

7

3.   Consider the model

$Q_t = \beta_1 P_t + \beta_2 W_t + Z_{1t}'\gamma + u_t$, $t=1, 2, \ldots, T$.

where P and W are endogenous and Z_1 is exogenous. Assume further that the first s

observations on W_t are all 0. Discuss the large sample properties of each of the following

three estimators, i.e. calculate their probability limits and discuss their asymptotic efficiency.

Assume you have another set of exogenous variables Z_2 and consider both the cases where

s below is a fixed number and when it is a constant fraction of T.

(a)   Regress P_t on all predetermined variables to form $\hat{P}_t$; regress only the last T-s values

of W_t on the last T-s ovservations of the predetermined variables to form

$\hat{W} = (0, \ldots, 0, \hat{W}_{s+1}, \ldots, \hat{W}_T)$. Then use OLS on (i).

(b)   Form $\hat{P}_t$ as in (a), but now regress all T values of W_t on the predetermined variables

and use this $\hat{W}_t^*$ in equation (i) and run OLS.

(c)   Again form $\hat{P}_t$ in the same way and form $\hat{W}_t^*$ as in (b). Now impose the zero

restrictions on the first s values of W_t so that $\hat{W}_t^{**} = (0, \ldots, 0, \hat{W}_{s+1}^*, \ldots, \hat{W}_T^*)$.

Use $\hat{W}_t^{**}$ in equation (i) and run OLS.

119

1. Suppose you have the nonlinear specification $y_i = \exp\{x_i'\beta\} + \epsilon_i$, where $E\epsilon_i = 0$, $V\epsilon_i = \sigma^2$.

   (i) Write out the form of the Newton-Raphson and the Gauss-Newton iterations. For the Gauss-Newton iteration see Amemiya (1985).

   (ii) Verify the asymptotic relationship between the $T^{-1}\sum_t \frac{\partial f_t}{\partial \beta} \frac{\partial f_t}{\partial \beta'}$ and $T^{-1}\frac{\partial^2 S_T}{\partial \beta \partial \beta'}$, by calculating the plims when computed at $\hat{\beta}$, the estimator which minimizes the sum of squares.

   (iii) Suppose that the specification arises from an underlying Poisson model so that $V(\epsilon_i) = \exp\{x_i'\beta\}$. Describe the properties of NLLS with this heteroskedasticity. How might one do Weighted NLLS (WNLLS) to account for the heteroskedasticity and what would be the steps of the iterative process?

2.

   (i) Suppose you have the model $y_{1i} = \beta_1 \log y_{2i} + \gamma_1 z_{1i} + \epsilon_{1i}$, where y_{2i} is correlated with ϵ_{1i}, but you have z_{2i} which is uncorrelated with ϵ_{1i} and $y_{2i} = \gamma_2 z_{2i} + \epsilon_{2i}$. Describe precisely an estimator for β_1 and show that it is consistent.

   (ii) Derive the properties of repeated least squares where you run OLS on the equation $y_{1i} = \beta_1 \log \hat{y}_{2i} + \gamma_1 z_{1i} + \eta_i$, where $\hat{y}_{2i}$ equals $P_z y_2$ and $z = [\ z_1\ \ z_2\ ]$.

3. Suppose you have the linear model $y_i = \beta_0 + \beta_1 x_i^* + \beta_2 (x_i^*)^2 + \beta_3 (x_i^*)^3 + \epsilon_i$, but you do not observe x_i^*, rather you observe $x_i = x_i^* + v_i$, where v_i is mean zero and independent of ϵ_i and x_i^*. Also suppose you have a z_i that is correlated with x_i^*, but is independent of ϵ_i.

   (i) Show that using z_i, its square and cube as instruments will not produce consistent estimates of the β's.

   (ii) Now consider the case where $\beta_3 = 0$. Show that in this very special case you can consistently estimate the β's using z_i and its square as instruments. You will need a slightly different approach to estimate β_0.

120

1. Consider the binary choice model $P(y_i = 1) = F(x_i'\beta)$ for some cumulative distribution

    function F.

(i)   If the true F is a cumulative standard normal and you use logit to estimate β what

           are the properties of your estimator? Hint: is the model Fisher consistent?

(ii)   Suppose the binary choice problem arises from an underlying model $y_i^* = x_i'\beta + \epsilon_i$,

           $y_i = 1$ if $y_i^* > 0$ and $y_i = 0$ otherwise, where ϵ_i is normally distributed, but is

           heteroskedastic, i.e. $Var(\epsilon_i | x_i)$ is not a constant. What are the properties of probit

           maximum likelihood here?

(iii)   Suppose ϵ_i in part (ii) is not heteroskedastic, but is serially correlated. What are the

           properties of probit maximum likelihood now?

2. Suppose the benefit to person i of cheating on his income tax is $x_i'\beta + \epsilon_i$, where ϵ_i is

    normally distributed and independent of x_i. Let the cost be a constant C which is unknown

    but is the same for all people. Assume a person decides to cheat if the benefits exceed the

    costs. Furthermore, assume that the IRS uses certain variables z_i (some of which may be in

    x_i) to determine whether or not to audit a return. As a result, a person is caught <u>conditional</u>

    on cheating if and only if $z_i'\gamma + \eta_i > 0$, where η_i is normally distributed and independent of ϵ_i,

    z_i, and x_i. Suppose you have a sample of N people that includes for each person an

    indicator for whether or not he is caught for income tax evasion, as well as x_i and z_i.

    (a)   Write out the likelihood function for the data.

    (b)   Explain how to estimate β and γ up to scale using nonlinear weighted least squares.

    (c)   Are β and γ identified up to scale if $x_i = z_i$ for all i? Explain.

3. Suppose $y_{ij}^* = x_{ij}'\beta_j + \epsilon_{ij}$, where $i = 1,...,N$ and $j = 1,2$. Assume that ϵ_{i1} and ϵ_{i2} are iid

    logistic random variables that are mutually independent. Also assume that you only observe

    x_{ij} and y_{ij} where $y_{ij} = 1$ if y_{ij}^* is positive and $y_{ij} = 0$ otherwise.

121

(a) Write out the likelihood function for the data and explain how you would estimate β_1 and β_2.

(b) Assume that $\beta = \beta_1 = \beta_2$. Suppose that for budgetary reasons the sampling rate in the second period is cut to half that in the first period, i.e. $i = 1,\ldots,N$ for $j = 1$ and $i = 1,\ldots,N/2$ for $j = 2$. How would you efficiently estimate β?

(c) Again assume that $\beta = \beta_1 = \beta_2$, but now also assume that $y^*_{ij} = x_{ij}'\beta + \alpha_i + \epsilon_{ij}$. Suppose that you do not observe α_i but estimate it by including a dummy variable for each i. What are the properties of this procedure?

(d) Under the assumptions of (c), consider the probability that $y_{i1} = 1$ given that $y_{i1} + y_{i2} = 1$. Does this suggest an estimation method with better properties than those in (c)? Explain.

Problem Set 8
Economics D80-3
5/26/93

1. You have a linear model $y_i = x_i'\beta + \epsilon_i$ where ϵ_i is distributed $N(0, \sigma^2)$. However, you only observe the data if $y_i > c$.

(i) Calculate the conditional expectation of y_i given x_i for $y_i > c$.

(ii) Write down the likelihood function for the sample.

(iii) Demonstrate Fisher consistency for the maximum likelihood estimates of β and σ^2.

2. Suppose a researcher wants to predict whether or not a household with a given set of characteristics purchases a car during a particular period of time. She has available data on a random set of households which includes various characteristics associated with each household and a discrete random variable indicating whether the household purchased a car. Assume the household buys a car when $y_i > 0$, with $y_i = x_i'\beta + u_i$ and u_i distributed uniformly on the interval $(-1,1)$. Let $\delta_i = 1$ if the household purchases a car and $\delta_i = 0$ otherwise. Assume that the absolute value of $x_i'\beta < 1$ for all i.

(i) Let $P_i = \Pr(\delta_i = 1$ given $x_i)$. Show that $P_i = (1 + x_i'\beta)/2$. Also show that δ_i is described by the linear probability model $\delta_i = P_i + \epsilon_i$, where $E(\epsilon_i$ given $x_i) = 0$.

(ii) Show that $\mathrm{Var}(\epsilon_i) = P_i(1-P_i)$ and explain why this implies the presence of heteroskedasticity.

(iii) Explain all of the steps in a procedure to efficiently estimate β.

122

3. Suppose your data consist of income and dollar purchases of automobiles for a large number of individuals obtained from a nationwide survey of automobile dealers. Assume that your observations include only those individuals making positive purchases and that expenditures greater than $20,000 are recorded as $20,000. Further assume that underlying latent expenditures are determined by the relationship $y_i^* = \beta x_i + \epsilon_i$, where y_i^* is desired purchases and x_i is income.

(a) Is the OLS estimator of the effect of income on asset purchases unbiased? Graph the relationships and explain any biases.

(b) Write out the likelihood function for the data under the assumption that ϵ_i is normally distributed.

(c) Suppose that instead of reporting expenditures continuously between $0 and $20,000, expenditures are only reported as being in one of three categories: $0-10,000, $10,000-20,000, $20,000 or more. Write out the likelihood function in this case under the assumption that ϵ_i is normally distributed.

Problem Set 8
Economics D80-3
5/26/93

1. You have a linear model $y_i = x_i'\beta + \epsilon_i$ where ϵ_i is distributed $N(0, \sigma^2)$. However, you only observe the data if $y_i > c$.

(i) Calculate the conditional expectation of y_i given x_i for $y_i > c$.

(ii) Write down the likelihood function for the sample.

(iii) Demonstrate Fisher consistency for the maximum likelihood estimates of β and σ^2.

2. Suppose a researcher wants to predict whether or not a household with a given set of characteristics purchases a car during a particular period of time. She has available data on a random set of households which includes various characteristics associated with each household and a discrete random variable indicating whether the household purchased a car. Assume the household buys a car when $y_i > 0$, with $y_i = x_i'\beta + u_i$ and u_i distributed

123

12

uniformly on the interval $(-1,1)$. Let $\delta_i = 1$ if the household purchases a car and $\delta_i = 0$ otherwise. Assume that the absolute value of $x_i'\beta < 1$ for all i.

(i)   Let $P_i = Pr(\delta_i = 1$ given $x_i)$. Show that $P_i = (1 + x_i'\beta)/2$. Also show that δ_i is described by the linear probability model $\delta_i = P_i + \epsilon_i$, where $E(\epsilon_i$ given $x_i) = 0$.

(ii)   Show that $Var(\epsilon_i) = P_i(1-P_i)$ and explain why this implies the presence of heteroskedasticity.

(iii)   Explain all of the steps in a procedure to efficiently estimate β.

3.   Suppose your data consist of income and dollar purchases of automobiles for a large number of individuals obtained from a nationwide survey of automobile dealers. Assume that your observations include only those individuals making positive purchases and that expenditures greater than \$20,000 are recorded as \$20,000. Further assume that underlying latent expenditures are determined by the relationship $y_i^* = \beta x_i + \epsilon_i$, where y_i^* is desired purchases and x_i is income.

(a)   Is the OLS estimator of the effect of income on asset purchases unbiased? Graph the relationships and explain any biases.

(b)   Write out the likelihood function for the data under the assumption that ϵ_i is normally distributed.

(c)   Suppose that instead of reporting expenditures continuously between \$0 and \$20,000, expenditures are only reported as being in one of three categories: \$0-10,000, \$10,000-20,000, \$20,000 or more. Write out the likelihood function in this case under the assumption that ϵ_i is normally distributed.

124

You have until 10:50. Answer all of the questions. Show your work and briefly justify your

conclusions.

1.   Consider the following system of equations: (i) $y_{1i} = \beta_{12}y_{2i} + \gamma_{11}x_{1i} + \gamma_{12}x_{2i} + \epsilon_{1i}$
(ii) $y_{2i} = \beta_{21}y_{1i} + \gamma_{21}x_{1i} + \epsilon_{2i}$,

where $i = 1,...,N$, x_{ji} is independent of ϵ_{kl} for all i,j,k,l, and $E[\epsilon_{1i}\epsilon_{2i}] \neq 0$.

(a) (15 points) Discuss identification and efficient estimation (if possible) of both equations.

(b) (15 points) Now suppose you know that $\gamma_{11} - \gamma_{21} = 0$. Discuss identification and
efficient estimation (if possible) of both equations.

2.   Suppose you have the panel data model $y_{it} = \beta x_{it} + u_{it}$ where $u_{it} = \mu_i + \lambda_t + \epsilon_{it}$ and
$i = 1,...,N$, $t = 1,...T$.

(a) (5 points) Write out the form of the covariance matrix for the errors u.

(b) (15 points) Suppose x_{it} is correlated with λ_t but uncorrelated with μ_i. Discuss consistent
and efficient estimation methods.

3.   Suppose you know that the true relationship you are modeling is $y_{it} = \beta x_{it} + \epsilon_{it}$, where
$i = 1,...,N$ and $t = 1,...,4$. However, you do not observe x_{it}, rather you observe $z_{it} = x_{it} + \eta_{it}$
$+ \eta_{i,t-1}$. Also assume that $x_{it} = x_i + \aleph_{it}$ and that η_{it} and $\aleph_{it}$ are i.i.d. across i and t and
independent of each other and all other variables.

(a) (10 points) What is the plim of the OLS estimator of β?

125

14

(b) (15 points) Discuss consistent and efficient estimation methods.

4. Suppose you estimate the equation $y_i = \beta x_i + \epsilon_i$ using instrumental variables z_{1i} and z_{2i} because you think x is correlated with ϵ.

(a) (7 points) Write out a test for whether $\beta = 4$.

(b) (10 points) Suppose you also obtain another estimate of β, call it $\tilde{\beta}$ by only using only z_1 as an instrument for x. Discuss a test which compares $\tilde{\beta}$ to the 2SLS estimate of β.

(c) (8 points) Discuss a test of overidentifying restrictions here.

University of Pennsylvania

ECON 6
INTRODUCTION TO ECONOMETRICS

ROBERTO S. MARIANO
SPRING 1995
U

COURSE DESCRIPTION

This course is designed to introduce the student to econometric techniques and their applications in economic and business analysis. The main objective of the course is to train the student in understanding

1. what these econometric techniques are,
2. why they work,
3. how they are implemented through the computer, and
4. how they are applied in practice in economics and business.

The course covers regression analysis, complications in the linear statistical model, simultaneous-equations econometric models, time-series and dynamic economic models, and applications in forecasting and policy analysis.

Microtsp will be used for computer-based calculations.

COURSE TEXT:

Griffiths, Hill and Judge (1993). **Learning and Practicing Econometrics**. J. Wiley.

Quantitative Micro Software (1994). EVIEWS (Microtsp For Windows and the Macintosh) User's Guide and Software Package.

COURSE OUTLINE

I. **THE SIMPLE LINEAR STATISTICAL MODEL (2 weeks; Required Readings: Chapters 5, 6, 7, 8 of Course Text)**

Basic concepts and model
Least squares and maximum likelihood estimation
Sampling characteristics and properties of estimators
Interval estimation, hypothesis testing, prediction
R^2, coefficient of determination
Choice of functional forms
Computer implementation and reporting regression results
Numerical examples and practical applications

II. **THE GENERAL LINEAR STATISTICAL MODEL** (2 weeks; Required Readings: Chapters 9, 10, 11 of Course Text)

Multiple linear regression model
Review of basic matrix algebra
Least squares estimators and their sampling properties
Using Microtsp
Confidence intervals
Testing hypotheses -- for a single coefficient and for some
    coefficients
ANOVA tests for linear restrictions
Testing a linear versus a log-linear model
Forecasting
Examples and applications in economics and business

III. **COMPLICATIONS IN THE GENERAL LINEAR MODEL** (2 weeks; Required Readings: Chapters 12, 13, 14 of Course Text)

Dummy variables and varying coefficient models
Multicollinearity
Models with random regressors
Large-sample behavior of least squares
Instrumental variable estimation
Applications

IV. **LINEAR MODELS WITH A GENERAL ERROR STRUCTURE** (2 weeks; Required Readings: Chapters 15, 16 of Course Text)

Properties of least squares in this general case
Generalized least-squares procedures
Heteroskedastic errors -- detection, estimation, computer implementation
Autocorrelated errors -- detection, estimation, computer implementation
Forecasting
Practical applications

V. **SIMULTANEOUS-EQUATIONS ECONOMETRIC MODELS** (3 weeks; Required Readings: Chapters 17, 18, 19 of Course Text)

Seemingly unrelated regressions
Examples of simultaneous-equations models
Structural and reduced-form equations
Identification
Estimation by two-stage least-squares and instrumental-variable methods
Validation and applications through model simulations
Computer implementation and practical examples through TSP

VI.   TIME-SERIES AND DYNAMIC ECONOMIC MODELS (1 week; Required
        Readings: Chapters 20, 21 of Course Text)

        Univariate time-series analysis and forecasting
        Distributed lag models
        Vector autoregressive processes
        Computer implementation and examples

COURSE REQUIREMENTS

The final grade for the course will be based on the following three items (with indicated weights:

1.   Mid-term exam 1, covering Topics I-II, to be given on February 21, 1995 (30%
     of final grade);

2.   Mid-term exam 2, covering Topics III-IV, to be given on March 30, 1995 (30%
     of final grade);

3.   A final exam, covering Topics IV-VI, to be given on the date scheduled in the
     University calendar for final exams (40% of final grade).

All mid-term and final exams are closed books and closed notes.

Homework exercises will be assigned throughout the semester. These exercises are meant to
be teaching rather than grading devices. Students are encouraged to form study groups of three
to discuss homework problems and submit homework solutions as a group. These solutions must
be submitted on specified due dates; late submissions will not be accepted. Timely submission
of homework exercises will be considered in determining final grades in marginal cases.

OFFICE HOURS

Roberto S. Mariano   Tuesday & Thursday;   10:00 - 11:30, 332 McNeil

ECON 705
Econometrics I

ROBERTO S. MARIANO
Fall 1994

COURSE OUTLINE   G

PROBABILITY, STATISTICS, AND REGRESSION ANALYSIS

I. FUNDAMENTALS OF PROBABILITY THEORY - REVIEW

Basic Probability Theory
Combinatorial Analysis
Random Variables
Univariate and Multivariate Probability Distributions
Mathematical Expectations and Moments

II. SPECIAL PROBABILITY DISTRIBUTIONS

Bernoulli, Binomial, Multinomial
Hypergeometric
Poisson
Geometric, Negative Binomial
Gamma
Gaussian/Normal
Chi-squared, t, F-distributions

III. DERIVING DISTRIBUTIONS OF FUNCTIONS OF RANDOM VARIABLES

Use of Moment-Generating Functions
Change-of-Variable Technique
Monte Carlo Simulations

IV. SAMPLING THEORY AND SAMPLING DISTRIBUTIONS

Random sampling
Distributions of sample mean and variance from a normal distribution
Distribution of sample mean from a non-normal distribution - analytical,
    Monte Carlo
Stochastic convergence and limiting distributions
Laws of large numbers
Central limit theorems

V. STATISTICAL ESTIMATION

Methods for finding point estimators - method of moments, generalized method of
    moments, maximum likelihood, least squares, Bayesian
Properties of point estimators - small samples: bias, precision, sufficiency, completeness,

efficiency
Properties of point estimators - large samples: consistency, limiting distribution, asymptotic efficiency
Interval estimation

VI.   HYPOTHESIS TESTING

Elements of a statistical test, critical region, size of a test, power of a test
Unbiased, consistent, similar tests
Likelihood ratio, Wald, and Lagrange multiplier tests: definitions, geometric interpretation
Asymptotic tests
Tests based on comparisons of alternative estimators
Tests based on conditional moment restrictions
Finite-sample properties of tests - equivalence of LR, W, LM tests in quadratic likelihood functions, optimality of certain tests in terms of highest power within a class of tests
Large-sample properties of tests
Examples and economic applications

VII.   BAYESIAN INFERENCE

Basic notions: prior and posterior distributions
Bayesian inference for the mean of a normal distribution with known variance
Bayesian point estimators
Bayesian inference for the mean and variance of a normal distribution

VIII.   GENERAL LINEAR STATISTICAL MODEL

Basic assumptions and the data generating process
Simple linear regression
Multiple linear regression
Components of the model and classical assumptions
Least squares estimation
Statistical properties of least squares estimators under normal and non-normal cases; Gauss-Markov theorem
Restricted least squares
Least squares and maximum likelihood estimation
Applications in economic analysis
Interval estimation
Prediction and prediction intervals
Tests of hypotheses about regression coefficients
Measuring goodness of fit of estimated regression line
Exact probability distributions of least squares estimators: analytical derivation and Monte Carlo simulation
Large-sample asymptotic distribution of least squares estimators
Functional forms in regression

LECTURE HOURS: TUESDAYS & THURSDAYS
10:30 - 12:00, 395 McNeil

TEXT: Richard Larsen and Morris Marx. **Introduction to Mathematical Statistics and Its Applications, Second Edition.** Prentice Hall, 1986.

ADDITIONAL REFERENCES

Bickel, Peter J. and Kjell A. Doksum. **Mathematical Statistics: Basic Ideas and Selected Topics.** Holden Day, 1977.

Cox, David R. and D.V. Hinkley. **Theoretical Statistics.** Chapman and Hall, 1979.

Freund, John E. and Ronald E. Walpole **Mathematical Statistics, Fifth Edition.** Prentice-Hall. 1992.

Goldberger, Arthur S. **A Course in Econometrics.** Harvard University Press, 1991.

Greene, William H. **Econometric Analysis, Second Edition.** Macmillan, 1993.

Hoel, Paul G. **Introduction to Mathematical Statistics, Fifth Edition.** J. Wiley, 1984.

Hoel, P.G., S.C. Port, and C.J. Stone. **Introduction to Probability Theory.** Houghton Mifflin, 1972.

Hoel, P.G., S.C. Port, and C.J. Stone. **Introduction to Statistical Theory.** Houghton Mifflin 1972.

*Hogg, Robert V. and Allen T. Craig. **Introduction to Mathematical Statistics, Fourth Edition.** Macmillan, 1978.

Judge, George et.al. **Introduction to the Theory and Practice of Econometrics Second Edition.** J. Wiley 1988.

Kelejian, Harry H. and Wallace E. Oates. **Introduction to Econometrics - Principles and Applications, Third Edition.** Harper & Row, 1989.

Lehman, Erich L. **Theory of Point Estimation.** J. Wiley, 1983.

Lehman, Erich L. **Testing Statistical Hypotheses, Second Edition.** J. Wiley, 1986.

Mood, Alexander J., Franklin A. Graybill, and Duane C. Boes. **Introduction to the Theory of Statistics, Third Edition.** McGraw-Hill, 1974.

COURSE REQUIREMENTS

The final grade for the course will be based on two mid-term exams, a final exam, and submission of solutions to homework exercises.

Homework exercises will be assigned throughout the course. Students are required to solve these exercises and submit solutions on time. These exercises are intended to be teaching rather than grading devices -- so students are encouraged to form study groups (of two or three) to discuss the homework problems and submit solutions as a team. Submitted solutions will not be graded but timeliness of submissions will be duly recorded.

Mid-term and final exams are <u>closed-book</u> and <u>closed-notes</u>, with the following schedule.

	% of Final Grade	Date	Coverage
Mid-term Exam 1	30%	Oct. 11	Topics II-IV
Mid-term Exam 2	30%	Nov. 10	Topics IV-VI
Final Exam	40%	Dec. 15-23	Topics V-VII

The mid-term exams will be given in class. The final exam will be given during the Final Examination period as scheduled by the University Registrar.

Northwestern University G
GRADUATE ECONOMETRICS III

ADMINISTRATIVE DETAILS:

1. Your grade will be based on your performance on approximately 8 problem sets (15%), the
    midterm exam (35%), and the final exam (50%). The midterm is on Monday, May 10
    during class and the final is on Monday, June 7, from 9-11.

2. The T.A. for this course is Katherine Czukas. She will meet with you on Friday from 9-11 in
    AAH G-192.

3. My office hours are Tuesday 1-3, and my office is AAH G-242.

PREREQUISITES: Economics D80-1,2.

COURSE DESCRIPTION: This course covers a wide variety of econometric tools needed for writing
and understanding empirical work in economics.

TEXTS:

Required:

J. Johnston, <u>Econometric Methods</u>, McGraw Hill, 1984. (Cited as "Johnston" below.)

William H. Greene, <u>Econometric Analysis</u>, Second Edition, Macmillan, 1993. (Cited as "Greene"
below.)

Takeshi Amemiya, <u>Advanced Econometrics</u>, Harvard University Press, 1985.   (Cited
as "Amemiya" below.)

Other Helpful Texts:

Zvi Griliches and Michael D. Intriligator, <u>Handbook of Econometrics</u>, North-Holland, 1983.
(Especially volumes I and II.)

George G. Judge, et al., <u>The Theory and Practice of Econometrics</u>, Second Edition, John Wiley &
Sons, 1985.

G. S. Maddala, <u>Limited-Dependent and Qualitative Variables in Econometrics</u>, Cambridge University
Press, 1983.

COURSE OUTLINE:

(1) Panel Data (3 lectures): error components models, random effects, fixed effects, within versus
between, quasi-differences, effects of relative size of variance components, asymptotics, efficiency,
testing, specification testing, Hausman-Taylor estimation.

> Johnston, 10.3.
> Greene, Chapter 16.
> Amemiya, 6.6.
> Jerry Hausman and William Taylor (1981): "Panel Data and Unobservable Individual
> Effects," <u>Econometrica</u> 49, pp. 1377-1398.

(2) Data Problems (1 lecture): measurement error bias in the univariate case, multivariate case and
panel data, missing data and proxy variables, solutions to measurement error problem using prior
information, ML.

112   1

Johnston, 10.6.
Greene, 9.3-9.5.
Zvi Griliches and Jerry Hausman (1986): "Measurement Error in Panel Data," Journal of
Econometrics, pp. 93-118.

(3) Introduction to Instrumental Variables (1 lecture): IV as a solution to the measurement error
problem, simple cases such as repeated observations, requirements on instruments.

(4) Simultaneous Equations, System Estimation and IV (4 lectures): SUR, the general form of the
simultaneous equations problem, two equation examples using supply and demand, ILS, uses of
other information, identification, just identification versus overidentification, estimation of
simultaneous equations, general exposition of IV, 2SLS, 3SLS, FIML, testing.

> Johnston, Chapter 11.
> Jerry Hausman, Chapter 7 in Handbook of Econometrics.
> Greene, Chapters 17 and 20.
> Amemiya, Chapter 7.

(5) Nonlinear Models (4 lectures): consistency and asymptotic normality of nonlinear least squares,
similarity to least squares with derivatives, nonlinear optimization approaches, one-step estimates,
maximum likelihood, testing in nonlinear models, nonlinear simultaneous equations, generalized
method of moments.

> Amemiya, Chapters 4 and 8.
> Takeshi Amemiya, Chapter 6 in Handbook of Econometrics.
> Greene, Chapters 11 and 12
> Lars Hansen (1982): "Large Sample Properties of Generalized Method of Moments
> Estimators," Econometrica, pp. 1029-1054.

(6) Discrete Choice Models (2 lectures): difficulties with OLS, probit, logit, NLLS versus ML,
multinomial models, ordered models.

> Amemiya, Chapter 9.
> Greene, Chapter 21.

(7) Limited Dependent Variable and Duration Models (2 lectures): bias of OLS, tobit models,
censoring or truncation, selection models, duration models.

> Amemiya, Chapters 10 and 11.
> Greene, Chapter 22.

Problem Set 1
Economics D80-3
3/31/93

1.   You have a sample of data for which you want to estimate the model

$y_{it} = x'_{it}\beta + \lambda_t + \epsilon_{it}$, where $i = 1, 2, \ldots, N_t$, and $t = 1, 2, \ldots, T$. Note that the number of

observations per time period is not identical. This type of situation is sometimes called the

"unbalanced" data case.

(i)   Derive formulae for unbiased estimates of the variance components, σ_λ^2 and σ_ϵ^2.

(ii)   Derive the form of the quasi-differenced model that can be easily used to obtain GLS estimates.

2.

(i)   For the regression model $y = X\beta + u$, X a Txk matrix, $Euu' = \Omega \neq \sigma^2 I$, show that GLS and OLS are equally efficient if and only if $\Omega X = X\Gamma$, where Γ is a kxk matrix of full rank.

(ii)   Show that OLS estimates on deviations from time means for the model of problem 1 are as efficient as GLS estimates on the deviations from time means. Note that the covariance matrix of the errors is singular so that you will need to use a generalized inverse.

Problem Set 2
Economics D80-3
4/07/93

1.   Consider writing the 2 error components model (2ECM) as

$y_{it} = (x_{it} - x_{i.})'\beta + x_{i.}'\delta + \mu_i + \epsilon_{it}$, where $i = 1, 2, \ldots, N$, and $t = 1, 2, \ldots, T$. Construct a Wald test of the hypothesis $H_0: \beta = \delta$. Show that this test is the same as the Specification Test which compares Fixed Effects and GLS estimates of β from the usual way of writing the 2ECM.

2.   Consider the 3 error components model from class:

$y_{it} = x_{it}'\beta + u_{it}$
$u_{it} = \mu_i + \lambda_t + e_{it},$ or
$y_{it} = x_{it}'\beta + \mu_i + \lambda_t + e_{it}$
$i = 1, 2, \ldots, N$
$t = 1, 2, \ldots, T$,

where the stochastic assumptions on error components are: $\{\mu i\}$, $\{\lambda t\}$, $\{\epsilon_{it}\}$ iid, mean zero, mutually independent with

$E\mu_i^2 = \sigma_\mu^2$, $E\lambda_t^2 = \sigma_\lambda^2$, $Ee_{it}^2 = \sigma_e^2$.

114

For simplicity, also assume x_{it} is nonstochastic and $\sum_i \sum_t x_{it} = 0$.

(a)   Show that the difference between the Fixed Effects and GLS covariance matrices for β is a positive semi-definite matrix.

(b)   Now assume that N and T both go to infinity in such a way that $N = aT$, for some positive constant a. Compare the efficiency of Fixed Effects and GLS in this case (hint: Fixed Effects and GLS are equally efficient). You may need to make plausible assumptions about X'X. Will estimates of μ_i and λ_t be consistent?

(c)   How would your answer to (b) change if N were fixed and T went to infinity? You may need to make additional assumptions about X'AX, and X'BX where $A = I_N \otimes J_T$ and $B = J_N \otimes I_T$.

Problem Set 3
Economics D80-3
4/14/93

1.   Derive equations (14) and (15) in Griliches and Hausman (1986).

2.   Suppose you estimate a wage equation for males born in the 1910's and 1920's and you think that being a veteran affects wages so you include a dummy variable for veteran status on the right-hand side. For example, you estimate $w_i = v_i \beta + x'_i \delta + \epsilon_i$, where w_i is the wage in 1970 for person i, $v_i = 1$ if person i is a veteran, and 0 otherwise, x_i is a set of additional variables affecting wages for person i, and $i = 1, \ldots, N$. You also believe that veteran status is correlated with the unobservable fitness of individuals because of the armed services selection procedure and you believe that fitness affects wages. In addition, you know each person's year and calendar quarter of birth.

i)   Men were drafted in WWII not by lottery number, but by date of birth. Men born January 1 were considered first, then those born January 2 and so on. In most years, most people born in the later months were not even considered for induction in the armed forces. Describe how you might consistently estimate the wage equation, and why it works.

115

4

(ii)   Suppose you think that years of education affects wages and that being a veteran increases the years of education completed because the government provides eductional subsidies to veterans that are not available to other individuals. Explain whether or not you still can consistently estimate the coefficient on veteran status in the wage equation.

3.   Consider the permanent income model of consumption, $C_{it} = \beta Y_i^* + \epsilon_{it}$, where $Y_{it} = Y_i^* + \nu_{it}$, $i = 1, 2, \ldots, N$, $t = 1, 2, \ldots, T$, C_{it} and Y_{it} are measured consumption and measured income for household i in period t and Y_i^* is unmeasured "permanent" income. Some possible estimators of β are (1) OLS regression of C_{it} on Y_{it} for $i = 1, 2, \ldots, N$, and $t = 1$, $2, \ldots T$, (2) OLS regression of $C_{i.}$ on $Y_{i.}$ for $i = 1, 2, \ldots, N$, where $C_{i.}$ and $Y_{i.}$ are the mean over all t of C_{it} and Y_{it}, and (3) IV estimation of $C_{it} = \beta Y_{it} + \epsilon_{it}$ using $\tilde{Y}_{it} = \dfrac{\sum_{s \neq t} Y_{is}}{T-1}$ as the instrument. Derive the properties (the plim and, when the estimator is consistent, the asymptotic distribution) of estimators (1) through (3) as N goes to infinity assuming $E(\nu_{it}) = 0$ and $E(\nu_{it}\nu_{ir}) = 0$.

4.   Suppose you have the model $y_t = x_t'\beta + \epsilon_t$, $t = 1, 2, \ldots, T$ where $E\epsilon\epsilon' = \sigma^2 I$, x_t' is a k dimensional vector and plim$(x'\epsilon/T) = 0$ and plim$(x'z/T)$ has column rank k.

(i)   Show that $\hat{\beta}_{IV} = (x' P_z x)^{-1} x' P_z y$ is consistent but inefficient here relative to OLS. $P_z = z(z'z)^{-1}z'$.

(ii)   Now suppose that we are uncertain that plim$(x'\epsilon/T)$ is in fact 0, but we are confident that plim $(z'\epsilon/T) = 0$ and plim $(x'z/T)$ exists and has column rank k. Suggest a test for the null hypothesis that plim $(x'\epsilon/T) = 0$.

1.   Consider the consumption function $C_t = a_1 + a_2 Y_t + \epsilon_t$. Consider Haavelmo's approach to

the problem. He treated income as endogenous, being determined through the identity $Y_t = C_t + Z_t$ where $Z_t = I_t + G_t$ was treated as an exogenous variable. I_t is investment and G_t is

government spending. Assume homoskedasticity and no serial correlation for ϵ_t.

(i)   Subtract off means from all the variables to make things simpler, and then compute

plim a_2 from OLS. What is the direction of the bias, and what is the intuition for this

result?

(ii)   Calculate the two reduced from equations (for C_t and Y_t) and find a_2 by indirect least

squares (ILS). Can one estimate a_2 using Z_t or its components as instruments?

Does I_t seem like a good instrument to use? Hint: Think of the accelerator model of

investment.

(iii)   Given the reduced form estimates calculate the asymptotic variance of the ILS or IV

estimate of a_2. Be sure to note the relationship between the reduced form errors.

(iv)   Is ILS or IV unbiased here in finite samples?

2.   Consider the system of equations:

$$\beta_{11} y_1 + \beta_{12} y_2 + \gamma_{11} x_1 + \gamma_{12} x_2 = u_1$$

$$\beta_{21} y_1 + \beta_{22} y_2 + \gamma_{21} x_1 + \gamma_{22} x_2 = u_2$$

where y_i, x_i, and u_i, $i = 1,2$ are Tx1 vectors and the x's and u's are uncorrelated.

(i)   Suppose a priori restrictions are $\gamma_{12} = 0$, $\gamma_{21} = 0$. In general, is the first equation

identified? What happens if $\gamma_{22} = 0$? Discuss both the rank and order conditions in

both situations. Then if γ_{22} does not equal zero, explicitly compute the parameters

of the structural first equation from the parameters of the reduced form.

(ii)   Now consider a priori restrictions $\gamma_{11} = 0$, $\gamma_{12} = 0$ and discuss identification of both

equations. Choosing the normalization $\beta_{11} = 1$, calculate β_{12} in terms of the reduced

form coefficients. If one were to estimate the reduced form coefficients and then

use them to solve for a unique β_{12} what restriction might one want to impose when

estimating the reduced form equations? Could we have used a subset of the

restrictions to identify the structural parameters of the first equation?

117

1. Suppose you have the simultaneous equations model

$$\text{(I)} \qquad y_t = \beta_{11}P_t + \epsilon_{1t}$$

$$\text{(II)} \qquad P_t = \beta_{21}y_t + \gamma_{21}z_{1t} + \gamma_{22}z_{2t} + \epsilon_{2t}$$

where $t = 1, 2, \ldots, T$, and z_{1t} and z_{2t} are uncorrelated with ϵ_{1t} and ϵ_{2t}.

(i) Derive the reduced form equations for y_t and P_t.

(ii) What is the bias of the estimator for β_{11} obtained from OLS applied to (I).

(iii) Write out the indirect least squares estimators for β_{11} and derive their asymptotic properties.

(iv) Write out the 2SLS estimator for β_{11} and compare its asymptotic variance to that of an optimal weighted average of the indirect least squares estimators from (iii).

2. Consider the Hausman and Taylor (1981) model:

$$y_{it} = x_{it}'\beta + z_i'\gamma + \mu_i + \epsilon_{it}, \quad i = 1, 2, \ldots, N, \; t = 1, 2, \ldots, T, \qquad x_{it}' = (x_{1it}' \; x_{2it}') \text{ and } z_i' =$$

$(z_{1i}' \; z_{2i}')$ where the dimensions of the vectors x_{1it}, x_{2it}, z_{1i} and z_{2i} are k_1, k_2, g_1, and g_2 respectively, x_{1it} and z_{1i} are uncorrelated with μ_i but x_{2it} and z_{2i} are correlated with μ_i. Give conditions under which γ can be consistently estimated and describe how to do it.

118

3. Consider the model

$$Q_t = \beta_1 P_t + \beta_2 W_t + Z_{1t}'\gamma + u_t, \quad t=1, 2, \ldots, T.$$

where P and W are endogenous and Z_1 is exogenous. Assume further that the first s observations on W_t are all 0. Discuss the large sample properties of each of the following three estimators, i.e. calculate their probability limits and discuss their asymptotic efficiency. Assume you have another set of exogenous variables Z_2 and consider both the cases where s below is a fixed number and when it is a constant fraction of T.

(a) Regress P_t on all predetermined variables to form $\hat{P}_t$; regress only the last T-s values of W_t on the last T-s ovservations of the predetermined variables to form $\hat{W} = (0, \ldots, 0, \hat{W}_{s+1}, \ldots, \hat{W}_T)$. Then use OLS on (i).

(b) Form $\hat{P}_t$ as in (a), but now regress all T values of W_t on the predetermined variables and use this $\hat{W}_t^*$ in equation (i) and run OLS.

(c) Again form $\hat{P}_t$ in the same way and form $\hat{W}_t^*$ as in (b). Now impose the zero restrictions on the first s values of W_t so that $\hat{W}_t^{**} = (0, \ldots, 0, \hat{W}_{s+1}^*, \ldots, \hat{W}_T^*)$. Use $\hat{W}_t^{**}$ in equation (i) and run OLS.

1. Suppose you have the nonlinear specification $y_i = \exp\{x_i'\beta\} + \epsilon_i$, where $E\epsilon_i = 0$, $V\epsilon_i = \sigma^2$.

(i) Write out the form of the Newton-Raphson and the Gauss-Newton iterations. For the Gauss-Newton iteration see Amemiya (1985).

(ii) Verify the asymptotic relationship between the $T^{-1}\sum_t \frac{\partial f_t}{\partial \beta} \frac{\partial f_t}{\partial \beta'}$ and $T^{-1} \frac{\partial^2 S_T}{\partial \beta \partial \beta'}$, by calculating the plims when computed at $\hat{\beta}$, the estimator which minimizes the sum of squares.

(iii) Suppose that the specification arises from an underlying Poisson model so that $V(\epsilon_i) = \exp\{x_i'\beta\}$. Describe the properties of NLLS with this heteroskedasticity. How might one do Weighted NLLS (WNLLS) to account for the heteroskedasticity and what would be the steps of the iterative process?

2.

(i) Suppose you have the model $y_{1i} = \beta_1 \log y_{2i} + \gamma_1 z_{1i} + \epsilon_{1i}$, where y_{2i} is correlated with ϵ_{1i}, but you have z_{2i} which is uncorrelated with ϵ_{1i} and $y_{2i} = \gamma_2 z_{2i} + \epsilon_{2i}$. Describe precisely an estimator for β_1 and show that it is consistent.

(ii) Derive the properties of repeated least squares where you run OLS on the equation $y_{1i} = \beta_1 \log \hat{y}_{2i} + \gamma_1 z_{1i} + \eta_i$, where $\hat{y}_{2i}$ equals $P_z y_2$ and $z = [\, z_1 \; z_2 \,]$.

3. Suppose you have the linear model $y_i = \beta_0 + \beta_1 x_i^* + \beta_2 (x_i^*)^2 + \beta_3 (x_i^*)^3 + \epsilon_i$, but you do not observe x_i^*, rather you observe $x_i = x_i^* + v_i$, where v_i is mean zero and independent of ϵ_i and x_i^*. Also suppose you have a z_i that is correlated with x_i^*, but is independent of ϵ_i.

(i) Show that using z_i, its square and cube as instruments will not produce consistent estimates of the β's.

(ii) Now consider the case where $\beta_3 = 0$. Show that in this very special case you can consistently estimate the β's using z_i and its square as instruments. You will need a slightly different approach to estimate β_0.

120

9

1. Consider the binary choice model $P(y_i = 1) = F(x_i'\beta)$ for some cumulative distribution function F.

(i) If the true F is a cumulative standard normal and you use logit to estimate β what are the properties of your estimator? Hint: is the model Fisher consistent?

(ii) Suppose the binary choice problem arises from an underlying model $y_i^* = x_i'\beta + \epsilon_i$, $y_i = 1$ if $y_i^* > 0$ and $y_i = 0$ otherwise, where ϵ_i is normally distributed, but is heteroskedastic, i.e. $Var(\epsilon_i | x_i)$ is not a constant. What are the properties of probit maximum likelihood here?

(iii) Suppose ϵ_i in part (ii) is not heteroskedastic, but is serially correlated. What are the properties of probit maximum likelihood now?

2. Suppose the benefit to person i of cheating on his income tax is $x_i'\beta + \epsilon_i$, where ϵ_i is normally distributed and independent of x_i. Let the cost be a constant C which is unknown but is the same for all people. Assume a person decides to cheat if the benefits exceed the costs. Furthermore, assume that the IRS uses certain variables z_i (some of which may be in x_i) to determine whether or not to audit a return. As a result, a person is caught <u>conditional</u> on cheating if and only if $z_i'\gamma + \eta_i > 0$, where η_i is normally distributed and independent of ϵ_i, z_i, and x_i. Suppose you have a sample of N people that includes for each person an indicator for whether or not he is caught for income tax evasion, as well as x_i and z_i.

(a) Write out the likelihood function for the data.

(b) Explain how to estimate β and γ up to scale using nonlinear weighted least squares.

(c) Are β and γ identified up to scale if $x_i = z_i$ for all i? Explain.

3. Suppose $y_{ij}^* = x_{ij}'\beta_j + \epsilon_{ij}$, where $i = 1, \ldots, N$ and $j = 1, 2$. Assume that ϵ_{i1} and ϵ_{i2} are iid logistic random variables that are mutually independent. Also assume that you only observe x_{ij} and y_{ij} where $y_{ij} = 1$ if y_{ij}^* is positive and $y_{ij} = 0$ otherwise.

(a) Write out the likelihood function for the data and explain how you would estimate β_1 and β_2.

(b) Assume that $\beta = \beta_1 = \beta_2$. Suppose that for budgetary reasons the sampling rate in the second period is cut to half that in the first period, i.e. $i = 1, \ldots, N$ for $j = 1$ and $i = 1, \ldots, N/2$ for $j = 2$. How would you efficiently estimate β?

(c) Again assume that $\beta = \beta_1 = \beta_2$, but now also assume that $y^*_{ij} = x_{ij}{}'\beta + \alpha_i + \epsilon_{ij}$. Suppose that you do not observe α_i but estimate it by including a dummy variable for each i. What are the properties of this procedure?

(d) Under the assumptions of (c), consider the probability that $y_{i1} = 1$ given that $y_{i1} + y_{i2} = 1$. Does this suggest an estimation method with better properties than those in (c)? Explain.

Problem Set 8
Economics D80-3
5/26/93

1. You have a linear model $y_i = x_i{}'\beta + \epsilon_i$ where ϵ_i is distributed $N(0, \sigma^2)$. However, you only observe the data if $y_i > c$.

(i) Calculate the conditional expectation of y_i given x_i for $y_i > c$.

(ii) Write down the likelihood function for the sample.

(iii) Demonstrate Fisher consistency for the maximum likelihood estimates of β and σ^2.

2. Suppose a researcher wants to predict whether or not a household with a given set of characteristics purchases a car during a particular period of time. She has available data on a random set of households which includes various characteristics associated with each household and a discrete random variable indicating whether the household purchased a car. Assume the household buys a car when $y_i > 0$, with $y_i = x_i{}'\beta + u_i$ and u_i distributed uniformly on the interval $(-1,1)$. Let $\delta_i = 1$ if the household purchases a car and $\delta_i = 0$ otherwise. Assume that the absolute value of $x_i{}'\beta < 1$ for all i.

(i) Let $P_i = Pr(\delta_i = 1$ given $x_i)$. Show that $P_i = (1 + x_i{}'\beta)/2$. Also show that δ_i is described by the linear probability model $\delta_i = P_i + \epsilon_i$, where $E(\epsilon_i$ given $x_i) = 0$.

(ii) Show that $Var(\epsilon_i) = P_i(1-P_i)$ and explain why this implies the presence of heteroskedasticity.

(iii) Explain all of the steps in a procedure to efficiently estimate β.

122

3.   Suppose your data consist of income and dollar purchases of automobiles for a large
      number of individuals obtained from a nationwide survey of automobile dealers. Assume
      that your observations include only those individuals making positive purchases and that
      expenditures greater than $20,000 are recorded as $20,000. Further assume that
      underlying latent expenditures are determined by the relationship $y^*_i = \beta x_i + \epsilon_i$, where y^*_i
      is desired purchases and x_i is income.

   (a)   Is the OLS estimator of the effect of income on asset purchases unbiased? Graph
          the relationships and explain any biases.
   (b)   Write out the likelihood function for the data under the assumption that ϵ_i is normally
          distributed.
   (c)   Suppose that instead of reporting expenditures continuously between $0 and
          $20,000, expenditures are only reported as being in one of three categories: $0-
          10,000, $10,000-20,000, $20,000 or more. Write out the likelihood function in
          this case under the assumption that ϵ_i is normally distributed.

Problem Set 8
Economics D80-3
5/26/93

1.   You have a linear model $y_i = x_i'\beta + \epsilon_i$ where ϵ_i is distributed $N(0, \sigma^2)$. However, you only
      observe the data if $y_i > c$.

(i)   Calculate the conditional expectation of y_i given x_i for $y_i > c$.

(ii)   Write down the likelihood function for the sample.

(iii)   Demonstrate Fisher consistency for the maximum likelihood estimates of β and σ^2.

2.   Suppose a researcher wants to predict whether or not a household with a given set of
      characteristics purchases a car during a particular period of time. She has available data on
      a random set of households which includes various characteristics associated with each
      household and a discrete random variable indicating whether the household purchased a car.
      Assume the household buys a car when $y_i > 0$, with $y_i = x_i'\beta + u_i$ and u_i distributed

123

12

uniformly on the interval $(-1,1)$. Let $\delta_i = 1$ if the household purchases a car and $\delta_i = 0$ otherwise. Assume that the absolute value of $x_i'\beta < 1$ for all i.

(i)   Let $P_i = Pr(\delta_i = 1$ given $x_i)$. Show that $P_i = (1 + x_i'\beta)/2$. Also show that δ_i is described by the linear probability model $\delta_i = P_i + \epsilon_i$, where $E(\epsilon_i$ given $x_i) = 0$.

(ii)   Show that $Var(\epsilon_i) = P_i(1-P_i)$ and explain why this implies the presence of heteroskedasticity.

(iii)   Explain all of the steps in a procedure to efficiently estimate β.

3.   Suppose your data consist of income and dollar purchases of automobiles for a large number of individuals obtained from a nationwide survey of automobile dealers. Assume that your observations include only those individuals making positive purchases and that expenditures greater than \$20,000 are recorded as \$20,000. Further assume that underlying latent expenditures are determined by the relationship $y_i^* = \beta x_i + \epsilon_i$, where y_i^* is desired purchases and x_i is income.

(a)   Is the OLS estimator of the effect of income on asset purchases unbiased? Graph the relationships and explain any biases.

(b)   Write out the likelihood function for the data under the assumption that ϵ_i is normally distributed.

(c)   Suppose that instead of reporting expenditures continuously between \$0 and \$20,000, expenditures are only reported as being in one of three categories: \$0-10,000, \$10,000-20,000, \$20,000 or more. Write out the likelihood function in this case under the assumption that ϵ_i is normally distributed.

124

You have until 10:50. Answer all of the questions. Show your work and briefly justify your

conclusions.

1. Consider the following system of equations: $\begin{array}{ll}(i) & y_{1i} = \beta_{12}y_{2i} + \gamma_{11}x_{1i} + \gamma_{12}x_{2i} + \epsilon_{1i} \\ (ii) & y_{2i} = \beta_{21}y_{1i} + \gamma_{21}x_{1i} + \epsilon_{2i} \;,\end{array}$

where $i = 1,...,N$, x_{ji} is independent of ϵ_{kl} for all i,j,k,l, and $E[\epsilon_{1i}\epsilon_{2i}] \neq 0$.

(a) (15 points) Discuss identification and efficient estimation (if possible) of both equations.

(b) (15 points) Now suppose you know that $\gamma_{11} - \gamma_{21} = 0$. Discuss identification and

efficient estimation (if possible) of both equations.

2. Suppose you have the panel data model $y_{it} = \beta x_{it} + u_{it}$ where $u_{it} = \mu_i + \lambda_t + \epsilon_{it}$ and

$i = 1,...,N$, $t = 1,...T$.

(a) (5 points) Write out the form of the covariance matrix for the errors u.

(b) (15 points) Suppose x_{it} is correlated with λ_t but uncorrelated with μ_i. Discuss consistent

and efficient estimation methods.

3. Suppose you know that the true relationship you are modeling is $y_{it} = \beta x_{it} + \epsilon_{it}$, where

$i = 1,...,N$ and $t = 1,...,4$. However, you do not observe x_{it}, rather you observe $z_{it} = x_{it} + \eta_{it}$

$+ \eta_{i,t-1}$. Also assume that $x_{it} = x_i + \tilde{x}_{it}$ and that η_{it} and $\tilde{x}_{it}$ are i.i.d. across i and t and

independent of each other and all other variables.

(a) (10 points) What is the plim of the OLS estimator of β?

125

(b) (15 points) Discuss consistent and efficient estimation methods.

4. Suppose you estimate the equation $y_i = \beta x_i + \epsilon_i$ using instrumental variables z_{1i} and z_{2i} because you think x is correlated with ϵ.

(a) (7 points) Write out a test for whether $\beta = 4$.

(b) (10 points) Suppose you also obtain another estimate of β, call it $\tilde{\beta}$ by only using only z_1 as an instrument for x. Discuss a test which compares $\tilde{\beta}$ to the 2SLS estimate of β.

(c) (8 points) Discuss a test of overidentifying restrictions here.

126

You have 1 hour and 50 minutes. Answer all 3 questions. The questions count equally. Show
your work and briefly justify your conclusions.

1.   (a) Suppose you posit the model $y_t = (\lambda x_t'\beta)^{\frac{1}{\lambda}} + u_t$, where u_t is mean zero and

homoskedastic given x_t. Explain what parameters are identified here and how you would
estimate them.

(b) Describe the ways that you could test if $\lambda = 1$.

(c) Suppose that instead of the model in (a) you have the model $\dfrac{(y_t)^\lambda - 1}{\lambda} = x_t'\beta + u_t$,

where λ is unknown but $\lambda \neq 0$, and again u_t is mean zero and homoskedastic given x_t.
Suggest an estimation technique for all the unknown parameters and give some indication
why it would work.

(d) Again assume you have the model of (c), but assume that x_t is correlated with u_t, but
you have a w_t that is correlated with x_t but is uncorrelated with u_t. Suggest an estimation
approach and explain why it would work.

2.   Suppose you have the 3 equation system:

(i) $y_1 = \gamma_{11}x_1 + \epsilon_1$

(ii) $y_2 = \beta_{23}y_3 + \gamma_{21}x_1 + \gamma_{22}x_2 + \epsilon_2$

(iii) $y_3 = \beta_{31}y_1 + \gamma_{31}x_1 + \gamma_{32}x_2 + \epsilon_3$

y_j, x_j, and ϵ_j are all Tx1 column vectors and ϵ_{1i} and ϵ_{2i} are correlated with each other but ϵ_{3i}
is uncorrelated with ϵ_{1i} and ϵ_{2i}.

129

18

(a)   Consider the case where $\beta_{23} = \beta_{31} = 0$. Describe consistent and efficient estimation methods for the 3 equations and the equivalences between possible estimators.

(b)   Instead of the assumptions in (a), assume $\beta_{23} \neq 0$, $\beta_{31} \neq 0$. Discuss identification and (if possible) consistent and efficient estimation of the 3 equations.

3.   Suppose you would like to learn about loan application, acceptance and amount decisions. You hypothesize that a person's desired borrowing is equal to $y^*_{1i} = x_{1i}'\beta_1 + \epsilon_{1i}$ and that the net profits to lenders for the loan are equal to $y^*_{2i} = x_{2i}'\beta_2 + \epsilon_{2i}$. Suppose that a person applies for a loan only if the desired loan amount is greater than K (because of a fixed fee). Assume that the lender accepts the application if net profits are positive and that the lender (conditional on acceptance) always gives the desired loan amount. Further assume that ϵ_{ji} conditional on x_{ji} is mean zero, normally distributed with variance σ_j^2, $j = 1,2$, and that ϵ_{1i} and ϵ_{2i} are independent of each other and independent over i.

(a)   Assume that you observe x_{1i} and x_{2i} for each person and whether or not a loan occurs, but you do not observe y^*_{ji}, $j = 1,2$, i.e. you do not observe the loan amount. Write out the likelihood function for the data and explain what parameters are identified. Consider both the case where K is known and the case where K is unknown. You should also say if your answer depends on whether x_{1i} and/or x_{2i} include a constant.

(b)   Instead of the assumptions in (a), now assume that you have a sample of only accepted loans and their loan amounts as well as the x_{1i} and x_{2i} for these accepted loans. Write out the likelihood function for the data and explain what parameters are identified. Consider both the case where K is known and the case where K is unknown.

130

1. (a) All parameters are identified and NLLS can be used to estimate them.

    (b) You could use any of the classical Wald, LR or LM tests as well as a specification test

    comparing OLS and NLLS.

    (c) Minimize $\sum_{t=1}^{T} \left[\dfrac{(y_t)^{\lambda}-1}{\lambda} - x_t'\beta \right]^2$ over β and λ.

    (b) Minimize $\left[\dfrac{y^{\lambda}-1}{\lambda} - X\beta \right]' W (W'W)^{-1} W' \left[\dfrac{y^{\lambda}-1}{\lambda} - X\beta \right]$ over β and λ.

2. (a) OLS on (iii) and SUR on (i) and (ii) together will be efficient. However, the OLS

    estimates of (i) will be the same as those from SUR.

    (b) (i) can be estimated by OLS. The residuals from (i) can be used as instruments for y_1 in

    (iii) to consistently estimate the parameters of that equation. The residuals from (iii) can

    now be used as an instrument for y_3 in (ii).

131

EC 331,EC332 - Econometrics I & II 1993/94 Session

Instructor : Süleyman Özmucur

U

Prerequisites : Ec 233, Ec 234 , Math 151, Math 152, Math 242

Textbook : Maddala, G.S. Introduction to Econometrics (2nd. ed.) Macmillan Publishing Company. New York. 1992.

Other books :

Johnston, J. *Econometric Methods*, 3rd. edition. McGraw-Hill. 1984.
Pindyck, R.S. & D. L. Rubinfeld, *Econometric Models &Economic Forecasts*, 3rd. ed.McGraw-Hill. 1991.
Kmenta, J. *Elements of Econometrics*, 2.nd ed. Macmillan. 1986.
Gujarati, D. *Basic Econometrics*. 2nd. ed. McGraw-Hill. 1988.
Intriligator, M.D. *Econometric Models, Techniques &Applications*. Prentice-Hall.1978.
Klein, L.R. *A Textbook of Econometrics*, 2nd ed. Prentice-Hall. 1974.
Klein, L.R. *An Introduction to Econometrics*. Prentice-Hall. 1962.
Maddala, G.S. *Econometrics*. McGraw-Hill. 1977.
Rao, P. & R.L. Miller, *Applied Econometrics*. Prentice-Hall. 1972.
Koutsoyiannis, A. *Theory of Econometrics*. 2nd. ed. Harper-Row. 1977.
Christ, C.F. *Econometric Models and Methods*. John Wiley & Sons. 1966.
Goldberger, A.S. *Econometric Theory*. John Wiley & Sons. 1964.
Theil, H. *Principles of Econometrics*. John Wiley & Sons. 1971.
Zellner, A.(ed.) *Readings in Economic Statistics and Econometrics*.Little, Brown and Company.1968.
Cramer, J.S. *Empirical Econometrics*. North-Holland. 1969.
Hebden, J. *Applications of Econometrics*. Philip Allan. 1983.
Bridge, J.L. *Applied Econometrics*. North-Holland. 1971.
Chow, G.C. *Econometrics*. McGraw-Hill. 1983.
Judge, G.J., R.C. Carter, W.E. Griffiths, H. Lütkepohl, T-C Lee. *Introduction to the Theory and Practice of Econometrics*. John Wiley&Sons. 1982.
Desai, M. *Applied Econometrics*. McGraw-Hill. 1976.
Harvey, A.C. *The Econometric Analysis of Time Series*. MIT Press. 1990.
Marchi, N. & C. Gilbert, *History and Methodology of Econometrics*. Clarendon Press. 1989.
Malinvaud, E. *Statistical Methods of Econometrics*. 2nd ed. North-Holland. 1970.

Class Hours

Monday   1 , 2   HKD 301
Wednesday 1 , 2   HKD 301
Friday   1 , 2   (reserved for problem sessions)

Office Hours

Monday   3   IB 503
Wednesday 3   IB 503
and by appointment (tel : 1804 or 1505)

Grading(First semester)		**Grading(Second semester)**	
Exam 1	30	Midterm Exam	30
Exam 2	30	Term paper	30
Final Exam	40	Final Exam	40

A detailed time-table for the term-paper will be given at the beginning of the second semester.

EC 331,EC332 - Econometrics I & II   1993/94 Session
Course Outline(Other readings will be given during the semester) :

1. Econometric Approach :

Maddala , Chps. 1, 2

2. Simple Regression

Maddala, Chp. 3

Exam 1 (November 17 th, Wednesday)

3. Multiple Regression

Maddala, Chp. 4

4. Multicollinearity

Maddala, Chp. 7

5. Dummy Variables

Maddala, Chp. 8

Exam 2 (December 22nd , Wednesday)

6. Heteroskedasticity

Maddala, Chp. 5

Final Exam (January 12, 1994, Wednesday, 12:00 - 15:00)

7. Serial Correlation

Maddala, Chp. 6

8. Lagged Variables and Models of Expectations

Maddala, Chp. 10

9. Errors in Variables

Maddala, Chp 11

10. Simultaneous Equations Models

Maddala, Chp. 9

11. Diagnostic Checking, Model Selection,and Specification Testing

Maddala, Chp. 12

12. Time Series Analysis

Maddala, Chp. 13, 14

EC 332 - Econometrics II   Course Outline   Spring 1993

EC 332 - Econometrics II
Instructor : Süleyman Özmucur

Prerequisite : Ec 331

Textbook : Johnston, J. *Econometric Methods*, 3rd. edition. McGraw-Hill. 1984.

Other books :
Pindyck, R.S. & D. L. Rubinfeld, *Econometric Models &Economic Forecasts*, 3rd. ed.McGraw-Hill. 1991.
Kmenta, J. *Elements of Econometrics*, 2.nd ed. Macmillan. 1986.
Gujarati, D. *Basic Econometrics*. 2nd. ed. McGraw-Hill. 1988.
Intriligator, M.D. *Econometric Models, Techniques &Applications*. Prentice-Hall.1978.
Klein, L.R. *A Textbook of Econometrics*, 2nd ed. Prentice-Hall. 1974.
Klein, L.R. *An Introduction to Econometrics*. Prentice-Hall. 1962.
Rao, P. & R.L. Miller, *Applied Econometrics*. Prentice-Hall. 1972.
Zellner, A.(ed.) *Readings in Economic Statistics and Econometrics*.Little, Brown and Company.1968.
Cramer, J.S. *Empirical Econometrics*. North-Holland. 1969.
Hebden, J. *Applications of Econometrics*. Philip Allan. 1983.
Bridge, J.L. *Applied Econometrics*. North-Holland. 1971.
Desai, M. *Applied Econometrics*. McGraw-Hill. 1976.
Harvey, A.C. *The Econometric Analysis of Time Series*. MIT Press. 1990.

Class Hours

Monday	1 , 2	IB 102
Wednesday	1 , 2	IB 102

Office Hours

Monday	3	IB 503
Wednesday	3	IB 503

and by appointment (tel : 1804 or 1505)

Grading

Midterm Exam	30
Termpaper	30
Final Exam	40

Important dates:

Midterm exam	April 14, Wednesday (8:30 - 10:00)
Final Exam	June 9, Wednesday (12:00 - 15:00)
Term Paper	

TP1.paper topic	February 24 , Wednesday
TP2.introduction,theory,literature survey,data sources	March 31, Wednesday
TP3.estimation results	April 21, Wednesday
TP4.final report	May 26, Wdnesday

Course Outline :

1. Generalized Least Squares(GLS)

Johnston , Chp. 8.1 - 8.3

2. Autocorrelation

Johnston, Chp. 8.5

3. Heteroscedasticity

Johnston, Chp. 8.4

4. Seemingly unrelated regression equations(SURE)

Johnston, Chp. 8.6

5. Maximum Likelihood Estimators(MLE) and Asymptotic distributions

Johnston, Chp. 7

6. Lagged Variables

Johnston, Chp. 9

7. Simultaneous equation systems

Johnston, Chp. 11

Suggested problems : all in Chapters 7,8,9, and 11

EC 531,EC532 - Econometrics I & II   1993/94 Session

Instructor : Süleyman Özmucur   **G**

Textbook :Greene, William H. *Econometric Analysis*(2nd ed.). Macmillan Publishing Company. New York. 1993.

Other books :
Johnston, J. *Econometric Methods*, 3rd. edition. McGraw-Hill. 1984.
Pindyck, R.S.   & D. L. Rubinfeld, *Econometric Models &Economic Forecast*s, 3rd. ed.McGraw-Hill. 1991.
Intriligator, M.D. *Econometric Models, Techniques &Applications*. Prentice-Hall.1978.
Klein, L.R. *A Textbook of Econometrics*, 2nd ed. Prentice-Hall. 1974.
Klein, L.R. *An Introduction to Econometrics*. Prentice-Hall. 1962.
Maddala, G.S. *Econometrics*. McGraw-Hill. 1977.
Rao, P. & R.L. Miller, *Applied Econometrics*. Prentice-Hall. 1972.
Christ, C.F. *Econometric Models and Methods*. John Wiley & Sons. 1966.
Goldberger, A.S. *Econometric Theory.* John Wiley & Sons. 1964.
Theil, H. *Principles of Econometrics*. John Wiley & Sons. 1971.
Zellner, A.(ed.) *Readings in Economic Statistics and Econometrics*.Little, Brown and Company.1968.
Cramer, J.S. *Empirical Econometrics*. North-Holland. 1969.
Bridge, J.L. *Applied Econometrics*. North-Holland. 1971.
Chow, G.C. *Econometrics*. McGraw-Hill. 1983.
Judge, G.J., R.C. Carter, W.E. Griffiths, H. Lütkepohl, T-C Lee. *Introduction to the Theory and Practice of Econometrics*. John Wiley&Sons. 1982.
Harvey, A.C. *The Econometric Analysis of Time Series*. MIT Press. 1990.
Marchi, N. & C. Gilbert, *History and Methodology of Econometrics*. Clarendon Press. 1989.
Malinvaud, E. *Statistical Methods of Econometrics*. 2nd ed. North-Holland. 1970.

Class Hours

Monday	5 , 6	YD 407
Wednesday	5	IB 203

Office Hours

Monday	3	IB 503
Wednesday	3	IB 503

and by appointment (tel : 1804 or 1505)

Grading(First semester)

Exam 1	30	November 17 th Wednesday
Exam 2	30	December 22 nd Wednesday
Final Exam	40	(January 6 th Thursday)

Grading(Second semester)

Midterm Exam	30
Term-paper	30
Final Exam	40

EC 531,EC532 - Econometrics I & II   1993/94 Session
Course Outline(Other readings will be given during the semester) :

1. Econometric Approach :
Greene , Chps. 1-4

2. Classical Least Squares
Greene, Chps. 5,6

3. Hypothesis Tests
Greene, Chp. 7

4. Functional Forms, Nonlinearity, and Specification
Greene, Chp. 8

5. Data Problems
Greene, Chp. 9

6. Large-Sample Results for the Classical Regression Model
Greene, Chp. 10

7. Nonlinear Regression Models
Greene, Chps. 11,12

8.Nonspherical Disturaances
Greene, Chp. 13

9. Heteroscedasticity
Greene, Chp. 14

10. Autocorrelation
Greene, Chp. 15

11. Models that use both cross-section and time-series data
Greene, Chp. 16

12. Systems of Regression Equations
Greene, Chp. 17

13. Lagged Variables
Greene, Chp. 18

14. Time-Series Models
Greene, Chp. 19

15. Simultaneous Equations Model
Greene, Chp. 20

16. Models with Discrete Dependent and Limited Dependent Variables
Greene, Chps. 21, 22

EC 535 - Forecasting Methods Course Outline Spring 1993

Instructor : Süleyman Özmucur
Prerequisites : Ec 331, Ec 332 or Ec 531, Ec 532 **G**

Textbook :

Makridakis, S.,S.C. Wheelwright, V.E. McGee, *Forecasting:Methods and Applications* (2nd ed.) John Wiley&Sons. 1983. (MWM)

Other books :

Box, G.E.P & G.M.Jenkins, *Time Series Analysis, Forecasting and Control*(revised ed.). Holden-Day.1976.
Granger,C.W.J.&P.Newbold,*Forecasting Economic Time Series*(2nd ed) Academic Press.1986
Klein, L.R. *Lectures in Econometrics*. North-Holland. 1983.
Hall, S.G. & S.G.B. Henry, *Macroeconomic Modelling*. North-Holland.1988.
Challen, D.W. & A.J. Hagger, *Macroeconometric Systems, Construction, Validation and Applications*. THe Macmillan Press. 1983.
Cuthbertson, K., S.G. Hall, M.P. Taylor, *Applied Econometric Techniques*. The University of Michigan Press. 1992.
Harvey, A.C. *The Econometric Analysis of Time Series*. MIT Press. 1990.
Intriligator, M.D. *Econometric Models, Techniques &Applications*. Prentice-Hall.1978.
Johnston, J. *Econometric Methods*. McGraw-Hill. 1984.
Pindyck, R.S. & D. L. Rubinfeld, *Econometric Models &Economic Forecasts*, 3rd. ed.McGraw-Hill. 1991.
Theil, H. *Economic Forecasts and Policy* . North-Holland. 1958
Zellner, A.(ed.) *Readings in Economic Statistics and Econometrics*.Little, Brown and Company.1968.
Özmucur, S. *Geleceği Tahmin Yöntemleri*. ISO Yayın No. 1990-2.
Neftçi, S. & S. Özmucur, *Türkiye Ekonomisi için TÜSİAD Öncü Göstergeler Endeksi*.1991

Class Hours

Wednesday 6,7,8 1B207

Office Hours

Monday 3 IB 503
Wednesday 3 IB 503
and by appointment (tel : 1526 or 1505)

Grading

Term paper 50
Final Exam 50

EC 535 - Forecasting Methods   Course Outline   Spring 1993
Course Outline (other readings will be given during the semester):

1.Basic Concepts
MWM, Chp. 1, 2, 11,14,15,16
Özmucur, Chp. 1

2. Smooting Methods
MWM, Chp. 3
Özmucur, Chp. 3

3. Decomposition Methods
MWM, Chp. 4
Özmucur, Chp. 2, 4

4. Modern Time series analysis
MWM, Chp.8,9, 10
Box-Jenkins. Chps. 1,2 3
Özmucur, Chp. 5

5. Econometric Models
MWM, Chp. 5,6,7
Johnston, Chp. 11
Klein, Chp. 7
Özmucur, Chp. 6,7,8

6. Vector Autoregression (VAR) Models
Sims,C. "Macroeconomics and Reality " *Econometrica.* 1980
Özmucur, Chp. 9

7. Leading indicators or Barometric forecasting
MWM, Chp. 12
Özmucur, Chp. 11
Neftçi &Özmucur

8.Forecasting with an Input/Output
Leontief, *The Structure of American Economy*
Özmucur,Chp. 10

9. Qualitative and technological forecasting
MWM, Chp. 13
Özmucur, Chp. 14

10. Combination of forecasts
Granger&Newbold, Chp. 9
Özmucur, Chp. 15

EC 536 - Econometric Model Building   Course Outline   Fall 1992

Instructor : Süleyman Özmucur
Prerequisites : Ec 331, Ec 332 or Ec 531, Ec 532

G

Textbooks :
Klein, L.R. *Lectures in Econometrics*. North-Holland. 1983.
Hall, S.G. & S.G.B. Henry, *Macroeconomic Modelling*. North-Holland.1988.

Other books :
Amemiya, T. *Advanced Econometrics*. Harvard University Press.1985
Bridge, J.L. *Applied Econometrics*. North-Holland. 1971.
Challen, D.W. & A.J. Hagger, *Macroeconometric Systems, Construction, Validation and Applications*. THe Macmillan Press. 1983.
Chow, G.C. *Econometrics*. McGraw-Hill. 1983.
Chow, G.C. & P.Corsi(eds.) *Evaluating the reliability of Macro-Economic Models*. John Wiley&Sons. 1982.
Christ, C.F. *Econometric Models and Methods*. John Wiley & Sons. 1966.
Cramer, J.S. *Empirical Econometrics*. North-Holland. 1969.
Cuthbertson, K., S.G. Hall, M.P. Taylor, *Applied Econometric Techniques*. The University of Michigan Press. 1992.
Desai, M. *Applied Econometrics*. McGraw-Hill. 1976.
Fair, R. *Specification, Estimation, and Analysis of Macroeconometric Models*. Harvard University Press. Cambridge. 1984.
Goldberger, A.S. *Econometric Theory*. John Wiley & Sons. 1964.
Griliches,Z.&M.D.Intriligator(eds.) *Handbook of econometrics*. North-Holland. 1983
Harvey, A.C. *The Econometric Analysis of Time Series*. MIT Press. 1990.
Hebden, J. *Applications of Econometrics*. Philip Allan. 1983.
Intriligator, M.D. *Econometric Models, Techniques &Applications*. Prentice-Hall.1978.
Johnston, J. *Econometric Methods*. McGraw-Hill. 1984.
Judge, G.J., R.C. Hill, W.E. Griffiths, H. Lütkepohl, T-C Lee. *Introduction to the Theory and Practice of Econometrics*. John Wiley&Sons. 1982.
Judge, G.J.,W.E. Griffiths, R.C. Hill, H. Lütkepohl, T-C Lee. *The Theory and Practice of Econometrics*.(2nd ed.) John Wiley&Sons. 1985.
Klein, L.R. *A Textbook of Econometrics*, 2nd ed. Prentice-Hall. 1974.
Klein, L.R. *An Introduction to Econometrics*. Prentice-Hall. 1962.
Kmenta, J. *Elements of Econometrics*, 2.nd ed. Macmillan. 1986.
Kmenta, J.&J.B.Ramsey(eds.) *Large-Scale Macro-Econometric Models.Theory and Practice*. North-Holland. 1981.
Maddala, G.S. *Econometrics*. McGraw-Hill. 1977.
Malinvaud, E. *Statistical Methods of Econometrics*. 2nd ed. North-Holland. 1970.
Marchi, N. & C. Gilbert, *History and Methodology of Econometrics*. Clarendon Press. 1989.
Pindyck, R.S. & D. L. Rubinfeld, *Econometric Models &Economic Forecasts*, 3rd. ed.McGraw-Hill. 1991.
Rao, P. & R.L. Miller, *Applied Econometrics*. Prentice-Hall. 1972.
Theil, H. *Principles of Econometrics*. John Wiley & Sons. 1971.
Theil, H. *Economic Forecasts and Policy* . North-Holland. 1958
Zellner, A.(ed.) *Readings in Economic Statistics and Econometrics*.Little, Brown and Company.1968.

Class Hours

Monday   5,6,7   IB207

EC 536 - Econometric Model Building   Course Outline   Fall 1992

Monday   3   IB 503
Wednesday 3   IB 503
and by appointment (tel : 1526 or 1505)

Grading
Term paper   50
Final Exam   50

Course Outline (other readings will be given during the semester):

1.Macroeconometric models

Klein, Chp. 1
Hall&Henry Chps. 1, 4
Intriligator, M."Economic and Econometric Models" Chp.3 of Griliches&Intriligator(eds.)
Handbook of econometrics. Vol 1.North-Holland. 1983
Özmucur, S. *A monthly econometric model for Turkey, January 1981-June 1991*
Klein, L.R. "The Statistical Approach to Economics" *Journal of Econometrics*. Vol. 37. 1988.
pp.7-26.
Reinhart, C.M. " A Model of Adjustment and Growth An Empirical Analysis" *IMF Staff
Papers*. Vol 37. March 1990. pp. 168-82.
Khan, M.S. & M.D.Knight."Stabilizaation Programs in Developing Countries:A Formal
Framework" *IMF Staff Papers*. Vol. 28. March 1981. pp. 1-53.
Haque, N.U., K. Lahiri, P.J. Montiel. "A Macroeconometric Model for Developing Countries"
IMF Staff Papers. Vol. 37. September 1990. pp. 537-559.
Journal of Econometrics. Vol. 37. No. 1. Annals. January 1988.

2.Identification and Parameter Estimation

Johnston, Chps. 11 , 12
Amemiya, Chp. 7, 8
Harvey, Chps. 3,4
Hsiao C."Identification" Chp.4 of Griliches&Intriligator(eds.) *Handbook of econometrics*. Vol
1.North-Holland. 1983
Amemiya, T. "Non-linear Estimation". Chp. 6 of Griliches.&Intriligator(eds.) *Handbook of
econometrics*. Vol 1.North-Holland. 1983
Quandt,R.E., "Computational Problems and Methods" Chp. 12 of Griliches.&Intriligator(eds.)
Handbook of econometrics. Vol 1.North-Holland. 1983
Marquardt,D.W. "An Algorithm for least-squares estimation of Nonlinear Parameters" *Journal
of Society for Industrial and Applied Mathematics*. Vol. 11. No. 2. June 1963. pp.431-441.
Amemiya, T. "The Nonlinear Two-stage Least-squares Estimator" *Journal of Econometrics*
Vol.2 (1974) pp. 105-110.
Amemiya, T. "The Nonlinear Limited-Information Maximum Likelihood Estimator and the
Modified Nonlinear Two-stage Least-squares Estimator" *Journal of Econometrics* Vol.3 (1975)
pp. 375-386.
Amemiya, T. "The Maximum Likelihood and the Nonlinear Three-stage Least-squares Estimator
in the general nonlinear Simultaneous equation model" *Econometrica* Vol.45(1977) pp. 955-
968.

EC 536 - Econometric Model Building   Course Outline   Fall 1992
3. Specification and Diagnostic Tests

Hall &Henry, Chp. 2
Harvey, Chp. 5
Leamer, E.E. "Model Choice and Specification Analysis" Intriligator, M."Economic and Econometric Models" Chp.5 of Griliches&Intriligator(eds.) *Handbook of econometrics*. Vol 1.North-Holland. 1983
Hausman, J.A. "Specification and Estimation of Simultaneous Equation Models" Chp.7 of Griliches&Intriligator(eds.) *Handbook of econometrics*. Vol 1.North-Holland. 1983
Engle, R.F. "Wald, Likelihood Ratio, and Langrange Multiplier Tests in Econometrics" Chp. 13 of Griliches.&Intriligator(eds.) *Handbook of econometrics*. Vol 2.North-Holland. 1984
Geweke, J. "Inference and Causality in Economic Time Series" Chp. 19 of Griliches.&Intriligator(eds.) *Handbook of econometrics*. Vol 2.North-Holland. 1984
Journal of Policy Modeling. Vol. 14. No.3 (June 1992) and No. 4 (August 1992)
Journal of Economic Dynamics&Control. Vol 12 No.2/3(June, September 1988)
Oxford Bulletin of Economics and Statistics. Vol. 48. No. 3. 1986.

4. Model Solutions

Hall&Henry, Chp. 5
Klein, Chp.2

5. Validation

Klein, Chp. 3
Fair, R.C. "Evaluating the predictive accuracy of Models" Chp. 33 of Griliches.&Intriligator(eds.) *Handbook of econometrics*. Vol 3.North-Holland. 1986.

6. Simulation

Klein, Chp. 2, 4

7. Forecasting
Klein, Chp. 6
Journal of Econometrics. Vol. 40. No. 1. Annals. January 1989.
Özmucur, *Geleceği Tahmin Yöntemleri*. ISO. 1990.

8. Policy evaluation and control

Hall &Henry, Chp. 7
Klein, Chp. 5
Taylor, J.B."New Econometric Approaches to Stabilization Policy in Stochastic Models of Macroeconomic Fluctuations" Chp. 34 of Griliches.&Intriligator(eds.) *Handbook of econometrics*. Vol 3.North-Holland. 1986.
Klein, L.R. "Economic Policy Formation:Theory and Implementation(Applied Econometrics in the Public Sector)" Chp. 35 of Griliches.&Intriligator(eds.) *Handbook of econometrics*. Vol 3.North-Holland. 1986.
Özmucur, *Policy simulations with a monthly econometric model*

9. Models of the world economy

Klein, Chp.7

Econ. 557b
Spring 1995

Peter C.B. Phillips

TIME SERIES ECONOMETRICS II

G

UNIT ROOTS AND COINTEGRATION

This course is a continuation of Time Series Econometrics I, but the necessary background material will be covered in a review session at the beginning of the course. The main subject is nonstationary time series. We plan to cover asymptotic methods for nonstationary processes, unit root tests, tests of stationarity, spurious regression, cointegrated systems, cointegrated tests, and estimation of models with cointegration. We also plan to look at methods of model determination and automated approaches to model selection and prediction with multiple time series models. Some empirical applications and simulations will be given in class.

0. General References (the reading guide of Time Series Econometrics I has a more complete list. The items below are largely supplementary to that general list).

Banerjee, A., J. Dolado, J.W. Galbraith and D.F. Hendry (1993) <u>Cointegration, Error-correction and the Econometric Analysis of Non-stationary Data</u>, Oxford: Oxford University Press.

Davidson, J. (1994) <u>Stochastic Limit Theory: An Introduction for Econometricians</u>, Oxford University Press.

Fuller, W.A. (1976) <u>Introduction to Statistical Time Series</u>, New York: Wiley.

Gallant, A.R. and H. White (1988) "A unified theory of estimation and inference for nonlinear dynamic models," Oxford: Basil Blackwell.

Hall, P. and C.C. Heyde (1980) <u>Martingale Limit Theory and its Applications</u>, New York: Academic Press.

Hamilton, J.D. (1994) <u>Time Series Analysis</u>, Princeton: Princeton University Press.

Lutkepohl, H. (1993) <u>Introduction to Multiple Time Series Analysis</u>, New York: Springer Verlag (2nd ed.).

Phillips, P.C.B. (1992) "Unit roots" in P. Newman, M. Milgate and J. Eatwell (eds), <u>The New Palgrave Dictionary of Money and Finance</u>, 726–730.

Phillips, P.C.B. (1995) "Unit roots and cointegration: Recent books and themes for the future," <u>Journal of Applied Econometrics</u>.

Rao, B.B. (1994) <u>Cointegration for the Applied Economist</u>, St. Martin's Press.

Reinsel, G. (1993) <u>Elements of Multivariate Time Series Analysis</u>, New York: Springer–Verlag.

Stock, J.H. (1995) "Unit roots, structural breaks and trends," in R.F. Engle and D. McFadden (eds.), Handbook of Econometrics, Vol. 4, Amsterdam: North Holland.

Watson, M. (1995) "Vector autoregressions and cointegration in R.F. Engle and D. McFadden (eds.), Handbook of Econometrics, Vol. 4, Amsterdam: North Holland.

White, H. (1994) Estimation, Inference and Specification Analysis, Cambridge: Cambridge University Press.

1. Review: Stationary Time Series, Limit Theory and Martingales

Beveridge, S. and R. Nelson (1981) "A new approach to decomposition of time series in permanent and transitory components with particular attention to measurement of the 'Business Cycle', Journal of Monetary Economics, 7, 151–174.

Hall and Heyde (1980) op.cit.

Phillips, P.C.B. (1989) Lecture Notes on Stationary and Nonstationary Time Series, Institute of Advanced Studies, Vienna.

Phillips, P.C.B. (1988) "Reflections on econometric methodology," Economic Record, 64, 334–359.

Phillips, P.C.B. and V.Solo (1992) "Asymptotics for Linear Processes" Annals of Statistics, 20, 971–1001.

White, H. (1984) Asymptotic Theory for Econometricians, New York: Wiley.

2. Functional Limit Theory and its Applications to Unit Root Asymptotics

Billingsley, P. (1968) Weak Convergence of Probability Measures, New York: Wiley.

Chan, N.H. and C.Z Wei (1987) "Asymptotic inference for nearly nonstationary AR(1) processes," Annals of Statistics, 15, 1050–1063.

Jeganathan, P. (1991) "On the asymptotic behavior of least squares estimators in AR time series with roots near the unit circle," Econometric Theory, 7, 269–306.

Jeganathan, P. (1995) "Some aspects of asymptotic theory with applications to time series models," Econometric Theory, (forthcoming).

Phillips, P.C.B. (1987) "Towards a unified asymptotic theory for autoregression," Biometrika, 74, 535–547.

Phillips, P.C.B. (1988) "Multiple regression with integrated time series," Contemporary Mathematics, 80, 79–105.

Phillips, P.C.B. and S.N. Durlauf (1986) "Multiple Time Series Regression with Integrated Processes," Review of Economic Studies, 53, 473–496.

3. Long Run Variance Matrix Estimation

Andrews, D.W.K. (1991) "Heteroskedasticity and autocorrelation consistent covariance matrix estimation," Econometrica, 59, 817–858.

Andrews, D.W.K. and J.C. Monahan (1990) "An improved heteroskedasticity and autocorrelation consistent covariance matrix estimator," Econometrica, 60, 953–966.

Billingsley, P. (1968) op.cit.

Hannan, E.J. (1970) Multiple Time Series, New York: Wiley.

Lee, C.C. and P.C.B. Phillips (1994) "An ARMA pre-whitened long run variance estimator," Yale University, Mimographed.

Newey, W.K. and K.D. West (1987) "A simple positive semi-definite, heteroskedasticity and autocorrelation consistent covariance matrix," Econometrica, 55, 703–708.

Parzen, E. (1957) "On consistent estimates of the spectrum of a stationary time series," Annals of Mathematical Statistics, 28, 329–348.

White, H. (1980) "A heteroskedasticity–consistent covariance matrix estimator and a direct test of heteroskedasticity," Econometrica, 48, 817–838.

White, H. (1984) op. cit.

4. Unit Root Tests and Applications

Banerjee, A., Lumsdaine, R. and Stock, J.H. (1992) "Recursive and sequential tests of the unit root and trend break hypotheses: Theory and international evidence," Journal of Business and Economic Statistics, 10, 271–288.

Bhargava, A. (1986) "On the theory of testing for unit roots in observed time series," Review of Economic Studies, 53(174), 369–384.

Bierens, H.J. and S. Guo (1993) "Testing stationarity and trend stationarity against the unit root hypothesis," Econometric Reviews, 12, 1–32.

145

Blough, S.R. (1992) "The relationship between power and level for generic unit root tests in finite samples," Journal of Applied Econometrics, 7, 295–308.

Campbell, J.Y. and P. Perron (1991) "Pitfalls and opportunities: What macroeconomists should know about unit roots," NBER Macroeconomics Annual, 141–200.

Cochrane, J.H. (1988) "How big is the random walk in GNP?" Journal of Political Economy, 96, 893–920.

Cochrane, J.H. (1991a) "A critique of the application of unit root tests," Journal of Economic Dynamics and Control, 15, 275–284.

Cochrane, J.H. (1991b) "Comment on Campbell and Perron" NBER Macroeconomics Annual, 1991, 5, 201–210.

DeJong, D.N., J.C. Nankervis, N.E. Savin and C.H. Whiteman (1992a) "Integration versus trend-stationarity in macroeconomic time series," Econometrica, 60, 423–434.

DeJong, D.N., J.C. Nankervis, N.E. Savin and C.H. Whiteman (1992b) "The power problems of unit root tests for time series with autoregressive errors," Journal of Econometrics, 53, 323–343.

Dickey, D.A. and W.A. Fuller (1979) "Distribution of the estimators for autoregressive time series with a unit root," Journal of the American Statistical Association, 74, 427–431.

Dickey, D.A. and W.A. Fuller (1981) "Likelihood ratio statistics for autoregressive time series with a unit root," Econometrica, 49, 1057–1052.

Dickey, D.A., D.P. Hasza, and W.A. Fuller (1984) "Testing for unit roots in seasonal time series," Journal of the Americal Statistical Association, 79, 355–367.

Dickey, D.A. and S.G. Pantula (1987) "Determining the order of differencing in autoregressive processes," Journal of Business and Economic Statistics, 5, 455–462.

Elliott, G., T.J. Rothenberg and J.H. Stock (1992) "Efficient tests for an autoregressive unit root," NBER Technical Working Paper No. 130.

Evans, G.B.A. and N.E. Savin (1984) "Testing for unit roots: 1," Econometrica, 49, 753–779.

Evans, G.B.A. and N.E. Savin (1984) "Testing for unit roots: 2," Econometrica, 52, 1241–1269.

Fuller (1976) op. cit.

Ghysels, E. and P. Perron (1993) "The effect of seasonal adjustment filters on tests for a unit root," Journal of Econometrics, 55, 57–98.

Hall, A. (1989) "Testing for a unit root in the presence of moving average errors," Biometrika, 76, 49–56.

Hall, A. (1992) "Testing for a unit root in time series using instrumental variable estimation with pretest data-based model selection," Journal of Econometrics, 54, 223–250.

Hall, R.E. (1978) "Stochastic implications of the life cycle — permanent income hypothesis: Theory and evidence," Journal of Political Economy, 86(6), 971–987.

Hylleberg, S., R.F. Engle, C.W.J. Granger and S. Yoo (1990) "Seasonal integration and cointegration," Journal of Econometrics, 44, 215–238.

Lee, C.C. and P.C.B. Phillips (1994) "Efficiency gains using GLS and OLS under nonstationarity," Yale University, Mimeographed.

Nelson, C.R. and C.I. Plosser (1982) "Trends and random walks in macroeconomic time series: Some evidence and implications," Journal of Monetary Economics, 10, 139–162.

Park, J. (1990) "Testing for unit roots and cointegration by variable addition," in G.F. Rhodes and T.B. Fomby (eds) Advances in Econometrics: Cointegration , Spurious Regressions and Unit Roots, Greenwich, CT: JAI Press.

Perron, P. (1988) "Trends and random walks in macroeconomic time series: Further evidence from a new approach," Journal of Economic Dynamics and Control, 12, 297–332.

Perron, P. (1989) "The great crash, the oil price shock and the unit root hypothesis," Econometrica, 57, 1361–1401.

Perron, P. and P.C.B. Phillips (1987) "Does GNP have a unit root? A reevaluation," Economic Letters, 23, 139–145.

Perron, P. and T.S. Vogelsang (1992) "Nonstationarity and level shifts with an application to purchasing power parity," Journal of Business and Economic Statistics, 10, 301–320.

Phillips, P.C.B. and P. Perron (1987) "Testing for a unit root in time series regression," Biometrika, 75, 335–346.

Quah, D. (1992) "The relative importance of permanent and transitory components: Identification and some theoretical bounds," Econometrica, 60(1), 107–118.

Robinson, P.M. (1994) "Efficient tests of nonstationary hypotheses," Journal of the American Statistical Association, forthcoming.

Said, S.E. and D.A. Dickey (1984) "Testing for unit roots in autoregressive–moving average models of unknown order," Biometrika, 71, 599–608.

Said, S.E. and D.A. Dickey (1985) "Hypothesis testing in ARIMA (p,1,q) models" Journal of the American Statistical Association, 80, 369–374.

Schmidt, P. and P.C.B. Phillips (1992) "LM tests for a unit root in the presence of deterministic trends," Oxford Bulletin of Economics and Statistics, 54, 257–287.

Schwert, G.W. (1987) "Effects of model misspecification on tests for unit roots in macroeconomic data," Journal of Monetary Economics, 20, 73–103.

Schwert, G.W. (1989) "Tests for unit roots: A Monte Carlo investigation," Journal of Business and Economic Statistics, 7, 147–159.

Solo, V. (1984) "The order of differencing in ARIMA models," Journal of the American Statistical Association, 79, 916–921.

Sowell, F.B. (1990) "Fractional unit root distribution," Econometrica, 58, 495–506.

Sowell, F.B. (1992) "Maximum likelihood estimation of stationary univariate fractionally integrated time series models," Journal of Econometrics, 53, 165–188.

Stock, J.H. (1991) "Confidence intervals for the largest autoregressive root in U.S. economic time series," Journal of Monetary Economics, 28(3), 435–460.

Stock, J.H. and M.W. Watson (1988) "Variable trends in economic time series," Journal of Economic Perspectives, 2(3), 147–174.

Tanaka, K. (1990) "The Fredholm approach to asymptotic inference in nonstationary and noninvertible time series models," Econometric Theory, 6(4), 411–432.

Watson, M.W. (1986) "Univariate detrending methods with stochastic trends," Journal of Monetary Economics, 18, 49–75.

West, K.D. (1987) "A note on the power of least squares tests for a unit root," Economics Letters, 24, 1397–1418.

West, K.D. (1988a) "Asymptotic normality when regressors have a unit root," Econometrica, 56, 1397–1418.

West, K.D. (1988b) "On the interpretation of near random walk behavior in GNP," American Economic Review, 78, 202–208.

Zivot, E. and Andrews, D.W.K. (1992) "Further evidence on the Great Crash, the oil price shock, and the unit root hypothesis," Journal of Business and Economic Statistics, 10, 251–270.

5. Testing Stationarity

Kwiatkowski, D., P.C.B. Phillips, P. Schmidt and Y. Shin (1992) "Testing the null hypothesis of stationarity against the alternatives of a unit root: How sure are we that economic time series have a unit root?," Journal of Econometrics, 54, 159–178.

Nabeya, S. and K. Tanaka (1988) "Asymptotic theory of a test for the constancy of regression coefficients against the random walk alternative," Annals of Statistics, 16, 218–235.

Nyblom, J. (1986) "Testing for deterministic linear trend in time series," Journal of the American Statistical Association, 81, 545–549.

Nyblom, J. (1989) "Testing for constancy of parameters over time," Journal of the American Statistical Association, 84, 223–230.

Saikkonen, P. and R. Luukkonen (1993a) "Testing for moving average unit root in autoregressive integrated moving average models," Journal of American Statistical Association, 88, 596–601.

Saikkonen, P. and R. Luukkonen (1993b) "Point optimal tests for testing the order of differencing in ARIMA models," Econometric Theory, 9(3), 343–362.

Tanaka, K. (1990b) "Testing for a moving average unit root," Econometric Theory, 6(4), 433–444.

6. Spurious Regression

Durlauf, S.N. and P.C.B. Phillips (1988) "Trends versus random walks in time series analysis," Econometrica, 56, 1333–1354.

Granger, C.W.J. and P. Newbold (1974) "Spurious regressions in econometrics," Journal of Econometrics, 2, 111–120.

Nelson, C.R. and H. Kang (1981) "Spurious periodity in inappropriately detrended time series," Econometrica, 49, 741–751.

Phillips, P.C.B. (1986) "Understanding supurious regressions in econometrics," Journal of Econometrics, 33, 311–340.

Phillips, P.C.B. (1989) "Partially identified econometric models," Econometric Theory, 5, 181–240.

7. Regression with Integrated Processes

Park, J.Y. and P.C.B.Phillips (1988) "Statistical inference in regressions with integrated processes: Part I," Econometric Theory, 4, 468–498.

Park, J.Y and P.C.B. Phillips (1989) "Statistical inference in regressions with integrated processes: Part II," Econometric Theory, 5, 95–132.

Phillips, P.C.B. (1988) op.cit.

Sims, C.A., J.H. Stock and M.W. Watson (1990) "Inference in linear time series with some unit roots," Econometrica, 58, 113–144.

8. Cointegration and Tests for Cointegration

Ahn, S.K. and G.C. Reinsel (1988) "Nested reduced rank autoregressive models for multiple time series," Journal of American Statistical Association, 83, 849–856.

Ahn, S.K. and G.C. Reinsel (1990) Estimation for partially nonstationary multivariate autoregressive models," Journal of the American Statistical Association, 85, 813–823.

Campbell, J.Y. and R.J. Shiller (1987) "Cointegration and tests of present value models" Journal of Political Economy, 95, 1062–1088. Reprinted in Long-Run Economic Relations: Readings in Cointegration, edited by R.F. Engle and C.W.J. Granger, Oxford University Press, New York, 1991.

Engle, R.F. and C.W.J. Granger (1987) "Cointegration and error correction: Representation, estimation and testing," Econometrica, 55, 251–276.

Johansen, S. (1988a) "Statistical analysis and cointegrating vectors," Journal of Economic Dynamics and Control, 12, 231–254.

Johansen, S. (1988b) "The mathematical structure of error correction models," Contemporary Mathematics, Structural Inference from Stochastic Processes, Vol. 80, N.U. Prabhu (ed.), American Mathematical Society: Providence, RI.

Johansen, S. (1991) "Estimation and hypothesis testing of cointegration vectors in Gaussian vector autoregressive models," Econometrica, 59, 1551–1580.

Johansen, S. (1992a) "Determination of cointegration rank in the presence of a linear trend," Oxford Bulletin of Economics and Statistics, 54, 383–397.

Johansen, S. (1992b) "A representation of vector autoregressive processes integrated of order 2," Econometric Theory, 8(2), 188–202.

Johansen, S. and K. Juselius (1990) "Maximum likelihood estimation and inference on cointegration — with applications to the demand for money," Oxford Bulletin of Economics and Statistics, 52(2), 169–210.

Johansen, S. and K. Juselius (1992) "Testing structural hypotheses in a multivariate cointegration analysis of the PPP and UIP of UK," Journal of Econometrics, 53, 211–244.

Phillips, P.C.B. (1991a) "Optimal inference in cointegrated systems," Econometrica, 59, 283–306.

Phillips, P.C.B. (1991b) "Error correction and long run equilibria in continuous time," Econometrica, 59, 967–980.

Phillips, P.C.B. and M. Loretan (1991) "Estimating long run economic equilibrium," Review of Economic Studies, 58, May 1991, 407–436

Phillips, P.C.B. and S. Ouliaris (1990) "Asymptotic properties of residual based tests for cointegration," Econometrica, 58, 165–193.

Stock, J.H. (1987) "Asymptotic properties of least squares estimators of cointegrating vectors," Econometrica, 55, 1035–1056.

Stock, J.H. and M.W. Watson (1988) "Testing for common trends," Journal of the American Statistical Association, 83(404), 1097–1107.

Econometric Reviews, (1994) [special issue].

Journal of Economic Dynamics and Control, Vol. 12 (1988) [special issue].

Oxford Bulletin of Economics & Statistics, Vol. 48 (1986) [special issue].

Oxford Bulletin of Economics & Statistics, Vol. 54 (1992) [special issue].

9. Causality Tests in Cointegrated Systems

Sims, C.A., J. Stock and M.W. Watson (1990) "Inference in linear time series models with unit roots," Econometrica, 58, 113–144.

Toda, H.Y. and P.C.B. Phillips (1993) "Vector autoregression and causality," Econometrica, 61, 1367–1394.

Toda, H.Y. and P.C.B. Phillips (1994a) "The spurious effect of unit roots on exogeneity tests in vector autoregressions: An analytical study," Journal of Econometrics, 59, 229–255.

Toda, H.Y. and P.C.B. Phillips (1994b) "Vector autoregression and causality: A theoretical overview and simulation study," Econometric Reviews, 13, 259–285.

10. Regression Estimation of Cointegrated Systems

Kitamura, Y. and P.C.B. Phillips (1994a) "Fully modified IV, GIVE and GMM estimation with possibly nonstationary regressors and instruments," Cowles Foundation Discussion Paper No. 1082.

Kitamura, Y. and P.C.B. Phillips (1994b) "Efficient IV estimation in nonstationary regression: An overview and simulation study," Yale University, Mimeographed.

Park, J.Y. (1992) "Canonical cointegrating regression," Econometrica, 60, 119–143.

Phillips, P.C.B. (1995) "Fully modified least squares and vector autoregression," Cowles Foundation Discussion Paper No. 1047. Forthcoming in Econometrica.

Phillips, P.C.B. and B.E. Hansen (1990) "Statistical inference in instumental variables regression with I(1) processes," Review of Economic Studies, 57, 99–125.

Saikkonen, P. (1991) "Asymptotically efficient estimation of cointegrating regressions," Econometric Theory, 7(1), 1–21.

Saikkonen, P. (1992) "Estimation and testing of cointegrated systems by an autoregressive approximation," Econometric Theory, 8(1), 1–27.

Stock, J.H. and M.W. Watson (1993) "A simple estimator of cointegrating vectors in higher order integrated systems," Econometrica, 61, 783–820.

11. Bayesian Approaches to Unit Root and Cointegration Analysis

Chao, J. and P.C.B. Phillips (1994) "Bayesian model selection in partially nonstationary vector autoregressive processes with reduced rank structure," Yale University, Mimeographed.

Econometric Theory, Vol. 10, No. 3&4, 1994 [special issue].

Journal of Applied Econometrics, Vol. 6, No.4, 1991 [special issue].

Le Cam, L. and G.L. Yang (1990) Asymptotics in Statistics: Some Basic Concepts. New York Springer–Verlag.

Geweke, J. (1988) "The secular and cyclical behavior of real GNP in nineteen OECD countries, 1957–1983," Journal of Business and Economic Statistics, 6, 479–486.

Phillips, P.C.B. (1991a) "To criticize the critics: An objective Bayesian analysis of stochastic trends," Journal of Applied Econometrics, 6(4), 333–364 (with discussion).

Phillips, P.C.B. (1991b) "Bayesian routes and unit roots: De rebus prioribus semper est disputandum," Journal of Applied Econometrics, 435–475.

Phillips, P.C.B. (1992) "The long-run Australian consumption function reexamined: An empirical exercise in Bayesian inference," in C. Hargreaves (ed.), Long Run Equilibrium and Macroeconomic Modelling, Cheltenham: Edward Elgar.

Phillips, P.C.B. and W. Ploberger (1994a) "An asymptotic theory of Bayesian inference for time series," Cowles Foundation Discussion Paper No. 1038.

Phillips, P.C.B. and W. Ploberger (1994b) "Posterior odds testing for a unit root with data-based model selection," Econometric Theory, 10, 774–808.

Sims, A. (1988) "Bayesian skepticism on unit root econometrics," Journal of Economic Dynamics and Control, 12, 463–474.

Sims, C.A. and H. Uhlig (1991) "Understanding unit rooters: A helicopter tour," Econometrica, 59(6), 1591–1600.

Zivot, E. and P.C.B. Phillips (1994) "A Bayesian analysis of trend determination in economic time series," Econometric Reviews, 13(3), 291–336.

12. Bayesian Vector Autoregressions, Model Determination and Prediction

Cooley, T.B. and S.F. LeRoy (1985) "A theoretical macroeconometrics: A critique," Journal of Monetary Economics, 16, 283–308.

Hamilton (1994) op. cit, Chs. 11, 12.

Litterman, R.B. (1986) "Forecasting with Bayesian vector autoregressions: Five years of experience," Journal of Business and Economic Statistics, 4, 25–38.

Litterman, R.B. and L. Weiss (1985) "Money, real interest rates, and output: A interpretation of postwar U.S. data," Econometrica, 53, 129–156.

Lutkepohl, H. (1990) "Asymptotic distributions of impulse response functions and forecast error variane decompositions of vector autoregressive models," Review of Economics and Statistics, 72, 116–125.

Lutkepohl, H. (1993) op.cit. Ch. 5.

Phillips, P.C.B. (1992) "Bayes methods for trending multiple time series with an empirical application to the U.S. economy," Cowles Foundation Discussion Paper No. 1025.

Phillips, P.C.B. (1994) "Model determination and macroeconomic activity," Cowles Foundation Discussion Paper No. 1083.

Phillips, P.C.B. (1994a) "Bayesian model selection and prediction with empirical applications," Journal of Econometrics (forthcoming).

Phillips, P.C.B. (1994b) "Bayesian prediction: A response," Journal of Econometrics (forthcoming).

Phillips, P.C.B. (1994c) "Bayes models and forecasts of Australian macroeconomic time series" in C. Hargreaves (ed.) Nonstationary Time Series Analysis and Cointegration. Oxford: Oxford University Press.

Runkle, D. (1987) "Vector autoregressions and reality," Journal of Business and Economic Statistics, 5(4), 437–432.

Schwarz, G. (1978) "Estimating the dimension of a model," Annals of Statistics, 6, 461–464.

Sims, C.A. (1980) "Macroeconomics and reality," Econometrica, 48, 1–48.

Todd, R.M. (1990) "Vector autoregression evidence on monetarism: Another look at the robustness debate," Federal Reserve Bank of Minneapolis Quarterly Review, 19–37.

Todd, R.M. (1995) "Improving economic forecasting with Bayesian vector autoregression," Federal Reserve Bank of Minneapolis Quarterly Review, 4, 18–29.

West, M. and P.J. Harrison (1989) Bayesian Forecasting and Dynamic Models. New York: Springer–Verlag.

Zellner, A. and C.K. Min (1992) "Bayesian analysis, model selection and prediction," University of Chicago, Mimeographed.

Take Home Examination

Consider the model

(1) $y_t = bt^d + u_t, \quad t = 1, \dots, n$.

1(a) Suppose that $d \geq 1/2$ in (1) and $\Delta u_t = C(L)\varepsilon_t, \quad \varepsilon_t \equiv iid(0, \sigma^2)$, where

(2) $C(L) = \sum_{j=0}^{\infty} c_j L^j, \quad \sum_{j=0}^{\infty} j^{1/2} |c_j| < \infty, \quad C(1) \neq 0$.

Find a limit theory for the ordinary least squares (OLS) estimator of b in (1).

1(b) Now suppose that $d \geq -1/2$ in (1) and $u_t = C(L)\varepsilon_t, \quad \varepsilon_t \equiv iid(0, \sigma^2)$, where $C(L)$ is as in (2). Find a limit theory for the OLS estimator of b in (1) in this case.

Question 2.

Consider the structural-break regression model

(3)
$$y_t = x_t' \beta_1 + u_t, \quad t = 1, \dots, k;$$
$$y_t = x_t' \beta_2 + u_t, \quad t = k+1, \dots, n;$$

where $u_t \equiv iidN(0, \sigma^2)$. Assume that the m-vector of regressors x_t in (3) is deterministic and that there exists a diagonal matrix D_n such that

(4) $D_n^{-1/2} x_{[nr]} \rightarrow g(r) \quad \text{as } n \rightarrow \infty$,

uniformly in $r \in [0,1]$, where $g(.)$ is a piecewise continuous function on the $[0,1]$ interval.

2(a) Show that the maximum likelihood estimator of the structural break point k is given by

$$\hat{k} = \arg\min_{m \leq k \leq n-m} \hat{\sigma}^2(k)$$

where

$$\hat{\sigma}^2(k) = n^{-1} \left\{ \sum_{1}^{k} (y_t - x_t' \hat{\beta}_1)^2 + \sum_{k+1}^{n} (y_t - x_t' \hat{\beta}_2)^2 \right\}$$

and where $\hat{\beta}_1$ and $\hat{\beta}_2$ are the OLS estimators of β_1 and β_2 in (3).

2(b) Now suppose that the data are generated by the unit root model $\Delta y_t = C(L)\varepsilon_t, \quad \varepsilon_t \equiv iid(0, \sigma^2)$, where $C(L)$ satisfies (2) above, but that model (3) is estimated instead.

Define

$$\hat{r} = \arg\min_{\bar{r} \leq r \leq \tilde{r}} \hat{\sigma}^2([nr])$$

where $\bar{r} > 0$, and $\tilde{r} < 1$. Find the limit distribution of $\hat{r}$.

2(c) (optional) For the case where the regressor in (3) is the scalar trend $x_t = t$, perform a simulation experiment in which you calculate the estimator $\hat{r}$ and use the simulation estimates to produce a kernel density estimate of the sampling distribution of the estimator.

Question 3.

Consider the model of heteroskedastic integration

(4) $y_t = (1 + v_t)y_{t-1} + u_t, \quad t = 1, \dots, n$

where $v_t \equiv iidN(0, \sigma_v^2)$, $u_t \equiv iidN(0, \sigma_u^2)$ and these errors are independent.

3(a) Find an LM statistic for testing the null hypothesis

$$H_0: \sigma_v^2 = 0$$

that (4) is a random walk.

3(b) Find the limit distribution of your test statistic.

Question 4.

4(a) Test each of the 14 extended Nelson Plosser series (see Schotman & van Dijk, 1991) for the null hypothesis of difference stationarity against the altenative hypothesis of trend stationarity using appropriate versions of the Z(a), Z(t) and ADF tests. See how sensitive your results are to the use of data-based versions of the Z-tests that employ automated rules for the calculation of the long run variance estimator versus versions of these tests that use a preassigned lag length or bandwidth parameter.

4(b) Use a model selection technique such as BIC or PIC to jointly determine the lag order, trend degree, and the presence or absence of a unit root in the model. Compare your results with those you obtained in part (a). (See Phillips & Ploberger (1994) for some related work in the published literature.)

NOTE: I have put the data on a diskette in ASCII format and you may copy it for your use in this assignment. It is available in Elizabeth's office (room 10, 30 Hillhouse).

References:

Schotman P & H van Dijk (1991) " On Bayesian routes to unit roots", *Journal of Applied Econometrics*, 6, 387-402.

Phillips P C B & W Ploberger(1994) "Posterior Odds testing for a unit root with data-based model selection" , *Econometric Theory*, 10, 774-808

TAKE HOME EXAMINATION

November 1994

1. The time series $(X_t)_{-\infty}^{\infty}$ is strictly stationary with zero mean and autocovariance function

$$E(X_t X_{t+h}) = \begin{cases} 1 & h = 0 \\ \rho & h \neq 0 \end{cases}$$

where $0 < \rho < 1$.

(a) Find the almost sure and mean square limit of $\bar{X} = n^{-1}\Sigma_{t=1}^n X_t$ as $n \to \infty$.

(b) Is X_t ergodic? Give an example of an invariant event with probability p, $0 < p < 1$.

(c) Find the Wold decomposition of X_t.

(d) Find the forecast error variances of the optimal linear one-step ahead and two-step ahead predictors of X_{n+1}.

2. (a) Let X_t be generated by the stationary autoregressive model

$$X_t = \theta X_{t-1} + u_t , \quad t = ..., -1, 0, 1, ...$$

with $|\theta| < 1$ and u_t an orthogonal sequence whose mean is zero and whose variance is $\sigma^2 > 0$. The initial conditions for X_t are in the infinite past. The data available for prediction is $\{X_1, X_2, ..., X_n\}$. Let $\hat{X}_{n+1}$ be the best linear predictor of X_{n+1} based on $X_1, ..., X_n$. Let $\theta_{n0} = 0$ and $\hat{X}_1 = 0$. Find $\theta_{n1}, ..., \theta_{nn}$ for which

$$X_{n+1} = \Sigma_{j=0}^n \theta_{nj}(X_{n+1-j} - \hat{X}_{n+1-j}) .$$

(b) Let X_t be generated by the model

$$X_t = u_t + \theta u_{t-1} , \quad t = ... -1, 0, 1, ...$$

with $|\theta| < 1$ and u_t an orthogonal sequence whose mean is zero and whose variance is $\sigma^2 > 0$. Again, the data available for prediction is $\{X_1, ..., X_n\}$, whereas X_t is initiated in the infinite past. The best linear predictor of X_{n+1} based on $X_1, ..., X_n$ is denoted $\hat{X}_{n+1}$. Let $\theta_{n0} = 0$ and $\hat{X}_1 = 0$. Find $\theta_{n1}, ..., \theta_{nn}$ for which

$$X_{n+1} = \Sigma_{j=0}^n \theta_{nj}(X_{n+1-j} - \hat{X}_{n+1-j}) .$$

3. (a) Write a GAUSS computer program to estimate an autoregression with trend of the general form

$$a(L)y_t = \sum_{j=0}^{\ell} c_j t^j + \varepsilon_t , \quad a(L) = \sum_{i=0}^p a_i L^i , \quad a_0 = 1 \tag{1}$$

where $\varepsilon_t = \text{iid}(0, \sigma^2)$. If $\ell = -1$ in (1) then there is no deterministic component in the autoregression.

(b) Write a GAUSS program to compute the spectral density of a stationary autoregressive time series such as (1) above with $\ell = -1$ and the characteristic polynomial $a(z)$ having all of its zero outside the unit circle.

(c) Use the programs you have written to obtain "autoregressive" spectral estimates of the following post war USA macroeconomic time series:
  (i) real GDP (gdpq)
  (ii) real consumption (gcnq)
  (iii) real investment (ginq)
  (iv) employment (ℓpmhu)
their per capita versions *and* growth rates of these variables.

(d) Examine the sensitivity of these spectra to alternative settings of the lag length (p) of the autoregression and the degree (ℓ) of deterministic trend elimination.

(e) Is there a "typical spectral shape" for these series in log-levels? Is there a "typical spectral shape" for the growth rates of these series?

(f) Compare your results in (e) with those obtained recently by King and Watson (1994)[**] for these data.

REFERENCE

King, R. G. and M. W. Watson (1994), "Money, prices, interest rates, and the business cycle," mimeographed, NBER.

---

[*]Quarterly data for these variables over the period 1947:1–1993:4 are available in the Citibase data base. The Citibase codes for the series are given in parentheses. The Citibase series for population is available as "p16" and can be used to compute the per capita versions of the series. I have put the data on a diskette in ASCII format and you may copy it for your use in this assignment. It is available in Elizabeth's office (Room 10, 30 Hillhouse).

[**]Copies of the King and Watson (1994) paper are available in Elizabeth's office.

Take Home Examination

1. In the model

$$X_t = (1/2 + \varepsilon_t)X_{t-1} , \quad t = 1, 2, \ldots$$

ε_t = iid(0, 1/4) and X_0 is a random variable with zero mean and finite variance $\sigma^2 > 0$.
[Hint: use the martingale convergence theorem on a suitable function of Z_t.] Show that $Z_t = 2^{t/2}X_t$ converges almost surely as $t \to \infty$. Hence show that $X_t \to_{a.s.} 0$ as $t \to \infty$.

2. A time series y_t is generated by the unit root model
   (1) $y_t = y_{t-1} + u_t$, $t = 1, 2, \ldots$
   where y_0 is a random variable and the shocks u_t are driven by the linear process

   $$u_t = \Sigma_{j=0}^{\infty} c_j \varepsilon_{t-j} , \quad \Sigma_0^{\infty} j^{1/2}|c_j| < \infty$$

   with ε_t = iid(0, σ_ε^2). However, the time series y_t is observed only intermittently at $t = mk$ for $m = 0, 1, \ldots, M$ and some fixed integer k, i.e. every k'th observation (y_0, y_k, y_{2k}, etc.) is available data.

   In place of a regression based on (1), the following least squares regression with the available data is obtained

   $$y_{mk} = \hat{\alpha}_k y_{(m-1)k} + \hat{v}_m , \quad m = 1, \ldots, M$$

   where $\hat{\alpha}_k = \sum_{m=1}^{M} y_{mk}y_{(m-1)k} / \sum_0^M y_{(m-1)k}^2$.

   (a) Find the limit distribution of the estimator $\hat{\alpha}_k$ as $M \to \infty$.

   (b) If the $Z(\alpha)$ unit root test is constructed in the usual way from $\hat{\alpha}_k$ and the intermittent observations $\{y_{mk}\}_{m=1}^{M}$, what is its limit distribution?

3. A time series y_t is generated by the unit root model

(1) $y_t = y_{t-1} + u_t$, $t = 1, ..., n$

where y_0 is a random variable and the shocks u_t are driven by the linear process

$$u_t = \sum_{j=0}^{\infty} c_j \varepsilon_{t-j} , \quad \sum_{0}^{\infty} j^{1/2} |c_j| < \infty$$

with $\varepsilon_t =$ iid$(0, \sigma_\varepsilon^2)$.

Two models are used for producing h-period ahead forecasts of y_{n+h} ($h = 1, ..., N$):

Model 1: $\bar{y}_{n+h} = y_n$,

Model 2: $\hat{y}_{n+h} = \hat{b}(n+h)$,

where in Model 2 $\hat{b}$ is the least squares coefficient from the fitted regression

(2) $y_t = \hat{b}t +$ error

that uses data generated by (1).

It is proposed to test model (1) by a "forecast-encompassing" test in which the prediction error from model (1), i.e., $y_{t+h} - \bar{y}_{t+h}$, is regressed on the predictions $\hat{y}_{n+h}$ from model (2) to determine whether the latter have any explanatory power. This is achieved by the regression

(3) $y_{n+h} - \bar{y}_{n+h} = \gamma^* \hat{y}_{n+h} +$ error $(h = 1, ..., N)$

where γ^* is the fitted coefficient and its t-ratio is t_γ. Suppose $N = n\tau$ for some fixed $\tau \in (0, 1)$.

Find the limit behavior of t_γ as $n \to \infty$. Discuss the implications of your result for this forecast-encompassing" test of model (1) against model (2).

ECONOMETRICS IV: TIME SERIES
TAKE HOME EXAMINATION

April 1993
Peter C. B. Phillips

Answer Both Questions: Any reference material allowed

Time Allowed: One week

Due Date: Wednesday 19 May 12 noon

1. Write the first introductory lecture in a course on NONSTATIONARY TIME SERIES. Be sure to give a SENSE of the subject matter, techniques and economic applications of the work that you discuss. Indicate how many lectures will be devoted to each topic in order to achieve your course objectives and outline your main source reference material. Keep your answer UNDER 15 pages (without references).

2. Consider the model

$$y_t = Bx_t + u_{0t} \tag{1}$$

$$\Delta^2 x_t = u_{xt} \tag{2}$$

where $u_t = (u'_{0t}, u'_{xt})'$ is a stationary time series that satisfies the functional central limit theorem

$$n^{-1/2} \Sigma_1^{[n\cdot]} u_t \longrightarrow_d B(\cdot) = BM(\Omega)$$

Partition $B( )$ and Ω conformably with u_t as $(B'_0, B'_x)'$ and

$$\Omega = \begin{bmatrix} \Omega_{00} & \Omega_{0x} \\ \Omega_{x0} & \Omega_{xx} \end{bmatrix}.$$

You may assume that Ω is positive definite.

(i)   Find the limit distribution of the least squares estimator of the matrix B in (1).

(ii) Construct a new fully modified least squares estimator of B using the information in equation (2) and show that your estimator has a mixed normal limit distribution.

(iii) See if you can find the limit distribution of the usual Phillips-Hansen (1990) fully modified estimator of B in (1).

ECON 120B
Winter 1995

Ramu Ramanathan
Course outline

U

TEXT: INTRODUCTORY ECONOMETRICS WITH APPLICATIONS,
Third Edition (1995), by Ramu Ramanathan (available at the bookstore)

MANUAL: INTRODUCTION TO UNIX FOR BEGINNERS
by Ramu Ramanathan (available from soft reserves under Econ 60)

COURSE CONTENT: In this quarter, we will study the theory and applications of econometric techniques, that is, estimation of economic relationships, tests of hypotheses, and forecasting.

ASSIGNMENTS: There will be three assignments, each of which will carry a weight of 5% towards the final grade. They will involve both theoretical and empirical work. Joint work and free discussion are strongly encouraged. If you work as a team (no more than three people per team), submit a single set of answers and identify the team members. Each member will get the same grade assigned to the answers. If your name does not appear on any assignment turned in, you cannot add it later. If your name appears on two papers, the LOWER grade will be chosen. LATE PAPERS WILL NOT BE ACCEPTED.

EXAMS: There will be two mid-term exams, one on the Thursday of the fifth week, February 9, 1995 (20% weight), and the second on the Thursday of the eighth week, March 2, 1995 (30% weight). The final exam (11:30 am to 2:30 pm, Monday, March 20, 1995) will have a 35% weight.

The exams will be closed book, but you can bring a 4" by 6" index card on which you may copy down (on both sides) formulas, etc. It must be HAND-WRITTEN; photo reducing and pasting is not permitted. Bring a calculator (just a simple one will do, no need for scientific or business calculator). If you bring a solar calculator, be sure to sit directly under a light. All grading problems must be rectified within a week from the time an exam or assignment is returned. NO REGRADING OF EXAMS WILL BE ALLOWED IF THEY WERE WRITTEN IN PENCIL. If you write in pencil, however, you can pick up the exam from the T.A. in his/her office, check the grading immediately, and take care of complaints before leaving the office.

MAKE-UP EXAMS: I will generally not give incompletes or make-up exams, especially if you have 3-exam conflicts on finals. If for some reason a make-up exam is given, 10% of the score will be deducted as penalty. There is no penalty for medical absence, but a doctor's certificate is required. I ought to warn you that my make-up exams are usually harder.

COURSE GRADE: The course grade will be assigned as follows. First, a weighted average of numerical scores will be obtained. If the mean class score is below 67.5 percent, points will be added to all scores to bring the mean score to 67.5 percent. Then letter grades will be assigned using the following percentage scale.

99-100	A+	85-89	B+	70-74	C+	45-54	D
95-98	A	80-84	B	65-69	C	< 45	F
90-94	A-	75-79	B-	55-64	C-		

OFFICE AND HOURS: My office is Room 324, ECON building, Marshall College (Phone 534-6787). My office hours will be from 1 to 2:15 pm on Tuesdays and Thursdays in Room ECON 324. I will also be available Monday and Thursday from 11 am to noon in Room ECON 114 (Undergraduate Advisor's office). However, during these times UG advisor's duties take priority over 120B students' questions. Variations from the above will be posted on the computer bulletin. The TAs' office hours will be posted on their doors and on the computer bulletin.

ELECTRONIC MAIL: We will be using the electronic mail (email) and bulletin board system extensively for communication purposes. After each class you should sign up on the computer and see if you have mail or bulletins. FAILING TO DO THAT MAY BE DISAS-TROUS BECAUSE YOU WILL MISS IMPORTANT ANNOUNCEMENTS. My email address is rramanat@ucsd or rramanat@weber.

READING LIST

Chapter 2 is a review of Econ 120A material and will not be discussed in class except as needed. Look for computer bulletins on this.

1.	Introduction (1 hour)	Chapter 1
2.	The Simple Linear Regression Model (7 hours)	Chapter 3
3.	Multiple Regression (4 hours)	Chapter 4
4.	Choosing Functional Forms (3 hours)	Chapter 5
5.	Multicollinearity (2 hours)	Chapter 6
6.	Qualitative or Binary Independent Variables (4 hours)	Chapter 7
7.	Heteroskedasticity (3 hours)	Chapter 8
8.	Serial Correlation (3 hours)	Chapter 9

I. (8 points)

"If a regression coefficient is significant at the 10 percent level (one-tail test), then it must also be significant at the 1 percent level." Is the above statement valid or invalid? Carefully justify your answer.

II. (16 points)

Suppose the true model is, $Y_t = \beta X_t + u_t$. In other words, $\alpha = 0$. I estimate β as $\overline{Y} / \overline{X}$ (call it $\tilde{\beta}$), where the bars indicate the sample means of X and Y.

(a) (10 points) Derive the expected value of $\tilde{\beta}$. Clearly state the assumptions you made to derive the expectation (points will be taken off for stating unnecessary assumptions). Is the estimate biased or unbiased?

(b) (6 points) The least squares estimate of β (call it $\hat{\beta}$) can be shown to be $(\Sigma X_t Y_t) / \Sigma X_t^2)$ [You need not prove this.]. *Without any derivations*, explain whether $\hat{\beta}$ or $\tilde{\beta}$ is more efficient. Explain your reasons.

III. (76 points)

Using annual data for 1959-1989 (making T = 31), the following model of timber harvest in Oregon was estimated.

$$\text{HARVEST} = \beta_1 + \beta_2 \text{ EXPORTS} + \beta_3 \text{ HOUSTART} + \beta_4 \text{ INDPROD}$$
$$+ \beta_5 \text{ TIMBPRIC} + \beta_6 \text{ PRODPRIC} + u_t$$

where HARVEST is total timber harvested in billion board feet, EXPORTS is the volume of timber exports to foreign countries in 100 million board feet, HOUSTART is total housing starts in the U.S. in millions, INDPROD is the index of industrial production for paper and wood products, TIMBPRIC is price of timber measured in dollars per 1000 board feet, and PRODPRIC is the producer price index for all commodities.

The following table has the estimates of the β's for three alternative models (if an entry is blank, it means that the variable is absent from the model).

	Model A		Model B		Model C	
	Coeff. (std.err)	Test Stat.	Coeff. (std.err)	Test Stat.	Coeff. (std.err)	Test Stat.
Constant	3.913 (0.574)	ignore	4.269 (0.376)	ignore	3.602 (0.533)	ignore
EXPORTS	0.108 (0.082)	_____				
HOUSTART	0.524 (0.355)	_____			0.618 (0.360)	_____
INDPROD	0.525 (0.127)	_____	0.694 (0.080)	_____	0.612 (0.091)	_____
TIMBPRIC	- 0.018 (0.011)	_____				
PRODPRIC	- 0.456 (0.087)	_____	- 0.556 (0.079)	_____	- 0.481 (0.089)	_____
d.f.		_____		_____		_____
Critical value		_____		_____		_____
ESS	6.22273		7.90322		7.1265	
ADJ RSQ	0.758		0.725		0.743	
SGMASQ	0.248909		0.282258		0.263945	
AIC	0.29562		0.309385		0.297571	
FPE	0.297085		0.309573		0.298002	
HQ	0.323613		0.323702		0.316071	
SCHWARZ	0.390185		0.355441		0.358054	
SHIBATA	0.278437		0.304286		0.289213	
GCV	0.308648		0.3125		0.303047	
RICE	0.327512		0.316129		0.309848	

(a) (10 points) In the above table, enter the appropriate values for the test statistics for testing whether or not each of the β's is significantly different from zero (exclude the constant terms).

(b) (6 points) Also enter the degrees of freedom (d.f.) for each of the models.

(c) (6 points) Next enter the critical values for a 10 percent level of significance (don't ask me whether the test is one-tailed or two-tailed, you decide what it is based on the information given above).

(d) (10 points) Near each of the test statistics you wrote for (a), write down whether the corresponding coefficient is significant or insignificant.

(e) (6 points) Which of the three models is the "best"? Explain what criteria you used and why you choose the model you did.

(f) (4 + 4 points) Based on your test for Model A only , would you say any of the variables should be considered as candidates for omission? If yes, which ones? Also state what the advantages of omitting the variables are.

Using Model A as the unrestricted model and Model B as the restricted model, test a relevant joint hypothesis by carrying out the following steps.

(g) (6 points) Write down the null hypothesis.

165

(h) (6 points) Write down the formula for the test statistic and compute it.

(i) (4 points) State its distribution under the null and d.f.

(j) (6 points) State the decision rule (for a 10 percent level) and your conclusion. Use numerical values, not symbols.

(k) (8 points) Suppose EXPORTS is measured in billion board feet. Write down the new numerical values (for Model A only) of the coefficients and standard errors that changed because of that. Be sure to justify how you arrived at the answer. How are the t-statistics, F-statistics, and R^2 affected by the change in units?

Econ 120B   Ramu Ramanathan
Spring 1994   First Midterm (20%)

I. (10 points)
In the model, $Y_t = \alpha + \beta X_t + u_t$, we have shown that the OLS estimator $\hat{\beta}$ is unbiased. Using this and other assumptions you should state, prove that $\hat{\alpha} = \overline{Y} - \hat{\beta}\overline{X}$ is also unbiased. [Points will be taken off for stating unnecessary assumptions.]

II. (5 + 5 points)
For each of the following equations, indicate whether the statement is correct as stated or is incorrect. Explain, using a diagram if necessary, why the statement is correct or incorrect.
($\hat{}$ indicates "estimated").

a) $\hat{Y}_t = \hat{\alpha} + \hat{\beta} X_t + \hat{u}_t$.

b) $\sum\limits_{\iota=1}^{t=T} X_t u_t = 0$, where the sum is for the sample observations.

III. (45 points)
Using quarterly data for ten years (making the number of observations 40), the following model of demand for new cars was estimated.

$$\text{NUMCARS} = \beta_1 + \beta_2 \text{ PRICE} + \beta_3 \text{ INCOME} + \beta_4 \text{ INTRATE} + \beta_5 \text{ UNEMP} + \hat{u}_t$$

where NUMCARS is the number of new car sales per thousand population, PRICE is the new car price index, INCOME is per capita real disposable income (in actual dollars), INTRATE is the interest rate, and UNEMP is the unemployment rate. The following table has the estimates of the β's for three alternative models.

	Model A	Model B	Model C
price	-0.071391	-0.079392	-0.024883
	(0.034730)	(0.011022)	(0.007366)
income	0.003159	0.00356	
	(0.001763)	(0.0006266)	
intrate	-0.153699	-0.146651	-0.204769
	(0.049190)	(0.039229)	(0.051442)
unemp	-0.072547		
	(0.298195)		
ESS	23.510464	23.550222	44.65914
ADJ RSQ	0.758	0.764	0.565
SGMASQ	0.671728	0.654173	1.207004
AIC	0.754701	0.719108	1.29716
FPE	0.755693	0.71959	1.297529
HQ	0.814563	0.764388	1.35795
SCHWARZ	0.932092	0.851414	1.472329
SHIBATA	0.734702	0.706507	1.28395
GCV	0.767689	0.726859	1.304869
RICE	0.783682	0.735944	1.313504

In Model A, test the joint hypothesis $\beta_3 = \beta_5 = 0$ by carrying out the following steps.

a) (7 points) Write down the formula for the test statistic and compute it.

b) (2 points) State its distribution and d.f.

c) (4 points) State the decision rule (for a 1 percent level) and your conclusion.

Next test each of the β's in <u>Model A only</u> whether or not it is significantly different from zero by carrying out the following steps.

d) (2 points) Write down the d.f. for the test statistic. _____

e) (2 points) Write down the critical value for a 10 percent level of significance (don't ask me whether the test is one-tailed or two-tailed, you decide what it is based on the information given above).

f) (8 points) Use the information in (e) and test whether each coefficient is significant or not. Clearly show your work and state your conclusion.

For UNEMP   For PRICE   For INTRATE   For INCOME

g) (2 + 2 points) Based on your test in (f), would you recommend any of the variables be omitted? If yes, which one? Also state what the advantages of omitting the variable(s) are.

h) (4 points) Suppose income is measured in thousands of dollars. Write down the new numerical values of the coefficients and standard errors that changed because of that.

i) (8 points) For each variable, explain whether the sign of the estimated regression coefficients is as you would expect or is it "the wrong sign"? (justify your answers carefully).

For UNEMP   For PRICE   For INCOME   For INTRATE

j) (4 points) Which of the three models is the "best". Explain what criteria you used and why you choose the model you did.

Econ 120B   Ramu Ramanathan
Winter 1994   First Midterm (20%)

MAXIMUM NUMBER OF POINTS = 55 + 15 = 70

Write your name and student ID on the paper. Read the questions (note that question II is on the next page) carefully and make sure that you do not misunderstand them. ALL THE INFORMATION YOU NEED IS THERE. Any one cheating in this or any other exam will get an F in the course and be reported to the Provost for disciplinary action.

I. (55 points)

The attached table presents estimates and related statistics (p-values in parentheses) for four models relating the number of private housing units authorized by building permits and their determinants. The data refer to 40 cities in the U.S. The model is

$$\text{HOUSING} = \beta_1 + \beta_2 \text{ VALUE} + \beta_3 \text{ INCOME} + \beta_4 \text{ LOCALTAX} + \beta_5 \text{ STATETAX}$$

$$+ \beta_6 \text{ POPCHANG} + \beta_7 \text{ UNEMPRT} + u$$

where HOUSING is the actual number of building permits issued, VALUE is the median value of owner-occupied homes (in hundreds of dollars), INCOME is median household income (in hundreds of dollars), LOCALTAX is average local taxes per capita (in dollars), STATETAX is average state tax per capita (in dollars), POPCHANG is the percent increase in population between 1980 and 1982, and UNEMPRT is the percentage of unemployment.

(a) (15) For each regression coefficient in Model A test whether it is zero or not at the 10 percent level. Based on your test would you say that the variable should be retained or should be a candidate to be dropped from the model?

(b) (20) In Model A test the joint hypothesis $H_0 : \beta_2 = \beta_4 = \beta_5 = 0$ at the 10 percent level. Be sure to state the alternative hypothesis, compute the test statistic, state its distribution under the null, and the criterion for acceptance/rejection. State your conclusion in words.

(c) (5) Which of the models is the "best"? Explain what criteria you used to choose the best model.

(d) (7) For each regression coefficient (ignore the constant term for this) in your best model state whether some of the coefficients are "wrong" in sign. State what sign you would expect and why. Then identify whether it has the right sign or not.

(e) (8) In Model D, suppose you measure HOUSING in thousands of units and at the same time measure income also in thousands of dollars. Write down the estimated coefficients of the new model, the corresponding p-values, and the new unadjusted R-square.

II (15 points)

For a two-variable model, prove that $\hat{Y}_t = \hat{\alpha} + \hat{\beta} X_t$ is unbiased, that is, show that $E(\hat{Y}_t) = E(Y_t)$. [no tedious derivations are needed.] In proving it, be sure to state the <u>minimum assumptions</u> on u_t needed to assure unbiasedness. [Points will be taken off for stating unnecessary assumptions.]

Values in parentheses are p-values for a two-sided alternative

Variables	Model A	Model B	Model C	Model D
constant	- 12005	-11648	-11409	- 8801
	(0.02)	(0.02)	(0.02)	(0.05)
VALUE	- 1.824			
	(0.53)			
INCOME	65.274	61.880	64.310	55.987
	(0.01)	(0.02)	(0.01)	(0.02)
LOCALTAX	3.011	3.283	3.853	
	(0.31)	(0.26)	(0.12)	
STATETAX	1.903	0.914		
	(0.52)	(0.71)		
POPCHANG	792.678	769.150	768.690	709.919
	(0.001)	(0.001)	(0.001)	(0.001)
UNEMPRT	350.912	376.852	391.395	358.487
	(0.105)	(0.074)	(0.057)	(0.084)
ESS	186.395	188.726	189.503	203.482
Unadj. R-sq.	0.516	0.510	0.508	0.472
$\hat{\sigma}^2$	5.648	5.551	5.414	5.652
AIC	6.613	6.369	6.083	6.213
FPE	6.637	6.383	6.091	6.218
HQ	7.358	6.980	6.567	6.605
SCHWARZ	8.887	8.205	7.513	7.357
SHIBATA	6.291	6.134	5.922	6.104
GCV	6.846	6.530	6.188	6.280
RICE	7.169	6.740	6.317	6.359

MAXIMUM NUMBER OF POINTS = 10 + 40 = 50

Write your name and student ID on the paper. Read the questions carefully and make sure that you do not misunderstand them. Any one cheating in this or any other exam will get an F in the course and be reported to the Provost for disciplinary action.

I. (8 + 2 points)

Suppose the true model is $Y_t = \alpha + \beta X_t + u_t$. I estimate β as $\beta^* = \overline{Y} / \overline{X}$, where the bar indicates sample mean. Compute the expected value of β^* making sure to state the assumptions you use to do that (points will be taken off for writing unnecessary assumptions). Is this estimator biased or unbiased? Explain.

II. (12 + 12 + 4 + 12 points)

The attached table presents estimates and related statistics (standard errors in parentheses) for four models relating the list price of an automobile to a number of characteristics, using 106 observations. The model is

price $= \beta_1 + \beta_2$ weight $+ \beta_3$ wbase $+ \beta_4$ length $+ \beta_5$ width $+ \beta_6$ height $+ \beta_7$ liters $+ u$

where price is in thousands of dollars, weight is the weight of the car in hundreds of pounds, wbase is wheelbase in inches, length, width, and height are in inches, and liters is the engine displacement in liters.

(a) (For Model A only) I believe that some of the coefficients are "wrong" in sign. For each regression coefficient (ignore the constant term for this) state what sign you would expect and why. Then identify whether it has the right sign or not.

(b) Test the joint hypothesis $H_0 : \beta_3 = \beta_7 = 0$ at the 5 percent level. Be sure to state the alternative hypothesis, compute the test statistic, state its distribution under the null, and the criterion for acceptance/rejection. State your conclusion in words.

(c) Which of the models is the "best"? Explain what criteria you used to choose the best model.

(d) Test Model A for <u>overall significance</u> at the 1 percent level. Be sure to state the null and alternative hypotheses, compute the test statistic, state its distribution, and the decision rule. What do you conclude? (You have all the information you need for this.)

Values in parentheses are standard errors

Variables	Model A	Model B	Model C	Model D
constant	43.463	43.096	42.258	42.715
	(10.35)	(10.14)	(9.97)	(10.08)
weight	1.016	1.006	0.951	0.822
	(0.16)	(0.15)	(0.11)	(0.08)
wbase	- 0.018			
	(0.09)			
length	- 0.066	- 0.071	- 0.066	
	(0.05)	(0.04)	(0.04)	
width	- 0.408	- 0.402	- 0.408	- 0.482
	(0.14)	(0.13)	(0.13)	(0.13)
height	- 0.364	- 0.376	- 0.356	- 0.430
	(0.17)	(0.16)	(0.15)	(0.15)
liters	- 0.238	- 0.222		
	(0.44)	(0.43)		
ESS	502.082	502.280	503.648	519.877
$\bar{R}^2$	0.677	0.680	0.683	0.676
$\hat{\sigma}^2$	5.072	5.023	4.987	5.097
AIC	5.405	5.306	5.221	5.289
FPE	5.406	5.307	5.222	5.289
HQ	5.805	5.641	5.494	5.509
SCHWARZ	6.445	6.170	5.920	5.848
SHIBATA	5.362	5.275	5.200	5.275
GCV	5.430	5.324	5.233	5.297
RICE	5.457	5.343	5.246	5.305

Any student found to cheat in this course will get an F in the course and be reported to the Dean.

Using 1980 census data for the 50 states, the following model was estimated (values in parentheses are standard errors).

(U) $\hat{PC}$ =   -0.365   -0.0009D   +0.0094 NW   +.0003Y
             (0.978)   (.0006)   (.0104)   (0.0001)

             -0.099 U   +1.519 COP   -0.0068 AGE1   +0.0077 AGE2
             (0.084)   (0.276)   (0.00034)   (0.0038)

$$R^2 = 0.557 \qquad \overline{R}^2 = 0.484 \qquad ESS = 33.41$$

where PC = property crime index, D = population density, NW = percent of non-white population, Y = per capita income in dollars, U = unemployment rate, COP = size of police force per thousand population, AGE1 = population (in thousands) in the age group 15-24 and AGE2 = population (in thousands) in the age group 25-34.

1) (25 points) Does the observed sign of each regression coefficient (ignore constant) agree with intuition. In other words, what sign would you expect a priori and why? Does any result surprise you?

2) (25 points) Test each coefficient (ignore constant) for statistical significance at the 5% level (two tails).

A second model was estimated and the results are given below (with standard errors in parenthesis).

(R) $\hat{PC}$ =   -.037   +0.0002Y   +1.428 COP   -0.0061 AGE1   +0.0068 AGE2
             (0.84)   (0.00008)   (0.266)   (0.0034)   (0.839)

$$R^2 = 0.512 \qquad \overline{R}^2 = 0.468 \qquad ESS = 36.85$$

3) (25 points) Using both the models U and R perform an appropriate test at 5% level. Be sure to (a) state the null and alternative hypotheses, (b) the test criterion for acceptance/rejection of the hypothesis and (c) the statistical distribution (including degrees of freedom *for your models*). What do you conclude from your test?

4) (25 points) For Model R, the F-statistic for overall goodness of fit is 11.8 and the corresponding p-value is 0.003. State the null hypothesis for this F-test. From the p-value would you accept or reject the null? Why?

172

I. (10 points)

"Adding an irrelevant variable (that is, one that has a truly zero coefficient) to a model has the same effect as high multicollinearity when it comes to the properties of unbiasedness, consistency, and efficiency of the OLS estimators of parameters." Carefully explain whether the statement is valid or not. If it is partially valid, indicate which parts they are.

II. (15 points)

1. (8 points) Derive the marginal effect of Y with respect to X $(\partial Y/\partial X)$ for the functional form (ignoring the error term) $\ln (Y) = \beta_1 + \beta_2 X + \beta_3 X^2 + \beta_4 (XZ)$. [Note: your answer should not depend on Y.]

2. (7 points) Derive the elasticity of Y with respect to X for the same.

III. (40 points)

Consider the Cobb-Douglas production function $Q_t = e^\alpha K_t^\beta L_t^\gamma e^{u_t}$. You have data on Q, K, and L.

1. (5 points)
Derive a model (call it Model R) that is estimable using the OLS procedure.

2. (6 + 5 points)
I suspect that the parameters α, β, and γ are not constant but "time-varying", that is, $\alpha = \alpha_1 + \alpha_2 t$ and similarly for β and γ, where t is time, going from 1 to T. Derive another model (call it U) that can be used to obtain the estimates of the new parameters just listed.

What variables would you generate to estimate this model?

3. (4 + 3 points)
State the joint hypothesis on Model U that will result in Model R being the restricted model. What is the alternative hypothesis?

4. (5 points)
Suppose you have 46 observations (T = 46). To use the Wald test write down an expression for the test statistic. Define all the symbols you use and be sure to put actual numerical values where available.

5. (3 + 3 points)
What is its distribution and d.f.?

6. (3 points)
Write down the numerical value of the critical value for a 5 percent test.

7. (3 points)
Describe the decision rule for your test.

IV. (25 points)

I have data on the sale price (PRICE) in thousands of dollars, square feet of living area (SQFT), and square feet of the yard size (YARD) for a sample of 59 single family homes sold recently. The basic model I first estimated was

$$PRICE = \beta_1 + \beta_2 \, SQFT + \beta_3 \, YARD + u$$

I suspect that the terms ln(SQFT) and ln(YARD) should be added to the above model. To perform an LM test for the addition of these variables, I obtained the following auxiliary regression.

$$\hat{u}_t = 3265 + 0.255 \, SQFT - 0.000485 \, YARD - 507 \, \ln(SQFT) + 6.765 \, \ln(YARD)$$
$$(0.01) \quad (0.012) \qquad (0.917) \qquad (0.011) \qquad (0.886)$$

173

Unadjusted Rsquare = 0.115, T = 59, and the values in parentheses are p-values for a two-tailed test.

1. (6 points) Carefully describe how I must have obtained $\hat{u}_t$ (you can do this verbally or give ecslib commands).

2. $(2 + 3 + 3$ points) Compute the test statistic and state its distribution and d.f.

3. $(3 + 3$ points) Use a 5 percent level of significance and actually carry out the test. What do you conclude?

4. (5 points) From the information given above, write down a model I should estimate. Carefully justify your choice (Note: this should not be "kitchen sink" model.)

Econ 120B   Ramu Ramanathan
Spring 1994   Second Midterm (30%)

I. (10 points) Consider the relationship (ignoring the error term)

$$Y = \beta_1 + \beta_2 X + \beta_3 \ln X + \beta_4 Z + \beta_5 (Z \ln X)$$

where X and Z are explanatory variables. Derive an algebraic expression for the elasticity of Y with respect to X (Note: your answer should not depend on Y).

II. (48 points) The attached table has the estimated coefficients and associated statistics (standard errors in parentheses) for the demand for cigarettes in Turkey. The data are annual for the years 1960-1988 (29 observations). The definitions of the variables are as follows:

LQ   = Logarithm of cigarette consumption per adult (dependent variable)
LY   = Logarithm of per capita real GNP in 1968 prices (in Turkish liras)
LP   = Logarithm of real price of cigarettes in Turkey liras per kg.
D82 = 1 for 1982 onward, 0 prior to that
D86 = 1 for 1986 onward, 0 prior to that
LYD1 = LY multiplied by D82
LYD2 = LY multiplied by D86
LPD1 = LP multiplied by D82
LPD2 = LP multiplied by D86

1) (24 points) In Model D , write down the numerical values of the income and price elasticities of demand for each of the three periods (enter them in the following table).

Period	Income elasticity	Price elasticity
1960-81		
1982-85		
1986-88		

174

(Entries in parentheses are the corresponding standard errors)

	Variable	Model A	Model B	Model C	Model D
$\hat{\beta}_1)$	Constant	- 4.997 (0.511)	- 4.800 (0.677)	- 4.186 (0.535)	- 4.997 (0.509)
$\hat{\beta}_2)$	D82	23.364 (5.547)	- 0.108 (0.207)	- 0.103 (0.026)	21.793 (5.254)
$\hat{\beta}_3)$	D86	- 36.259 (12.859)	- 0.406 (0.236)	- 0.103 (0.037)	- 28.291 (9.433)
$\hat{\beta}_4)$	LY	0.732 (0.069)	0.705 (0.091)	0.621 (0.071)	0.732 (0.068)
$\hat{\beta}_5)$	LYD1	- 2.798 (0.661)			- 2.602 (0.623)
$\hat{\beta}_6)$	LYD2	4.251 (1.516)			3.298 (1.098)
$\hat{\beta}_7)$	LP	- 0.371 (0.097)	- 0.337 (0.129)	- 0.201 (0.090)	- 0.371 (0.097)
$\hat{\beta}_8)$	LPD1	0.405 (0.206)	0.016 (0.246)		0.288 (1.787)
$\hat{\beta}_9)$	LPD2	- 0.236 (0.258)	0.288 (0.250)		
$\overline{R}^2$		0.921	0.859	0.852	0.921
ESS		0.018645	0.036444	0.04195	0.019427

Use the above table to construct a test for the null hypothesis "there has been no structural change in the price and income elasticities over the three periods 1960-81, 1982-1985, and 1986-1988. To do this, complete the following.

2) (4 points) The unrestricted model is _____ and the restricted model is _____.

3) (4 points) Write down the null hypothesis in terms of the β's.

4) (4 points) Compute the numerical value of the test statistic.

5) (3 points) State its distribution and d.f.

6) (5 points) Now actually carry out the test and state whether you would accept the null hypothesis or reject it. Use a 1 percent level of significance.

7) (4 points) Based on your test, would you say there has been a significant structural change in the elasticities or not? Explain.

III. (42 points) Here you are to describe how to carry out a Lagrange multiplier test. Consider the basic model

$$LQ_t = \alpha + \beta\, LY_t + \gamma\, LP_t + u_t$$

You want to use the LM test to examine whether or not the entire relation is different across the three time periods for which D82 and D86 are defined.

1) (10 points) Derive another model that will enable you to carry out the LM test.

2) (6 points) In your model, write down the null hypothesis for "there has been no structural change in the relation".

3) (10 points) Carefully describe what regression(s) you will run. [Your answer should say "regress y against x1, x2, x3, ... where y, x1, x2, etc. should be actual variable names in your model. Don't use vague terms such as estimate model, compute test statistic, and so on.]

4) (4 points) Describe the test statistic to compute.

5) (4 points) What is its distribution (including d.f.) under the null hypothesis?

6) (4 points) Write down the numerical value of the critical value (for a 10 percent level) for your test statistic (explain where you got it from).

7) (4 points) Describe the decision rule for your test.

Econ 120B   Ramu Ramanathan
Winter 1994   Second Midterm (30%)

MAXIMUM NUMBER OF POINTS = 20 + 40 = 60

Read the questions carefully and make sure that you do not misunderstand them. ALL THE INFORMATION YOU NEED IS THERE. If the number of minutes you spend on any part is more than the number of points, you are wasting time. If you get stuck somewhere, don't waste time but move on.

I. (20 points)
Consider the following double log model of timber harvest in Oregon estimated with annual data for the 31 years 1959-1989.

$$\ln(HARVEST) = \beta_1 + \beta_2 \ln(HOUSESTART) + \beta_3 \ln(INDPROD) + \beta_4 \ln(PRODPR) + u$$

The estimated coefficients are given below. The last column is the coefficient divided by its standard error.

Indep. variable	Coeff. ($\hat{\beta}$)	$\hat{\beta}$ / std. err
CONSTANT	0.856	7.228
ln (HOUSESTART)	0.157	2.073
ln (INDPROD)	0.807	7.721
ln (PRODPR)	− 0.415	− 6.105

where HOUSESTART is total housing construction in the U.S. in millions, INDPROD is an index of industrial production for paper and wood products, and PRODPR is an index of producer price for all commodities.

1) For the elasticity of INDPROD only (call it β) test whether or not it is equal to 1. To do this, be sure to carry out the following steps.

   a) (2 points) State the null and alternative hypotheses.

   b) (5 points) Compute the test statistic.

   c) (3 points) State its distribution and the numerical value of the d.f.

   d) (3 points) State the decision rule for a 5% level of significance.

   e) (2 points) State you conclusion whether the effect is elastic, inelastic, or unitary elastic.

2) (5 points) Suppose HOUSESTART is measured in thousands instead of millions. How will this affect the coefficients (that is, the β's)? If anything is changed, write down the new value.

177

II. (40 points)

Consider the consumption function $C = \alpha + \beta Y + u$, where C is the consumption expenditures of a family and Y is its disposable income (income after taxes). I hypothesize that (a) α will depend on whether the family owns its residence or rents it, and (b) β will depend linearly on both the level of Y and whether or not the family owns its residence. You have data for 50 households.

1) (10 points) Carefully derive another model that will enable you to test both the above hypotheses.

2) (5 points) State the null and alternative hypotheses to test that "there is no difference in the consumption relation between a home owner and a renter. (Note: the "relation" means both the intercept and the slope terms)

3) (10 points) Describe what regression(s) you will run and what test statistic you would compute.

4) (5 points) State its distribution and the numerical value(s) of the d.f.

5) (5 points) Describe how you will go about deciding whether to accept the hypothesis or not (at the 5 percent level).

6) (5 points) In your model in II.1, derive the algebraic expression for the marginal propensity to consume (that is, for the marginal effect of Y on C).

Any one cheating in this or any other exam will get an F in the course and be reported to the Provost for disciplinary action.

MAXIMUM NUMBER OF POINTS IS 35 + 15 = 50

I. (35 points)

Consider the household consumption function in double log form

$$\ln(C) = \alpha + \beta \ln(Y) + u \qquad T = 40$$

where $\ln(C)$ is the logarithm of consumption expenditures and $\ln(Y)$ is the logarithm of household income in a given period. I believe that the parameters α and β are not constant but depend on the number of people (N) in the household, that is, on its size.

a. (5) Formulate another econometric model that will enable me to allow for the parameters to vary with the family size (clearly define any additional variables I should use).

b. (10) In the new model, derive an expression for the elasticity of consumption (that is, of C) with respect to family size (that is, N).

c. (5) State the null and alternative hypotheses in the new model to test the hypothesis that the size of the household does not affect consumption.

d. (10) To use the Lagrange Multiplier (LM) test, describe what regression(s) are to be run and how the test statistic is to be computed. Unless your answers are specific to the above model, you will not get points especially if all you have done is copied from the index card.

d. (5) Describe the distribution of the test statistic (including the numerical values of the d.f.) and how I can apply the p-value approach with 10% level for acceptance or rejection.

II. (15 points) Consider the following relationship between the amount of money spent by a state on welfare programs (Y) and the state's revenue (X):

$$Y = \alpha_1 + \alpha_2 D1 + \alpha_3 X + \alpha_4(D1*X) + u$$

where D1 is a dummy variable that takes the value 1 if the state legislature is controlled by Democrats and 0 otherwise, and * means multiplication.

My research assistant decided to define another dummy variable D2 which takes the value 1 if the legislature is controlled by non-Democrats and 0 otherwise, and estimate the following model instead.

$$Y = \beta_1 D1 + \beta_2 D2 + \beta_3(D1*X) + \beta_4(D2*X) + u$$

Describe step by step how I can obtain estimates of the α's from those of the β's, *without running another regression*. That is, you should derive expressions for the α's in terms of the β's.

Any one cheating in this or any other exam will get an F in the course and be reported to the Provost for disciplinary action.

MAXIMUM NUMBER OF POINTS IS 50

I. (10+5+10+5+10 points)

I want to study the determinants of commercial television market shares and have the following basic specification (for simplicity, the t subscript is omitted):

$$\text{SHARE} = \alpha + \beta \, \text{NSTAT} + \gamma \, \text{CABLE} + u \qquad T = 40$$

where SHARE is the market share (in %) of a station, NSTAT is the number of competing television stations in the area, and CABLE is the percent of households wired for cable television. I also know whether the station is VHF or not and its network affiliation (ABC, CBS, NBC, or none of these). I believe that the coefficient for NSTAT will depend on the qualitative variables just listed. Carefully describe how I can use the Lagrange Multiplier test to verify that belief. More specifically:

a. (10) Formulate another econometric model that will enable me to test the hypothesis (clearly define any additional variables I should use).

b. (5) State the null and alternative hypotheses in that model.

c. (10) Describe what regression(s) are to be run and how the test statistic is to be computed.

d. (5) Describe the distribution of the test statistic (including the numerical values of the d.f.) and state the criterion for acceptance or rejection.

e. (10) Describe how I can select new variables to add to the basic model and what I should do thereafter to continue the analysis.

II. (4+6 points)

The Planning Department of a city obtained the following estimated relationship.

$$\ln H = 1.12 + 1.14 \ln Y + 0.96 \ln P$$

where H is the total number of single family dwellings, Y is total income of the city (in dollars corrected for inflation), and P is the city's population. Suppose I used per capita income (Y/P) instead of Y and estimated the following model.

$$\ln H = \beta_1 + \beta_2 \ln (Y/P) + \beta_3 \ln P + u$$

a) (4) Calculate the numerical values of the estimates of the β's. [You have all the information you need.]

b) (6) The model is misspecified because it omits the interest rate and a price measure both of which will affect the number of housing units. Write down the properties of the above estimates in terms of (i) unbiasedness, (ii) consistency, and (iii) validity of tests of hypotheses.

Your name _____   Your Id No. _____

NOTE THAT CAMPUS RULES FORBID REGRADING THE FINAL EXAMS. Therefore, read the questions carefully and answer all points. For each part, confine your answers to the specific question. Marks will be taken off for irrelevant or redundant answers. Answers must be specific to the model in the problem. Simply copying down formulas from the index card without applying them to the problem will get you zero points. Don't use general terms such as "estimate basic model", "compute TRsquare statistic", "use weighted least squares", etc. Clearly state exactly what they are FOR THE SPECIFIC QUESTION. Think of your answers as explaining to a Research Assistant exactly how to proceed.

CHECK AND MAKE SURE THAT ALL 9 PAGES ARE LEGIBLE. IF ANY OF THEM IS MISSING, GET A NEW COPY.

ANYONE CHEATING IN THIS EXAM WILL GET AN F IN THE COURSE AND BE REFERRED TO THE PROVOST FOR DISCIPLINARY ACTION.

MAXIMUM NUMBER OF POINTS   60 + 30 + 30 = 120

I.

In the second homework, you estimated the following model of women's labor force participation rate using 1980 Census data for the 50 states.

$$WLFP = \beta_1 + \beta_2\,YF + \beta_3\,YM + \beta_4\,EDUC + \beta_5\,UE + \beta_6\,MR$$
$$+ \beta_7\,DR + \beta_8\,URB + \beta_9\,WH + u$$

WLFP = Percent of women in the labor force (dependent variable)
YF   = Median earnings in dollars by females
YM   = Median earnings in dollars by males
EDUC = Percentage of female high school graduates over 24 years of age
UE   = Unemployment rate (%)
MR   = Marriage rate (%) of women at least 16 years of age
DR   = Divorce rate (%)
URB = Percentage of urban population in State
WH   = Percentage of females over 16 years who are white

Lois Cruz, a former Econ 120B student, just finished an independent study in which he gathered the data for the same variables but from the 1990 Census. An interesting question is "has there been a structural change in the relationship specified above (that is, is the entire relation different)?" To address this, define the dummy variable D which takes the value 1 for the 1990 year and 0 for the

1980 year. Stack the data together to get a total of 100 observations. The table below has the estimated coefficients for three models. Note that interaction terms are also included there. The values in parentheses are standard errors.

VARIABLE	MODEL A COEFF (STDERR)	MODEL B COEFF (STDERR)	MODEL C COEFF (STDERR)
β_1) constant	50.881 (11.676)	58.777 (8.482)	39.335 (3.209)
β_2) YF	0.00452 (0.0012)	0.000427 (0.000408)	0.00538 (0.00065)
β_3) YM	-0.0000111 (0.000548)	-0.000355 (0.00031)	
β_4) EDUC	0.278 (0.067)	0.397 (0.057)	0.259 (0.039)
β_5) UE	-1.119 (0.292)	-0.940 (0.254)	-1.325 (0.184)
β_6) MR	-0.224 (0.164)	-0.311 (0.133)	
β_7) DR	0.227 (0.188)	0.178 (0.174)	
β_8) URB	-0.06 (0.032)	-0.011 (0.024)	-0.065 (0.019)
β_9) WH	-0.128 (0.035)	-0.116 (0.032)	-0.137 (0.025)
β_{10}) D	-6.371 (14.923)		
β_{11}) D x YF	-0.00353 (0.0013)		-0.00461 (0.000605)
β_{12}) D x YM	-0.000163 (0.000634)		
β_{13}) D x EDUC	0.00721 (0.118)		
β_{14}) D x UE	-0.492 (0.437)		
β_{15}) D x MR	0.146 (0.243)		
β_{16}) D x DR	0.211 (0.327)		0.287 (0.203)
β_{17}) D x WH	0.041 (0.054)		0.049 (0.030)
β_{18}) D x URB	-0.024 (0.047)		
ESS	416.026	731.251	451.609
R^2	0.862	0.758	0.850

1. First carry out a Wald test for the null hypothesis that the structure is the same between 1980 and 1990. To do this, answer the following questions.

(2 points) Write down the null hypothesis. _____

(2 points) To use the Wald test, compute the numerical value of the test statistic.

(2 points) What is its distribution including d.f.? _____

(2 points) Write down the numerical value (or range) of the critical value for a 1 percent test.

(3 points) Carry out the test and indicate what you conclude as to whether the structure has significantly changed or not.

2. In Model C, test whether each of the regression coefficients (excluding the constant term) is individually (that is, not jointly) significantly different from zero or not, at the 10 percent level, by carrying out the following steps.

(8 points) Compute the values of the test statistic.

(2 points) State the distribution of the test statistic and its d.f. _____

(2 points) Write down the critical value (or range) for a 10 percent test.

(8 points) In the table on Page 3, write down whether the coefficient is significant or insignificant.

3. (5 points) Using Model C, write down the complete estimated relation for the dependent variable for the 1990 period (note that this must be in the standard way all estimated econometric models are written and involve only the original variables in the basic model).

4. In Model C, I want to test the joint null hypothesis that in 1990 , the coefficients for YF and WH are both zero.

(4 points) State the null hypothesis for this joint test. Do this carefully because you will get very little partial credit for the remaining parts of question I.4 if you get the null hypothesis wrong.

(5 points) Using Model C as the unrestricted model, derive a restricted model (it must be in terms of parameters and not numerical values) for testing the hypothesis you stated above. Show all your derivations.

(3 points) Write down an expression for the Wald test statistic (define any symbols you use). Be sure to put in numerical values where available.

(2 points) Indicate its distribution under the null and the numerical value(s) of the d.f.

5. Suppose you start with Model B as the basic model and want to use the LM test to test whether the dummy variable and interaction terms in Model A should be added.

(4 points) Describe the regression(s) to be run and any new variables to be generated.   183

(2 points) Write down the numerical value of the critical value for this test at the 5 percent level.

II.

Consider the model $\quad PRICE_t = \beta_1 + \beta_2 \ln(SQFT_t) + \beta_3 \ln(YARD_t) + u_t$.

where PRICE is the sale price of a house in dollars, SQFT is the living area in square feet, and YARD is the size of the yard in square feet.

1. (10 points) I know from past studies that the variance of u is proportional to the size of the yard. Describe step by step how I should apply the weighted least squares procedure (WLS) that makes use of this information. Be sure to state what variables to generate and what regressions to run.

(4 points) Show how you will compute the LM test statistic and indicate what its distribution is under the null, including the d.f.

(2 points) In what way are the WLS estimates better than OLS estimates?

3. In the above model, suppose the nature of the heteroscedasticity is unknown.

(3 points) Write down the most general form of the auxiliary equation for the error variance so that I can apply the White's test.

(2 points) State the null hypothesis that there is no heteroscedasticity.

(7 points) Describe what regression(s) I should run, how I should compute the test statistic, what its distribution is and the numerical value of the d.f.

Suppose there is heteroscedasticity and I want to apply the WLS procedure using the auxiliary equation you stated above.

(6 points) In the next page, describe how I should compute the weights and how I should apply them to obtain WLS estimates (assume that the negative variance problem does not arise).

III.

Consider the double-log model of farm output

$$\ln(Q_t) = \beta_1 + \beta_2 \ln(K_t) + \beta_3 \ln(L_t) + \beta_4 \ln(A_t) + \beta_5 \ln(F_t) + \beta_6 \ln(S_t) + u_t$$

where Q is output, K is capital, L is labor, A is the acreage planted, F is the amount of fertilizers used, and S is the amount of seed planted. Using annual data for the years 1949 through 1988, the above model was estimated and the Durbin-Watson statistic was 1.409.

1. (2 points) Write down the auxiliary equation for the error term for using the DW statistic as the test statistic.

(3 points) State the null hypothesis you will test and the alternative most common in economics.

(4 points) Write down the critical values for the DW test, actually carry out the test and state what the test result is.

<u>Course Outline</u>

1.   Statistical Review

2.   Regression Under Ideal Conditions
     a.   Simple Regression Model
     b.   Multiple Regression Model

3.   Non-Ideal Conditions and Related Topics
     a.   Non-normal Disturbances
     b.   Restrictions
     c.   Multicollinearity
     d.   Specification Error
     e.   Generalized Least Squares
     f.   Heteroskedasticity
     g.   Autocorrelation
     h.   Stochastic Regressors

4.   Seemingly Unrelated Regressions

<u>Reading List</u>

1.   (STATISTICAL REVIEW) Greene, Ch. 2-4; Schmidt, appendix; Amemiya, Ch. 3;
     Goldberger, Ch. 2-12; Kmenta, Ch. 1-6.

2A. (SIMPLE REGRESSION) Greene, Ch. 5; Kmenta, Ch. 7; Johnston, Ch. 1-3.

2B. (MULTIPLE REGRESSION) Greene, Ch. 6-7, 10.1-10.3; Schmidt, Ch. 1; Fomby,
     Hill and Johnson, 2.1-2.4, Ch. 3, 4.1-4.3; Amemiya, Ch. 1; Johnston, Ch.
     5,7; Kmenta, 10.1-10.2; Goldberger, Ch. 19-22.

3A. (NON-NORMAL ERRORS) Judge, Ch. 20; Schmidt, 2.4; Amemiya, 2.3; Kmenta,
     8.1; Fomby, Hill and Johnson, 4.4; Greene, 10.5; Koenker, <u>Econometric</u>
     <u>Reviews</u>, No. 2, 1982.

3B. (RESTRICTIONS) Fomby, Hill and Johnson, Ch. 6; Judge, Ch. 3; Kmenta,
     11.2.

3C. (MULTICOLLINEARITY) Schmidt, 2.3; Greene, 9.2; Goldberger, Ch. 23; Fomby,
     Hill and Johnson, Ch. 13; Amemiya, 2.2; Judge, Ch. 22; Johnston, 6.5;
     Kmenta, 10.3.

3D. (SPECIFICATION ERROR) Schmidt, 2.2; Fomby, Hill and Johnson, 18.2, 18.3;
     Greene, 8.3-8.5; Kmenta, 10.4.

3E. (GENERALIZED LEAST SQUARES) Fomby, Hill and Johnson, 8.1-8.3; Amemiya,
     6.1, 6.2; Greene, Ch. 13; Schmidt, 2.5; Johnston, 8.1-8.3; Kmenta, 12.1.

3F. (HETEROSKEDASTICITY) Greene, Ch. 14; Judge, Ch. 11; Amemiya, 6.5; Fomby,
     Hill and Johnson, Ch. 9; Johnston, 8.4.

3G. (AUTOCORRELATION) Judge, Ch. 8; Greene, Ch. 15; Fomby, Hill and Johnson,
     Ch. 10; Amemiya, 6.3; Harvey, Ch. 6; Kmenta, 8.3.

3H. (STOCHASTIC REGRESSORS) Schmidt, Ch. 3; Fomby, Hill and Johnson, Ch. 5,
     11; Greene, 10.4; Kmenta, 8.4, 9.1; Johnston, 10.6.

4.   (SEEMINGLY UNRELATED REGRESSIONS) Schmidt, 2.6; Greene, Ch. 17; Judge,
     Ch. 12.   **185**

2. Next you are asked to carry out an LM test for AR(2), that is, second order autocorrelation.

(4 points) Write down the auxiliary equation for the error term and state the null hypothesis of no serial correlation.

The auxiliary equation was estimated, after suppressing the 1949 and 1950 data, and the unadjusted R^2 was 0.687.

(2 points) Compute the test LM test statistic _____

(2 points) State its distribution and d.f. _____

(3 points) Write down the critical value for the 0.001 level and carry out the test. What do you conclude about serial correlation?

3. (10 points) I want to use the Generalized Cochrane-Orcutt procedure for taking account of AR(2) in the errors. Carefully describe the steps I should ask my Research Assistant to take to obtain the estimates.

Your name _____   Your Id No. _____

NOTE THAT CAMPUS RULES FORBID REGRADING THE FINAL EXAMS. Therefore, read the questions carefully and answer all points. For each part, confine your answers to the specific question. Marks will be taken off for irrelevant or redundant answers. Answers must be specific to the model in the problem. Simply copying down formulas from the index card without applying them to the problem will get you zero points. Don't use general terms such as "estimate basic model", "compute TRsquare statistic", "use weighted least squares", etc. Clearly state exactly what they are FOR THE SPECIFIC QUESTION.

CHECK AND MAKE SURE THAT THERE ARE 6 PAGES. IF ANY OF THEM IS MISSING, GET A NEW COPY.

ANYONE CHEATING IN THIS EXAM WILL GET AN F IN THE COURSE AND BE REFERRED TO THE PROVOST FOR DISCIPLINARY ACTION.

MAXIMUM NUMBER OF POINTS $35 + 25 + 20 + 35 = 115$

I. (35 points)

Consider the model

$$PRICE_t = \beta_1 + \beta_2 SQFT_t + \beta_3 YARD_t + \beta_4 POOL_t + u_t$$

where PRICE is the sale price of a house, SQFT is the living area in square feet, YARD is the size of the yard, and POOL is a dummy variable that takes the value 1 if the house has a swimming pool and 0 otherwise. I suspect that the model exhibits heteroscedasticity, but the form is unknown.

1. (10 points)
Write down the <u>most general form</u> of the auxiliary equation for error variance σ_t^2 so that you can use White's test.

2. (5 points)
Formally write down the null hypothesis "there is no heteroscedasticity" that corresponds to your equation in (1).

3. (10 points)
To carry out White's test, describe the regression(s) to be run and the variables to generate. (This should be like "regress y against 0, x1, x2, ... " where y and the x's must be specific to the above model.)

187

4. (5 points)
Describe the test statistic to compute, its distribution, and d.f.

5. (5 points)
Describe how you would use the p-value approach to decide on acceptance or rejection of the null hypothesis.

II. (25 points)

Consider the model $S_t = \alpha + \beta A_t + u_t$, in which S_t is the average sales and A_t is the average advertizing budget for industry t (t = 1, 2, ..., T) at a point in time (that is, it is cross section). The average is computed for all the firms in the industry. This makes the variance of u_t not constant but equal to σ^2/N_t, where N_t is the known number of firms in the industry. You have data on S_t, A_t, and N_t.

1. (17 points)
Carefully describe, step by step, how you would obtain weighted least squares (WLS) estimates of α and β. Your instructions should be clear and specific as though to a research assistant. In particular, describe what variables to generate and how the ols method can be used to obtain WLS estimates (show all your work below).

2. (2 points) Are the WLS estimates biased or unbiased? _____

3. (2 points) Are they consistent? _____

4. (2 points) Are they BLUE? _____

5. (2 points) Are the tests of hypotheses on WLS estimates valid? _____

III. (20 points)

Consider the following double-log model of the demand for ice cream.

$$LD_t = \beta_1 + \beta_2 LY_t + \beta_3 LP_t + \beta_4 T_t + u_t$$

where L denotes logs, D is demand, Y is income, P is price, and T is temperature. In order to test for higher order serial correlation, the following auxiliary regression was estimated, where ut1 = uhat(t-1), ut2 = uhat(t-2), and ut3 = uhat(t-3).

```
        OLS ESTIMATES USING THE 27 OBSERVATIONS 4-30
                Dependent variable  - ut

   VARIABLE          COEFFICIENT       STDERROR      T STAT     PROB t > |T|

  0) constant         -0.51069        1.515891     -0.336891    0.739709
 10) ut1               0.552587       0.246655      2.240318    0.036585 **
 11) ut2              -0.204653       0.297275     -0.688429    0.499091
 12) ut3              -0.064952       0.290782     -0.223372    0.825512
  6) LY                0.140065       0.285781      0.490114    0.629387
  7) LP                0.142403       0.632046      0.225304    0.824029
  8) LT                0.017987       0.081584      0.220473    0.827738


Error Sum of Sq (ESS)     0.17808    Std Err of Resid. (sgmahat)     0.094361
Unadjusted R-squared      0.233      Adjusted R-squared              0.003
Durbin-Watson Stat.       1.883646   First-order auto corr coeff    -0.049
```

1. (5 points) Write down the auxiliary equation for the error term implied by the above equation.

2. (2 points) Write down the null hypothesis for no autocorrelation.

3. (2 points) Write down the numerical value of the test statistic.

4. (2 points) Write down its distribution and d.f.

5. (2 points) Write down the critical value for a 10 percent test.

6. (3 points) State the decision rule and the conclusion.

7. (4 points) Based on your conclusion, are ols estimates of the parameters of the model,

> unbiased? _____   consistent? _____
>
> efficient? _____   are tests valid? _____

IV. (35 points)

A general version of the capital asset pricing model (CAPM) used in finance literature is the following.

$$(A) \quad SR_t = \beta_1 + \beta_2 MR_t + \beta_3 RFR_t + u_t$$

where SR is the rate of return of a company's stock, MR is the rate of return of a market average portfolio (such as the Standard and Poor stock average), and RFR is the return of a risk free asset (such as, for example, the three-month Treasury bill). You have data on SR, MR, and RFR for a company for a number of periods.

1. (5 points) A more commonly used version of CAPM is the following.

$$(B) \quad SR_t - RFR_t = \alpha (MR_t - RFR_t) + v_t$$

Write down the null hypotheses on the β's (which should not involve α) that will make (B) the restricted model (Model A would be the unrestricted model).

189

2. (5 points)
To use Wald test on your hypotheses, describe the variables to generate and the regressions to run.

3. (3 points) Describe how you would compute the test statistic.

4. (2 points) Write down its distribution and d.f.

5. (20 points)
Suppose the data are time series, you have used appropriate tests and found that there is serial correlation of the first order in the residuals, that is, AR(3). Describe, step by step, how you would go about using the mixed (that is, hybrid) Hildreth-Lu and Cochrane-Orcutt procedure to estimate the parameters of <u>Model A</u>

I. (20 points)
Consider the relation $P_t = \alpha + \beta S_t + u_t$, where P is profits and S is sales of a certain firm. You have quarterly time series data for 10 years (40 observations). To allow for seasonal differences, I define three dummy variables, $D_1 = 1$ for fall only, $D_2 = 1$ for spring only, and $D_3 = 1$ for summer only, winter being the control.

(a) (4 points)
I believe that both the coefficients are different across seasons. Derive the most general model (U) that incorporates that belief (show your intermediate steps below).

(b) (3 points)
I want to test the null hypothesis "there is no difference in the relation between fall and spring." Carefully write down the null hypothesis for this test.

(c) (4 points)
Derive the restricted model.

(d) (4 points)
Describe the regressions to be run for this test.

(e) (5 points)
Write down the expression for the test statistic, its distribution including the numerical value(s) of the d.f.

II. (25 points)
The attached partial computer printout relates to the model $EXPTRAV_t = \alpha + \beta \, INCOME + u_t$ that was used as an example in the chapter on heteroscedasticity (HSK). EXPTRAV is the expenditure on travel and INCOME is the total income, both measured in billions of dollars for the 50 states and the District of Columbia (51 observations).

(a) (2 points)
Write down the auxiliary equation for the error variance implicit in the print out.

190

(b) (2 points) Next state the null hypothesis that there is no HSK.

(c) (2 points) Calculate the numerical value of the test statistic (show your work).

(d) (2 points) Write down the distribution and its d.f.

(e) (7 points) Actually carry out the test (at 5 percent) and state whether HSK is present or not.

(f) (10 points)

Regardless of your answer to (e) above, suppose you want to use the weighted least squares procedure to estimate the parameters. Your research assistant is a good programmer, but does not know any econometrics. Describe step by step how your R.A. should proceed to estimate the model by weighted least squares. Note that your description must be specific to the model and estimated auxiliary equation (with numerical values from the computer printout wherever available). For simplicity, assume that there is no negative or zero variance problem.

PARTIAL COMPUTER PRINTOUT FOR QUESTION II

```
?ols exptrav const income  ;

          OLS ESTIMATES USING THE 51 OBSERVATIONS 1-51
                 Dependent variable  - exptrav


 VARIABLE          COEFFICIENT        STDERROR      T STAT    PROB t > |T|

 0) constant          0.26649         0.32944       0.809     0.4225
 2) income            0.06754         0.00350      19.288     0.0000 ***

Error Sum of Sq (ESS)    157.90707    Std Err of Resid. (sgmahat)    1.79516
Unadjusted R-squared        0.884    Adjusted R-squared                0.881

?genr usq=uhat*uhat
Generated var. no. 4 (usq)
?square pop  ;
Created sq_pop = pop squared  as var no. 5

?ols usq const pop sq_pop  ;

          OLS ESTIMATES USING THE 51 OBSERVATIONS 1-51
                 Dependent variable  - usq


 VARIABLE          COEFFICIENT        STDERROR      T STAT    PROB t > |T|

 0) constant         -1.37791         2.24070      -0.615     0.5415
 1) pop               1.37239         0.67147       2.044     0.0465 **
 5) sq_pop           -0.04124         0.03086      -1.337     0.1877

Error Sum of Sq (ESS)   3684.47761    Std Err of Resid. (sgmahat)    8.76128
Unadjusted R-squared        0.119    Adjusted R-squared                0.082
```

191

III. (25 points)

According to basic macroeconomic theory, the equilibrium gross national product (Y_t) depends on a number of policy variables and other independent variables: money supply (M_t), government expenditure (G_t), taxes (T_t), and exports (X_t). The attached computer printout presents the results of an analysis conducted with quarterly U.S.data using the ECSLIB program.

(a) (8 points)

What signs would you expect for each of the regression coefficients (ignore the constant term)? Justify your answers from economic theory.

$$M_t \qquad X_t \qquad T_t \qquad G_t$$

(b) (2 + 2 points)

Which of the signs do not agree with your intuition? Do you have any explanation for them?

(c) (7 points)

Test (two-tailed) the model for first-order serial correlation at 5 percent. Based on your results, write down the properties of the OLS estimates, their standard errors, R-squared values, validity of tests etc.

d) (6 points)

Use the information provided to test the model for the most general fourth order serial correlation at the 1 percent level. Be sure to write down the equation for the error term and the null hypotheses.

e) (10 points)

Based on your test in (d) describe to your Research Assistant the exact procedure (this must be for your model) for using the Generalized CORC procedure.

PARTIAL COMPUTER PRINTOUT FOR QUESTION III

```
List of variables
  0) const       1) Period     2) Yt        3) Mt         4) Gt .
  5) Tt          6) Xt

?corr Mt Gt Tt Xt  ;

        CORRELATION COEFFICIENTS (USING THE OBSERVATIONS 1960.1-1984.4)
               (missing values denoted by -999 will be skipped)


        3) Mt          4) Gt         5) Tt         6) Xt

        1.000          0.998         0.993         0.961      (3
                       1.000         0.992         0.963      (4
                                     1.000         0.981      (5
                                                   1.000      (6


?ols Yt const Mt Gt Tt Xt  ;
```

OLS ESTIMATES USING THE 104 OBSERVATIONS 1959.1-1984.4
Dependent variable   - Yt

VARIABLE	COEFFICIENT	STDERROR	T STAT	PROB t > |T|
0) constant	74.31764	8.24521	9.013	< 0.0001 ***
3) Mt	0.24260	0.01925	12.601	< 0.0001 ***
4) Gt	-0.55270	0.18354	-3.011	0.0033 ***
5) Tt	2.20909	0.20321	10.871	< 0.0001 ***
6) Xt	2.92166	0.94278	3.099	0.0025 ***

Error Sum of Sq (ESS)	77577.59973	Std Err of Resid. (sgmahat)	27.99307
Unadjusted R-squared	0.999	Adjusted R-squared	0.999
Durbin-Watson Stat.	0.401	First-order auto corr coeff	0.812

```
?genr ut = uhat
?lags ut  ;
Created ut_1 = ut(-1)  as var no. 8
Created ut_2 = ut(-2)  as var no. 9
Created ut_3 = ut(-3)  as var no. 10
Created ut_4 = ut(-4)  as var no. 11
List of variables
  0) const      1) Period      2) Yt        3) Mt        4) Gt
  5) Tt         6) Xt          7) ut        8) ut_1      9) ut_2
 10) ut_3      11) ut_4
```

```
?smpl 1960.1 ;
?ols ut const ut_1 ut_2 ut_3 ut_4 Mt Gt Tt Xt  ;
```

OLS ESTIMATES USING THE 100 OBSERVATIONS 1960.1-1984.4
Dependent variable   - ut

VARIABLE	COEFFICIENT	STDERROR	T STAT	PROB t > |T|
0) constant	20.10843	5.63716	3.567	0.0006 ***
8) ut_1	0.69513	0.10285	6.758	< 0.0001 ***
9) ut_2	0.12626	0.12583	1.003	0.3183
10) ut_3	0.02876	0.12837	0.224	0.8232
11) ut_4	0.10275	0.10652	0.965	0.3373
3) Mt	-0.01209	0.01146	-1.054	0.2945
4) Gt	0.35455	0.12331	2.875	0.0050 ***
5) Tt	-0.40493	0.13139	-3.082	0.0027 ***
6) Xt	1.24866	0.56477	2.211	0.0295 **

Mean of dep. var.	0.74138	S.D. of dep. variable	27.73337
Error Sum of Sq (ESS)	24136.15496	Std Err of Resid. (sgmahat)	16.28596
Unadjusted R-squared	0.683	Adjusted R-squared	0.655
F-statistic (8, 91)	24.511	Prob. F > 24.511 is < 0.00001	
Durbin-Watson Stat.	1.742	First-order auto corr coeff	0.098

NOTE THAT CAMPUS RULES FORBID REGRADING THE FINAL EXAMS. Therefore, read the questions carefully and answer all points. Marks will be taken off for irrelevant or redundant answers. Answers must be specific to the model in the problem. Simply copying down formulas from the index card without applying them to the problem will get you zero points. Don't use general terms such as "estimate basic model", "compute TRsquare statistic," etc. Clearly state exactly what they are FOR THE SPECIFIC QUESTION.

MAXIMUM NUMBER OF POINTS $35 + 35 = 70$

I. (30 points)
Consider the following model relating profits to sales of a number of firms.

$$LP_t = \beta_1 + \beta_2 LS_t + \beta_3 D_t + u_t$$

where $LP = \ln(\text{profits})$, $LS = \ln(\text{sales})$, and $D = 1$ if the company is in the manufacturing industry and 0 otherwise.

(a) (5 points) Write down the most general form of the auxiliary equation for the variance of u_t so that you can carry out White's test for heteroscedasticity (HSK).

(b) (5 points) State the null hypothesis that there is no HSK.

(c) (10 points) Describe the regressions to be run to conduct the test (be very specific to your model).

(d) (5 points) What is the test statistic, its distribution, and d.f.?

(e) (5 points) What is the decision rule?

(f) (5 points) Are the WLS estimates unbiased, consistent, and efficient?

II. (30 points)
Consider the following double-log model of the demand for a commodity.

$$LQ_t = \beta_1 + \beta_2 LP_t + \beta_3 LY_t + u_t$$

where $LQ = \ln(\text{per capita quantity demanded})$, $LP = \ln(\text{price per unit})$, and $LY = \ln(\text{per capital real income})$.

(a) (6 points) Write down the general auxiliary equation for AR(4) error specification and formally state the null hypothesis of no serial correlation.

(b) (12 points) Describe step by step, for the above model, how you would test for fourth-order serial correlation. Be sure to describe the regressions to run, how you will compute the test statistic, and what its distribution and d.f. are.

(c) (12 points) Suppose you find significant AR(4) in the residuals. Describe the steps for using the Generalized Cochrane-Orcutt estimation procedure for the above model.

(d) (5 points) Are the estimates unbiased, consistent, and efficient?

NOTE THAT CAMPUS RULES FORBID REGRADING THE FINAL EXAMS. Therefore, read the questions carefully and answer all points. Marks will be taken off for irrelevant or redundant answers. Answers must be specific to the model in the problem. Simply copying down formulas from the index card without applying them to the problem will get you zero points. Don't use general terms such as "estimate basic model", "compute TRsquare statistic," etc. Clearly state exactly what they are FOR THE SPECIFIC QUESTION.

MAXIMUM NUMBER OF POINTS 30 + 50 + 20 = 100

I. (30 points)
Consider the model

$$PRICE_t = \beta_1 + \beta_2 SQFT_t + \beta_3 \ln(SQFT_t) + \beta_4 YARD_t + \beta_5 \ln(YARD_t) + u_t$$

where PRICE is the price in dollars of a house, SQFT is the living area in square feet, and YARD is the size of the yard in square feet.

(a) (5 points) I suspect that the marginal effect of SQFT on PRICE decreases as SQFT increases and similarly that the marginal effect of YARD on PRICE decreases as YARD increases. If these hypotheses were true, what signs would you expect for β_3 and β_5? Carefully justify your answers.

(b) (10 points) I know from past studies that the variance of u is proportional to the size of the yard. Describe step by step how I would apply the weighted least squares procedure that makes use of this information. Be sure to state what variables to generate and what regressions to run.

(c) (5 points) In what way(s) is the WLS procedure better than the OLS procedure?

(d) (10 points) In the basic model, suppose the nature of the heteroscedasticity is unknown. Carefully describe the steps to be taken to perform the White's test for the above model. To do this, first write the auxiliary equation for the error variance (you may ignore the crossproduct terms) and state the null hypothesis of no heteroscedasticity. Then describe the regressions to run, how you will compute the test statistic, and what its distribution and d.f. are.

II. (50 points)
Consider the model

$$AIR_t = \beta_1 + \beta_2 PRICE_t + \beta_3 INCOME_t + \beta_4 ACCID_t + u_t$$

where AIR is the per capita passenger miles of air travel, PRICE is the average price per mile, INCOME is per capita income, and ACCID is the number of accidents per passenger mile, all at time t. You have annual data for the 41 years 1947-1987.

(a) (2 points) Write down the auxiliary equation for AR(3) error specification and formally state the null hypothesis of zero serial correlation.

195

(b) (10 points) Describe step by step, for the above model, how you would test for third-order serial correlation of the errors. Be sure to describe the regressions to run, how you will compute the test statistic, and what its distribution and d.f. are.

(c) (13 points) Suppose you find significant AR(3) in the residuals. Describe the steps for using the Generalized Cochrane-Orcutt estimation procedure for the above model.

Prior to 1979, the airline companies were regulated strictly and from 1979 onward they were operating under deregulation. We can therefore suspect that the entire relationship between air travel and its determinants will have undergone a structural change since 1979. [In answering the following questions assume that there is no serial correlation.]

(d) (10 points) Write down another model that will enable you to test whether there has been a structural change. Be sure to define all the new variables you need to create.

(e) (2 points) State the null hypothesis for no structural change, formally in terms of the parameters in your model.

(f) (13 points) Carefully describe the steps to be taken to perform a Wald test for structural change. In particular, describe the regressions to run, the test statistic to compute, its distribution and d.f., and the decision rule.

III. (20 points)
Suppose I estimate the model $Y_t = \beta X_t + u_t$, using the OLS procedure.

(a) (10 points) Show that the OLS estimate of β (call it $\hat{\beta}$) is given by

$$\hat{\beta} = \frac{\Sigma X_t Y_t}{\Sigma X_t^2}$$

Now suppose that the true model should have used Z_t instead of X_t so that the real data generating process is given by $Y_t = \beta Z_t + v_t$, where v_t are "well-behaved" errors with all the nice properties we need.

(b) (10 points) Derive the expected value of $\hat{\beta}$ and show that it is biased.

Michigan State University

ECONOMICS 420
FALL, 1994

U

Instructor: Peter Schmidt
Office: 108 Marshall Hall, 355-8381
Office hours: Monday-Thursday, 9:00-10:00. However, the Monday
                morning time may often be preempted by meetings of
                a college-wide committee of which I am a member.

This is a course in econometrics. This means that it is
essentially a course in statistics, with an emphasis on those
topics that are most useful in economics and related fields.
Basically it will cover linear regression and related topics.
The course will emphasize the relevance of statistical methods in
economic applications, and real data in economics and elsewhere
will be analyzed. However, the fundamental point of the course
is to understand statistical procedures and their potential
applications, not to learn which buttons to push on the computer
to make results appear.

The prerequisite for the course is one course in statistics,
at least at the level of Statistics 315 or 421. This is a
serious prerequisite, since the statistical review at the
beginning of the course will be brief. Knowledge of calculus or
matrix algebra is not presumed.

There will be two exams during the semester, on September 29
and November 3. There will be some take-home problem sets as
well. The final is on Thursday, December 15, 7:45-9:45 AM.

There will be two TA's for the course: Hailong Qian and
Kyle Vrieze. Mr. Qian will primarily handle questions about the
course material. His office is 305 Marshall Hall, and his office
hours are Tuesday and Thursday, 1:30 - 3:30. Mr. Vrieze will
primarily handle computer questions. His office hours are Monday
and Wednesday, 2:10 - 3:10, in the library on the 3rd floor of
Marshall Hall. The phone number for both TA's is 355-3432.

The text for the course is Griffiths, Hill and Judge,
Learning and Practicing Econometrics. Please read the
appropriate sections, as indicated on the course schedule.

TOPIC	APPROXIMATE NUMBER OF CLASSES	CHAPTERS IN TEXT
Statistical Review	6	1, 2, 3, 4
Simple Regression	6	5, 6, 7, 8
Multiple Regression	5	9, 10, 13
Functional Form and Specification	3	12
Autocorrelation/Heteroskedasticity	2	15, 16
Time Series and Dynamic Models	2	20, 21

Michigan State University

ECONOMICS 820

Spring, 1995   **G**

Instructor:	Peter Schmidt
Office:	108 Marshall Hall
Phone:	355-8381
Office Hours:	Tuesday, Wednesday and Thursday, 9:00 - 10:00

Office Hours for TAs: Qian, Hailong: Monday and Wednesday, 2:00-4:00
                             William Horrace: Tuesday and Thursday, 10:00 - 12:00

This is a course in theoretical econometrics. This means that it covers statistical topics that are of particular interest in economics and related fields. Basically it will cover linear regression analysis of single-equation and multiple-equation models. The course is intended as an introduction to econometric methods, and to be a useful prerequisite to further study in theoretical econometrics (Economics 821 and 822) or applied econometrics (Economics 823).

The prerequisites for the course are a basic knowledge of statistics and of matrix algebra. Students should have had at least one semester course in statistics, using calculus, such as Statistics 430 or Statistics 441-442. Statistics without calculus, such as Statistics 421-422, is not an adequate preparation for the course. There is no specific course prerequisite in matrix algebra, but some familiarity with matrices and the ability and willingness to manipulate them algebraically are required.

There will be a midterm exam on Wednesday, February 22, and a final exam on Monday, May 1 at 12:45 PM. There will also be some problems sets to do during the term. Please note that the last date to drop the course without a grade reported is March 1, and mid-term grades will be available before then to serve as an early warning to any students who may not be doing well in the course. I do not intend to give deferred grades or to let students drop the course after March 1 without a grade reported.

The text for the course is Greene, <u>Econometric Analysis</u>, 2nd edition, MacMillan, 1993. The following four books will also be referred to fairly often. Buy as many of them as you can afford, or share copies with a friend.

Schmidt, <u>Econometrics</u>, Marcel Dekker, 1976
Amemiya, <u>Advanced Econometrics</u>, Harvard Press, 1985
Fomby, Hill and Johnson, <u>Advanced Econometric Methods</u>, Springer-Verlag, 1984
Judge, et al., <u>The Theory and Practice of Econometrics</u>, 2nd edition, Wiley, 1984

Additional reference will be made to:

Goldberger, <u>A Course in Econometrics</u>, Harvard Press, 1991
Griliches and Intriligator, <u>Handbook of Econometrics</u>, North Holland, 1983
Harvey, <u>The Econometric Analysis of Time Series</u>, 2nd edition, MIT Press, 1990
Johnston, <u>Econometric Methods</u>, 3rd edition, McGraw Hill, 1984
Kmenta, <u>Elements of Econometrics</u>, 2nd edition, Macmillan, 1986
Sargan, <u>Lectures on Advanced Econometric Theory</u>, Basil Blackwell, 1988

SYLLABUS AND COURSE OUTLINE

TEXTS:
"BL": Ben-Akiva , Moshe, and Steven R.Lerman, <u>Discrete Choice Analysis: Theory and Application to Travel Demand</u>, MIT Press, 1985.

Train: Train, Kenneth, <u>Qualitative Choice Analysis: Theory, Econometrics, and an Application to Travel Demand</u>, MIT Press, 1986.

Maddala: Maddala, G.S., <u>Limited-Dependent and Qualitative Variables in Econometrics</u>, Cambridge University Press, 1983.

I. INTRODUCTION AND BACKGROUND MATERIAL (Weeks 1-2)

   A. Introduction to Discrete Choice

      BL, Chpt. 1
      Train, Chpt. 1
      Small, Kenneth A., "Discrete Choice Econometrics", book review in <u>Journal of Mathematical Psychology</u>, vol. 32, no. 1 (March, 1988), pp. 80-87.

   B. Review of Mathematical Statistics

      BL, Chpt. 2
      (Also review your favorite statistics textbook)

   C. Theories of Individual Choice Behavior

      BL, Chpt. 3

II. BASIC BINOMIAL AND MULTINOMIAL CHOICE MODELS (Weeks 2-5)

   A. Logit, Probit, Nested Logit Models

      Train, Chpt. 2-4
      BL, Chpt. 4-5
      Brownstone, David, and Kenneth A. Small, "Efficient Estimation of Nested Logit Models", <u>Journal of Business and Economic Statistics</u>, vol. 7, no. 1 (Jan. 1989), pp. 67-74.

Thursday January 27th: Meet in Soc Sci Computer Lab

   B. Forecasting and Testing

      Train, Chpt. 6
      BL, Chpt. 7
      McFadden, Daniel, Kenneth Train, and William B. Tye, "An Application of Diagnostic Tests for the Independence from Irrelevant Alternatives Property of the Multinomial Logit Model", <u>Transportation Research Record</u>, no. 637 (1977), pp. 39-46.
      Small, Kenneth A., and Cheng Hsiao, "Multinomial Logit Specification Tests", <u>International Economic Review</u>, vol. 26, no.3 (Oct. 1985), pp. 619-627.
      McFadden, Daniel, "Regression-Based Specification Tests for the Multinomial Logit Model", <u>Journal of Econometrics</u>, vol. 34 (1987), pp. 63-82 (optional)

III. NON-RANDOM SAMPLES AND LARGE CHOICE SETS (Week 6)

  BL, Chpt 8

** MID-TERM EXAM: THURSDAY FEBRUARY 17TH (IN CLASS)

IV. GENERALIZED EXTREME VALUE (GEV) MODELS (Week 7)

  McFadden, Daniel, "Modelling the Choice of Residential Location", in Anders Karlqvist et al., eds., Spatial Interaction Theory and Planning Models (North-Holland, 1978), pp. 75-96.

  Small, Kenneth A., "A Discrete Choice Model for Ordered Alternatives", Econometrica, vol. 55, no. 2 (March 1987), pp. 409-424.

  Small, Kenneth A., "Approximated Generalized Extreme Value Models of Discrete Choice", working paper, UC Irvine, Oct. 1992 (forthcoming, Journal of Econometrics).

V. SIMULTANEOUS DISCRETE AND CONTINUOUS CHOICES (Week 8)

  Train, Chpt. 5
  The following three articles are optional reading:

  Giuliano, Genevieve, and Charles Lave, "The High Cost of A Bargain: Winning the Right to Use Part-Time Transit Drivers", Transportation Research, vol. 23A, no. 2, (1989), pp. 151-159.

  Dubin, Jeffrey A., and Daniel L. McFadden, "An Econometric Analysis of Residential Electric Appliance Holdings and Consumption", Econometrica, vol. 52, no. 2 (March, 1984), pp. 345-362.

  Mallar, Charles D., "Notes and Comments: The Estimation of Simultaneous Probability Models", Econometrica, vol. 45, no. 7 (Oct., 1977), pp. 1717-1722.

VI. APPLICATIONS (Week 9)

  BL, Chpt. 11
   OR
  Train, Chpt. 8-9

VII. CENSORING AND TRUNCATION (Week 10)

  Maddala, Chpt. 1, pp. 1-11
  Maddala, Chpt. 6, pp. 149-153, 165-167

***SECOND EXAM: THURSDAY MARCH 17TH (IN CLASS)

*** TERM PAPER DUE TUESDAY MARCH 22ND, 4:00 P.M.

Problem Set 3
Due Tuesday February 8, 1994
(Week 5)

You will be provided a data set describing a fictitious survey of
N=80 automobile commuters who are asked the following questions:

What is your occupation: laborer, clerical, managerial, or
professional?

Do you normally arrive at work early, on time, or late (compared
to your employer's standard working hours)?

How long would it take to travel to work if you were to arrive

$$\begin{array}{ll}
\text{Early?} & \underline{\hspace{3cm}} \text{ minutes} \\
\text{On Time?} & \underline{\hspace{3cm}} \text{ minutes} \\
\text{Late?} & \underline{\hspace{3cm}} \text{ minutes}
\end{array}$$
(Please fill in all three blanks).

The answers are coded as follows, for each respondent n=1, ...,
80:

$$k(n) = \text{CHOICE} = \begin{cases} 1 \text{ if arrive early} \\ 2 \text{ if arrive on time} \\ 3 \text{ if arrive late} \end{cases}$$

T_{in} = TIME = travel time for choice i

$$L_n = \text{LABCLER} = \begin{cases} 1 \text{ for laborer or clerical} \\ 0 \text{ for managerial or professional} \end{cases}$$

1. Suppose you believe that people don't actually distinguish
    between "early" and "on time" in this survey. Estimate a
    binary logit model as follows.

    $$s(n) = \text{BICHOICE} = \begin{cases} a & \text{if } k(n) = 1 \text{ or } 2 \\ b & \text{if } k(n) = 3 \end{cases}$$

    $$t_{sn} = \text{BITIME} = \begin{array}{l} 1/2 \ (T_{1n} + T_{2n}) \quad \text{for } s = a \\ T_{3n} \quad \text{for } s = b \end{array}$$

    Try the following specifications:

    $$V_{sn} = \beta_1 t_{sn} + \beta_2 d_{bs} + \beta_3 L_n d_{bs} \qquad \text{for } s = a,b$$

    $$\text{where } d_{bs} = \begin{cases} 0 & \text{if } s = a \\ 1 & \text{if } s = b \end{cases}$$

    (We call d_{bs} an "alternative-specific dummy" and $(L_n d_{bs})$ a
    "socioeconomic variable interacted with an alternative-
    specific dummy")

    (a) Report the coefficient estimates, standard errors, and
         log-likelihood value. Are the signs of coefficients
         what you expected?

    (b) Perform a 1-sided test of the null hypothesis $\beta_1 = 0$
         against the alternative hypothesis $\beta_1 < 0$.

(c) Perform a test of the joint hypothesis that $\beta_2 = \beta_3 = 0$

(d) Can you draw qualitative conclusions about the importance of travel time relative to other factors in determining time-of-day choice?

2. Repeat problem 1 with a binary probit model. In addition,

(e) Compare the coefficients estimated using logit with those using probit, taking care to rescale the former to equalize the variance in the random utility for the two models.

(f) Which model, logit or probit, achieves a higher log-likelihood, and by how much?

3. Now estimate a trinomial logit model using all three choices and the following specification:

$$V_{in} = \beta_1 T_{in} + \beta_2 D_{2i} + \beta_3 L_n D_{3i}$$

$$\text{where} \quad D_{2i} = \begin{cases} 1 & \text{if } i = 2 \\ 0 & \text{otherwise} \end{cases}$$

$$D_{3i} = \begin{cases} 1 & \text{if } i = 3 \\ 0 & \text{otherwise} \end{cases}$$

Answer the same questions (a) - (d) as for the binomial logit model.

(e) Do you feel this is a better model than the binomial logit? Why?

(f) Try one or two variants to see if you can improve the fit.

Problem Set 4
Due Tuesday February 22, 1994
(Week 7)

This continues estimation on the data set provided in your computer lab and used in the last problem set.

1. Estimate a trinomial nested logit model with the same utility specification as in the trinomial logit model of problem 3 of the last problem set, namely

$$V_{in} = \beta_1 T_{in} + \beta_2 D_{2i} + \beta_3 L_n D_{3i}$$

$$\text{where} \quad D_{2i} = \begin{cases} 1 & \text{if } i = 2 \\ 0 & \text{otherwise} \end{cases}$$

$$D_{3i} = \begin{cases} 1 & \text{if } i = 3 \\ 0 & \text{otherwise} \end{cases}$$

Assume the first two alternatives are grouped together; i.e., $B_a = \{1,2\}$ and $B_b = \{3\}$. Estimate the model using both the sequential and the maximum likelihood estimator and compare results. For the sequential estimates you need not correct the standard errors.

202

2. Repeat problem 1 using the larger data set HW4.DAT, which has 200 observations.

3. From the results of problem 2, perform three different statistical tests for the hypothesis that the true model is logit. Include at least one 1-sided test and at least one 2-sided test.

4. Using the maximum-likelihood results from problem 2, forecast the percentage of St. Louis workers arriving late under three difference scenarios:

    (a) Base case: current conditions as represented by the 30 individuals in data file "POP.DAT" whose variables are: L_n, $k(n)$, T_{1n}, T_{2n}, T_{3n}.

    (b) Worse congestion: everyone's travel time in period 2 goes up by 5 minutes.

    (c) No congestion: everyone's travel time is equalized across the three periods.

    d) How does the change from scenario (a) to scenario (b) compare with what would be predicted by pivot-point analysis?

5. Using the maximum-likelihood results from problem 2 as the "true" model, generate 10 new dependent variables (each of size N = 200) using the random number generator in TSP. Do not change the independent variables. Estimate the trinomial logit model on each of these 10 replications (knowing that it is misspecified because the true model is nested logit), and compute the empirical mean and standard deviation of the estimated coefficients. How biased are the estimated coefficients and their estimated errors?

    Hint: to generate a random choice s(n) with probabilities P_{in} of selecting alternatives i =1,2,3 first generate a uniform random variable x on the unit interval [0,1] and then set

    $s(n) = 1$ if $0 \leq x < P_{1n}$

    2 if $P_{1n} \leq x < P_{1n} + P_{2n}$

    3 if $P_{1n} + P_{2n} \leq x \leq 1$

ECONOMETRICS

U

REQUIRED READING

Pindyk, Robert S. & Daniel L. Rubinfeld, **Econometric Models & Economic Forecasts,**
Fourth Edition, McGraw Hill, New York, 1993.
Ramsey, James B. and Gerald Musgrave, **APL-STAT,** Wadsworth Inc., California, 1981.
Wykoff, Frank C., **Econometrics Handouts** - to be distributed, Pomona College.

RECOMMENDED READING

Berndt, Ernst R. **The Practice of Econometrics: Classic and Contemporary,** Addison-
Wesley, Reading, MA., 1991.
Chiang, Alpha, **Fundamental Methods of Mathematical Economics,** Third ed., McGraw Hill,
N.Y., 1984.
Deaton, Angus and John Muellbauer, **Economics and Consumer Behavior,** Cambridge, Uni-
versity Press, 1983.
Gilman, Leonard and Allen J. Rose, **APL An Interactive Approach,** Second ed., John Wiley
& sons, New York, 1976.
Intriligator, Michael D., **Econometric Models, Techniques, & Applications,** Prentice Hall,
Inc., Englewood Cliffs, N.J., 1978.
Kelejian, Harry and Wallace Oates, **Introduction to Econometrics,** Third ed., Harper &
Rowe, New York, 1989.
Lucas, Robert and Thomas Sargeant, **Rational Expectations and Econometric Practice,** Uni-
versity of Minnesota Press, Minneapolis, 1981.
Smith, Gary, **Statistical Reasoning,** 1988.

TOPICS, OUTLINE & READINGS

1. LINEAR REGRESSION: Three Weeks.

We will review advanced topics from Economics 103, beginning with the relationship between economic theories and empirical evidence. We discuss the formal
definition of econometrics and develop two prototypical econometric models, one
based on microeconomics and one on macroeconomics. We will then study basic
linear regression analysis with one independent variable. We will develop the capacity
to implement regression using APL on the IBM Personal System computers. This
material forms an essential foundation for all subsequent work in the course.

Please read the following material:

1. An economics statistics text of your choice as review. I recommend Smith's **Statistics for Economists**.
2. Pindyck & Rubinfeld--Chapters 1-3.
3. Ramsey & Musgrave, APL-STAT, relevant portions & exercises to familiarize yourself with APL.

****
NOTE: PAPER 1 DUE

While working on this module, each student is **required** to begin work on a term project. A **short paper** is due at the end of this module. This paper forms the first portion of a term project report. Two steps must be undertaken at this time: First, the student must prepare an economic theory, expressed in quantitative terms, dealing with an empirical economic issue. (The theory need not be original.) Second, the student must collect some data that is physically put on computer diskette and readable in APL. This must be done at this time and is a course requirement. The paper will have three parts: (1) A thesis statement of a paragraph to a page explaining the economic model that forms the theoretical basis for the problem being studied; (2) a brief description of the data to be used in the study; and (3) a list of key references for the study including data sources and theoretical references.
****

2. MATRIX ALGEBRA, CALCULUS, PROBABILITY THEORY & STATISTICAL INFERENCE:
Three weeks.

The material to be covered in this module consists of several corner stones needed before one can learn econometrics at a reasonably advanced level. We will prove various mathematical relations, involving linear algebra and then verify these relations in APL with each student using his own data base. Each student will be expected to understand and to be able to reproduce various proofs. This material will be exploited frequently in subsequent weeks, so it is essential to keep up and try to follow as much as you can. For some students, much of this material will be familiar from various other courses in math, especially Math 157. However, the applications and orientation are fresh, so you should find the material challenging.

Please read the following:

Johnston--Chapter 4 to be distributed.

****
NOTE: PAPER 2 DUE

You should by this point in the course be reasonably conversant in APL and you should have a viable data base fully operational on diskette. You will submit a second **short paper** at the end of this module. This paper will be an extension of paper 1. This paper should include a statistical display and analytic description of the important features of your data-not data dump but summary tabulations of your data. You should also prepare a separate section of your paper covering, with your data, key illustrations of proofs covered in the class. You may, but need not, also take this opportunity to refine and up date your first paper, so that this new paper is a coherent combination of paper 1 and paper 2 as an early beginning to you final project report.
****

****
MIDTERM EXAM
****

3. THE GAUSS MARKOV THEOREM: Five weeks.

This topic is the theoretical core of the course. We will pull together all the topics and tools developed so far into analysis of the key theorem of classical econometrics-the Gauss Markov Theorem. Everything in the field is built around this theorem. It forms the justification for drawing causal inferences from empirical analysis based on regression methods.

Please read the following:

Pindyck & Rubinfeld--Chapters 4 & 5.
Wykoff--handouts.

****
NOTE: PAPER 3 DUE

Your third **short paper** is due at the end of this module. It will consist of a discussion of your theory, model and data, in light of your understanding of the Gauss Markov Theorem. You are to discuss the nature of your data and your model in comparison to the ideal of the assumptions of the Gauss Markov Theorem. Think of this paper as a discussion of the research you would have undertaken had you known what you now know at the beginning of the course. How would you ideally improve on your data, how would you revise the key questions you would address or how would you modify your model if you could. Refer back to the thesis sentence of your first paper to see how well you are able to focus on the key questions.

****

4. MULTICOLLINEARITY, HETEROSCEDASTICITY, AUTOCORRELATION: Two weeks.

The general failure of economic data to meet the strict requirements of the Gauss Markov Theorem will become evident, and we will study several frequently encountered problems with data and introduce some methods for detecting these problems, interpreting results of studies that do not solve these problems, and we will discuss how to deal with these problems in a systematic fashion. We will learn the method of Generalized Least Squares.

Please read the following:

Pindyck & Rubinfeld--Chapters 6, 9 & 11.
Wykoff--handouts.

5. SPECIFICATION ANALYSIS, EXPERIMENTAL DESIGN, TWO STAGE LEAST SQUARES AND INSTRUMENTAL VARIABLES: One or two weeks.

We introduce basic economic reasoning and models back into the analysis at this point and explore our thinking about econometric model building. We will discuss some of your models and some famous critiques of econometric methods by Lucas, Leamer, and others. We will learn two new techniques: two stage least squares and instrumental variables. We may have time for qualitative variable models, probit and logit, and for non-linear models, such as Box-Cox. We may also briefly consider time series models.

Please read the following:
Pindyck & Rubinfeld--Chapters 7, 8, 10.
Pindyck & Rubinfeld--Chapters 14-16. TIME PERMITTING
Wykoff--handouts.

****
NOTE: PAPER 4 DUE

You will turn in your final paper one week before the end of classes. It will combine all your previous papers, updated as appropriate. This report will also contain all homework assignments and all APL proofs and illustrations. In addition, you will have your theory section, your data section and discussion, your econometric model, some regression analysis of your problem using your data. (This latter must include at least 5 regressions, using different functional forms, different variables, or different techniques. Each regression must be a multiple regression containing at least 2 independent variables.)

You must run a model with at least one dummy variable and must test at least three hypotheses with your data. I would also like you to test for serial correlation if you have time series data or for heteroscedasticity if you have cross section data. Finally, some discussion of specification analysis and experimental design must be contained in the paper.
****

STUDENT RESPONSIBILITY & GRADE DETERMINATION

Course work includes homework, a series of short papers, independent research, data collection, computer analysis as well as class attendance, reading, midterm exam and a final. **ALL WORK MUST BE DONE BY YOU ONLY AND MUST BE TURNED IN ON TIME.** You are not to lean on other faculty, graduate students, friends, etc. The work you submit is to be your own. This course depends on each one of you following a very strict **HONOR CODE**. I and your peers depend on you to do this.

Course grades will be determined both from material turned in and from my evaluation of your effort and performance throughout the course. This includes attendance, turning in assignments on time, effort on computer work, attitude, participation, and progress. I care very much about effort, because I know much of the material is difficult and that at times you will feel lost.

The following weights approximate the relative importance of assigned material:

Midterm	1/6
Homework	1/6
Project	1/3
Final	1/3

Business 326   Autumn Quarter, 1994
Introduction to Econometrics   Mr. Zellner

Course Information

Business 326 course meetings will be held on Tuesdays, 6:00-9:00 PM in Rosenwald Hall, Room 15. The course is designed to give students an introduction to econometric methods and their applications to business and economic problems. There will be mid-quarter and end-of-quarter examinations. In addition, problem sets will be assigned that will be discussed at weekly problem section meetings (to be arranged) with Jeff Currie, Teaching Assistant who will assist you with computer programs, data bases, etc.

The text for the course is: D.N. Gujarati, *Basic Econometrics* (2nd ed.), McGraw Hill, 1988, denoted DNG below. Also, papers included in the Bus 326 Course packet will be assigned for reading.

Office Hours: Mondays, 1:30-3:00, Ro 205D and by appt.
Email: FAC_AZELLNER@GSBVAX.UCHICAGO.EDU (for pressing questions)

Course Topics and Reading Assignments

I.   Econometrics and Business

   A. Definition of Econometrics

      1. Measurement, Data, Economic and Business Theory, Statistics and Computers

         a. Accuracy of measurements (Get the Facts!)
         b. Measurement without theory and theory without measurement
         c. Usual, unusual and ugly facts
         d. Data $\leftrightarrows$ Theory

      2. Objectives: Learning from Data and Experience and Solving Practical Problems

         a. Generalizations and models that are reliable in explanation, prediction and solution of practical problems

            (1)   KISS (keep it sophisticatedly simple)

      3. Examples of Econometric Analyses in Business

         a. What is the problem?
         b. Why is it important?
         c. How can the problem be solved?

Readings: DNG, 1-9
      A. Zellner, "The Philosophy and Objectives of Econometrics"[*]
      "Statistical Analysis of Econometric Models"[*] Section 1,2.1,4 Comments
        and Rejoinder.
     Background references: R.J. Epstein, *A History of Econometrics*, North-
        Holland, 1987, and M.S. Morgan, *The History of Econometric Ideas*,
        Cambridge U. Press, 1990.

II.   Econometric Models for One or Two Variables

   A. Models to Represent "Random Variation"
       ("All variation is random unless shown otherwise.")

      1. Random sequences and random walk models for stock prices and exchange
         rates
      2. Coin-flipping and forecasting turning-points
      3. "Bench-mark" models

   B. Simple Correlation (x $\leftrightarrows$ y) and Two Variable or Simple Regression (x $\rightarrow$ y) with
      Applications

      1. Correlation, regression and causation
      2. Interpretation of correlation and regression models
        a. "Descriptive" versus "Causal"

     Readings: DNG, Chs. 1-2
        A. Zellner, "Notes on Simple Correlation and Regression"
        A. Zellner, "Some Properties of the Durations of Economic Expansions
          and Contractions."[*]
        F.X. Diebold, "Are Long Expansions Followed by Short Contractions?"[*]

   C. Estimation of Parameters and Goodness of Fit

      1. Random walk models
      2. Two variable regression
      3. Methods of estimation
        a. Least-squares, etc.
        b. Maximum-likelihood
        c. Bayes
        d. Bayesian and Non-Bayesian Method of Moments

---

[*]Included in Course Packet.

4. Properties of estimates and estimators

Readings: DNG, Chs. 3-4

D. Random Walk and Two Variable Regression Model: Interval Estimation, Hypothesis Testing and Prediction

Readings: DNG, Chs. 5-6
        A. Zellner and B.R. Moulton, "Bayesian Regression Diagnostics with Applications to International Consumption and Income Data."[*]

III. Multiple Regression Model and Applications ($x_1, x_2, ..., x_k \rightarrow y$)

    A. Interpretation of model and its assumptions
    B. Estimation and testing procedures
    C. Prediction procedures

    Readings: DNG, Chs. 5-6
        D.A. Conway and H.V. Roberts, "Reverse Regression, Fairness and Employment Discrimination."[*]

IV. Special Problems in Regression Analysis

    <u>M</u>ulticollinearity
    <u>A</u>utocorrelation
    <u>L</u>eft-out variables and faulty functional form
    <u>T</u>ime-series complications
    <u>H</u>eteroscedasticity
    <u>U</u>nobserved variables and measurement errors
    <u>S</u>imultaneous-equation problems

    Readings: DGN, Chs. 10-13

V. Special Topics and Other Important Models

    A. Dummy Variables and Functional Forms for Relations
    B. Logit and Probit Models for Discrete Random Variables
       ($y = 1$ buy; $y = 0$ don't buy, etc.)
    C. Two-Part Models

---

[*]Included in Course Packet.

211

Readings: DGN, Chs. 14-15
>>> Y. Mundlak, "Empirical Production Function Free of Management Bias."[*]

D. Autoregressive, Distributed Lag and Forecasting Models

Readings: DGN, Ch. 16
>>> A. Garcia-Ferrer, et al., "Macroeconomic Forecasting Using Pooled International Data."[*]
>>> A. Zellner and C. Hong, "Forecasting International Growth Rates Using Bayesian Shrinkage and Other Procedures."[*]

VI. Simultaneous Equation Model

A. Interpretation of Model and Examples
B. Identification Problem
C. Estimation, Testing and Prediction Procedures
D. Applications and Evaluation

Readings: DGN, Chs. 17-19
>>> A. Zellner and S.C. Peck, "Simulation Experiments with a Quarterly Macroeconometric Model of the U.S. Economy," in A. Zellner, *Basic Issues in Econometrics*, U. of Chicago Press, 1984.
>>> S.K. McNees, "Forecasting Accuracy of Alternative Techniques: A Comparison of U.S. Macroeconomic Forecasts," *Journal of Business and Economic Statistics* 4 (1986), 5-15.

VII. Summary and Overview

Readings: A. Zellner, "Past, Present and Future of Econometrics," Invited Address, Notre Dame U., 1991.

Additional General References
>>> E.R. Berndt, *The Practice of Econometrics*, Addison-Wesley, 1990.
>>> W.H. Greene, *Econometric Analysis*, Macmillan, 2nd ed., 1993.
>>> Z. Griliches and M. Intriligator, *Handbook of Econometrics*, Vols. I-III, North-Holland, 1983, 1984 and 1986.
>>> J. Johnston, *Econometric Methods*, 3rd ed., McGraw-Hill, 1984.
>>> G.G. Judge et al., *The Theory and Practice of Econometrics*, 2nd ed., Wiley, 1985.
>>> G.S. Maddala, *Introduction to Econometrics* (2nd ed.), Macmillan, 1992.

>>> A. Zellner, *An Introduction to Bayesian Inference in Econometrics*, Wiley, 1971 (reprinted by Krieger, 1987).
>>> A. Zellner, *Basic Issues in Econometrics*, U. of Chicago Press, 1984.

---

[*]Included in Course Packet.

Topics and Readings[*]   G

I. Philosophy, Objectives and Policy Uses of Econometrics

Readings:
AZN: "Philosophy and Objectives of Econometrics"+ and "Perspectives on
        Mathematical Models in the Social Sciences" in A. Zellner, *Basic Issues
        in Econometrics*, U. of Chicago Press, 1984.
AZ: Ch.I.
AZSTE: pp.68-74.
A. Zellner, "Causality and Causal Laws in Economics," in D.J. Aigner and A.
   Zellner (eds.), *Causality, J. of Econometrics*, Sept./Oct. 1988, 6-21.

II. Univariate Regression Models: Assumptions and Interpretation

Readings:
AZN: "Notes on Simple Regression and Correlation"+ and "Notes on
        Mathematical Analysis of the Multiple Regression Model (MRM)"+.
JGHLL: Ch.2.
WHG: Ch.5.
A. Zellner, "Bayesian Method of Moments/Instrumental Variable (BMOM/IV)
   Analysis of Mean and Regression Models.+"

---

[*]**Abbreviations:**
AZN: A. Zellner, Class Notes.
AZR: A. Zellner (ed.), *Readings in Econometrics and Economic Statistics*, Little, Brown
         and Co., 1968.
AZ: A. Zellner, *An Introduction to Bayesian Inference in Econometrics*, 1971, reprinted
         by Krieger Publishing Co., 1987.
AZBIE: A. Zellner, *Basic Issues in Econometrics*, U. of Chicago Press, 1984 and 1987
         (paperback ed.).
AZSTE: A. Zellner, "Statistical Theory and Econometrics," in Z. Griliches and M.D.
         Intriligator (eds.), *Handbook of Econometrics*, Vol. I, Ch.2, Amsterdam: North-
         Holland, 1983.
JGHLL: Judge, Griffiths, Hill, Lutkepohl and Lee, *The Theory and Practice of Econometrics*,
         2nd ed., Wiley, 1985.
MRM: Multiple Regression Model.
MVRM: Multivariate Regression Model.
SEM: Simultaneous Equation Model.
SURM: Seemingly Unrelated Regression Model.
WHG: W.H. Greene, *Econometric Analysis*, Macmillan, 1993.
+:   Included in course packet.

III. **Estimation and Testing Procedures for the MRM**

Readings:
AZN: "Notes on the MRM," Sections A.4a, A.4b, A.4c, and A.4d+.
AZSTE: Sect. III, 77-131.
JGHLL: Chs.3 and 4.
WHG: Chs.6 and 7.
S.F. Arnold, *The Theory of Linear Models...*, Chs.5 and 6.
A. Zellner, "Bayesian Method of Moments/Instrumental Variable (BMOM/IV) Analysis of Mean and Regression Models, ms., 1994+
A. Zellner and W. Vandaele, "Bayes-Stein Estimators for k-Means, Regression and Simultaneous Equation Models," Sections 1, 2 and 3.1, in S.E. Fienberg and A. Zellner (eds.), *Studies in Bayesian Econometrics and Statistics*, North-Holland, 1975.
A. Zellner, "Posterior Odds Ratios for Regression Hypotheses: General Considerations and Some Specific Results," Ch.3.7 in AZBIE.
P.L. Smith, "Splines as a Useful and Convenient Statistical Tool," *American Statistician*, May 1979, 57-62.
D.E.A. Giles and A.C. Rayner, "The Mean Squared Errors of the Maximum Likelihood and Natural-Conjugate Bayes Regression Estimators," *J. of Econometrics*, Oct. 1979, 319-330.
A. Zellner, "Bayesian Estimation and Prediction Using Asymmetric Loss Functions," *J. Am. Stat. Assoc.*, June 1986.
A. Zellner, "Bayesian and Non-Bayesian Estimation Using Balanced Loss Functions," in S.S. Gupta and J.O. Berger (eds.), *Statistical Decision Theory and Related Topics V*, New York: Springer-Verlag, 1994, 377-390.
J.M. Abowd, B.M. Moulton and A. Zellner, "The Bayesian Regression Analysis Package: BRAP User's Manual Version 2.0, May 1987".

IV. **Prediction Procedures for the MRM**

Readings:
AZN: "Notes on the MRM," Section A.4e+.
D.S. Salkever, "The Use of Dummy Variables to Compute Predictions, Prediction Errors and Confidence Intervals," *J. of Econometrics*, Nov. 1976, 393-398.
AZ: Ch.III, 72-75.
A. Zellner, C.Hong and C. Min, "Forecasting Turning Points in International Output Growth Rates...," *J. of Econometrics*, July/August 1991, 275-304+.

V. Asymptotic Theory, Variants of the MRM and Selected Applications

Readings:

A. Asymptotic Theory

JGHLL: Chs.5, 17 and 18.
WHG: Ch.10.

AZSTE: pp.110-117.
P. Schmidt, *Econometrics*, 64-72.
J. Johnston, *Econometric Methods* (2nd ed.), 1972, Ch.6, 176-192.
C.C. Heyde and I.M. Johnstone, "On Asymptotic Posterior Normality for Stochastic Processes," *J. Royal Statistical Society, B*, 1979, 184-189.
C-F. Chen, "On Asymptotic Normality of Limiting Density Functions with Bayesian Implications," *J. Roy. Stat. Soc.*, 47, 1985, 540-546.

B. Variants of the MRM

WHG: Ch.9.
A. Zellner, "Bayesian and Non-Bayesian Analysis of the Log-Normal Distribution and Log-Normal Regression," *J. Am. Stat. Assoc.*, June 1971, 327-330 and in AZBIE.
A. Zellner, "Bayesian and Non-Bayesian Analysis of the Regression Model with Multivariate Student-t Errors," *J. Am. Stat. Assoc.*, June 1976, 400-405 and in AZBIE.
T. Amemiya, "Qualitative Response Models," *Annals of Economic and Social Measurement*, 4/3, 1975, 363-372.
A. Zellner and P.E. Rossi, "Bayesian Analysis of Dichotomous Quantal Response Models," *J. of Econometrics*, 25, 1984, 365-393+.
WHG: Ch.21.
A. Pagan, "Econometric Issues in the Analysis of Regressions with Generalized Regressors," *Int. Econ. Review*, 25, Feb. 1984, 221-247+.
A.M. Pole and A.F.M. Smith, "Bayesian Analysis of Some Threshold Switching Models," *J. of Econometrics*, 29, 1985, 97-119.
A. Zellner, "Estimation of Functions of Populations Means and Regression Coefficients...: A Minimum Expected Loss (MELO) Approach," *J. Econometrics* Jan., 1978+

C. Selected Applications

E.R. Berndt, *The Practice of Econometrics*, Addison-Wesley, 1991: Ch.2 Capital Asset Pricing Model; Ch.3 Cost, Learning Curves and Scale Economics; Ch.4 Measurement of Quality Change; Ch.5 Determination of Wages and Measuring Wage Discrimination.

M.C. Lovell, "Seasonal Adjustment of Economic Time Series," in AZR, 50-69.

A. Zellner, "Model-Based Approaches to Seasonal Analysis and Adjustment," Sept. 1979.

Z. Griliches, "Hedonic Price Indexes for Automobiles: An Econometric Analysis of Quality Change," in AZR, 103-130.

M. Nerlove, "Returns to Scale in Electricity Supply," in AZR, 409-439.

VI. MRM: Analysis of Departures from Specifying Assumptions

Readings:

AZN: "Notes on the MRM," Sect.A.5+, and A. Zellner, "Bayesian Analysis of Regression Error Terms," *J. Am. Stat. Assoc.*, March 1975, 138-144.

JGHLL: Chs.8, 11 and 22.

P. Schmidt, *Econometrics*, 35-64.

J. Johnston, *Econometric Models* (3rd ed.), 1984, Chs.8 and 9.

J.M. Dufour, "Rank Tests for Parameter Instability," Jan. 1978 and "Predictive Tests for Structural Change and the St. Louis Equation," ms., 1982.

D.M. Wu, "Alternative Tests of Independence Between Stochastic Regressors and Disturbances," *Econometrica*, 41, July 1973, 733-750.

R. Reynolds, "Posterior Odds for the Hypothesis of Independence Between Stochastic Regressors and Disturbances," *Int. Econ. Rev.*, June 1982, 479-490.

T.B. Fomby and D.K. Guilkey, "On Choosing the Optimal Level of Significance for the Durbin-Watson Test and the Bayesian Alternative," *J. of Econometrics*, 1978, 203-213+.

A. Zellner and B.R. Moulton, "Bayesian Regression Diagnostics with Applications to International Consumption and Income Data," *J. of Econometrics*, 29, 1985, 187-211+.

H.K. Ryu, "Maximum Entropy Estimation of Density and Regression Functions," wp#91-98, Working Paper Series in Economics and Econometrics, GSB, U. of Chicago, 1991 and in *J. of Econometrics*, April, 1993, 397-440.

VII. Nonlinear Models

Reading:

JGHLL: Ch.6.

WHG: Ch.11.

T. Amemiya, "Nonlinear Regression Models," in Z. Griliches and M.D. Intriligator (eds.), *Handbook of Econometrics*, Vol. I, North-Holland, 1983, Ch.6.

AZ: Ch.6.

A.R. Gallant, *Nonlinear Statistical Models*, Wiley, 1987.

A. Zellner and H. Ryu, "Production, Cost and Returns to Scale Functions: Parametric and Semi-Parametric Approaches," ms., U. of Chicago, GSB, May, 1994.

VIII.   Model Selection Procedures

Reading:
JGHLL: Ch.21.
B.R. Moulton, "A Bayesian Approach to Regression Selection and Estimation...," *J. of Econometrics*, July-Aug. 1991, 169-193.

IX.   Selected Time Series Problems

Readings:
JGHLL: Chs.9 and 10.
WHG: Ch.18.
AZ: Ch.7, Sects.7.1, 7.3, 7.4, and 7.5.
D.J. Aigner, "A Compendium on Estimation of the Autoregressive-Moving Average Model from Time Series Data," *Int. Econ. Rev.*, Oct. 1971, 348-371.
D.F. Nicholls et al., "The Estimation and Use of Models with Moving Average Disturbance Terms: A Survey," *Int. Econ. Rev.*, Feb. 1975, 113-134.
C.W.J. Granger and P. Newbold, *Forecasting Economic Time Series*, Academic Press, 2nd ed., 1986.
A. Garcia-Ferrer et al., "Macroeconomic Forecasting Using Pooled International Data," *J. of Bus. and Econ. Statistics*, 5, 1987, 53-67.
A. Zellner and C. Hong, "Forecasting International Growth Rates Using Bayesian Shrinkage and Other Procedures," *J. of Econometrics*, 40, 1989, 183-202+.

X.   Multivariate Regression Models and Seemingly Unrelated Regression Models

Readings:
JGHLL: Ch.12.
WHG: Ch.17.
T.E. Dielman, "Pooled Cross-Sectional and Time Series Data: A Survey of Current Statistical Methodology," *American Statistician*, May 1983, 111-122.
H. Theil, *Principles of Econometrics*, 1971, Ch.7, 294-317 and 322-325.
P. Schmidt, Econometrics, 1976, 72-85.
V.K. Srivastava and D.E.A. Giles, *Seemingly Unrelated Regression Equations Models*, Dekker, 1987.

V.K. Srivastava and T.D. Dwivedi, "Estimation of Seemingly Unrelated Regression Equations: A Brief Survey," *J. of Econometrics*, Apr. 1979, 15-32.

A.K. Srivastava and D.S. Tracy, "Computation of Standard Errors in Seemingly Unrelated Regression Equation Models," *Communications in Statistics*, A15 (1986), 3583ff.

H.D. Vinod and A. Ullah, *Recent Advances in Regression Methods*, Dekker, 1981, Ch.10.

A. Zellner, "An Error-Components Procedure (ECP) for Introducing Prior Information About Covariance Matrices and Analysis of Multivariate Regression Models," *Int. Econ. Rev.*, Oct. 1979, 679-692+.

F. Palm and A. Zellner, "Large Sample Estimation Procedures for Dynamic Equation Systems," *J. of Econometrics*, Apr. 1980, 251-283 and "Rejoinder," *J. of Econometrics*, Sept. 1981, 131-138.

D.L. Hoffman, "Two-Step Generalized Least Squares Estimators in Multi-Equation Generated Regression Models," *Rev. of Economics and Statistics*, LXIX, May 1987, 336-351+.

R.C. Blattberg and E.I. Geroge, "Shrinkage Estimation of Price and Promotional Elasticities: Seemingly Unrelated Equations," *J. Am. Stat. Assoc.*, June, 1991, 304-315+.

P.E. Rossi, "Testing Hypotheses in Multivariate Regression: Bayes vs. Non-Bayes Procedures", ms., (1980)+.

XI.   Combined Cross-Section and Time Series Models

Readings:
JGHLL: Ch.13.
WHG: Ch.16.

H.Y. Izan, "To Pool or Not to Pool? A Reexamination of Tobin's Food Demand Problem," *J. of Econometrics*, 13 (1980), 391-402+.

A.C. Harvey, "The Estimation of Time-Varying Parameters from Panel Data," in *Proceedings of the International Conference on the Econometrics of Panel Data*, INSEE, Paris, 1977, 203-226.

C. Hsiao, *Analysis of Panel Data*, Cambridge U. Press, 1986.

A. Zellner and C. Hong, "Forecasting International Growth Rates Using Bayesian Shrinkage and Other Procedures," *J. of Econometrics*, 40, 1989, 183-202+.

R.C. Blattberg and E.I. George, "Shrinkage Estimation of Price and Promotional Elasticities: Seemingly Unrelated Equations," *J. Am. Stat. Assoc.*, 1991, 304-315.+

XII.   Introduction to the Simultaneous Equation Model (SEM)

Readings:
WHG: Ch.19.
H. Theil, *Principles of Econometrics*, Ch.9.
E. Berndt, Ch.8
M.D. Intriligator, "Economic and Econometric Models," in Z. Griliches and M.D. Intriligator (eds.), *Handbook of Econometrics*, Vol. I, North-Holland, 1983, Ch.3.
M. Morishima and M. Saito, "A Dynamic Analysis of the American Economy, 1902-1952," in AZR, 680-718.
A. Zellner and F. Palm, "Time Series Analysis and Simultaneous Equation Models," *J. of Econometrics*, May 1974, 17-54.
A. Zellner, "Statistical Analysis of Econometric Models," invited paper with discussion, *J. Am. Stat. Assoc.*, Sept. 1979, 628-651, reprinted in AZBIE.

Business 429/Economics 416   Spring Quarter, 1994
Bayesian Inference in Econometrics   Mr. Zellner

Course Outline and Readings   G

Readings will include papers in the literature and selected sections of the following:

1. A. Zellner, *An Introduction to Bayesian Inference in Econometrics*, Wiley, 1971, reprinted by Krieger Publishing Co., 1987, denoted by AZ below.
2. G.E.P. Box and G.C. Tiao, *Bayesian Inference in Statistical Inference*, Addison-Wesley, 1973, denoted by BT below.
3. D.V. Lindley, *Introduction to Probability Theory from a Bayesian Viewpoint*, Part Two, Inference, Cambridge U. Press, 1965, denoted by DVL below.
4. H. Raiffa and R. Schlaifer, *Applied Statistical Decision Theory*, Harvard, 1961, denoted by RS below.
5. S.E. Fienberg and A. Zellner (eds.), *Studies in Bayesian Econometrics and Statistics in Honor of Leonard J. Savage*, North-Holland, 1975, denoted by FZ below.
6. E.E. Leamer, *Specification Searches*, Wiley, 1978.
7. A. Zellner (ed.), *Bayesian Analysis in Econometrics and Statistics: Essays in Honor of Harold Jeffreys*, North-Holland, 1980, denoted by ZJ below.
8. J.O. Berger, *Statistical Decision Theory*, Springer-Verlag, 2nd ed., 1985.
9. A. Zellner, *Basic Issues in Econometrics*, U. of Chicago Press, 1984, denoted by AZBIE below.
10. B429/E416, *Course Packet*.

The following bibliographies are useful: R.B. Miller, "A Selected Bayesian Statistics Bibliography," Tech. Report 214, Dept. of Statistics, U. of Wisconsin, Madison, 1969; bibliography in D.V. Lindley, *Bayesian Statistics, A Review*, SIAM, 1971, 75-83; L.J. Savage, "Reading Suggestions for the Foundations of Statistics," *American Statistician*, Oct. 1970, 23-27; bibliography in M.H. DeGroot, *Optimal Statistical Decisions*, McGraw-Hill, 1970, 447-471, and "Papers Associated with the NBER-NSF Seminar on Bayesian Inference in Econometrics," U. of Chicago, 1975. See Also reference lists in 1-10 above and entries in the annual issues of the ASA/IMS *Current Index to Statistics* under the key words *Bayes* and *Bayesian*.

The following papers describe computer programs that are useful in applied Bayesian analyses:

J. Abowd, B.R. Moulton and A. Zellner, "The Bayesian Regression Analysis Package: BRAP User's Manual, Version 2.0 of 12/03/85," H.G.B. Alexander Research Foundation, U. of Chicago, May 1987.

B.R. Moulton, "NUMINT: Simpson's Rule and Monte Carlo Integration," H.G.B. Alexander Research Foundation, U. of Chicago, 1983.

B.R. Moulton and A. Zellner, "MELO Structural Coefficient Estimation Using the CM Computer Package," H.G.B. Alexander Research Foundation, U. of Chicago, 1983.

S.J. Press, "Bayesian Computer Programs," published in ZJ, 1980 and in S.J. Press, *Bayesian Statistics*, Wiley, 1989.

C.J. Silva, "Installation Guide for PCBRAP, Version 2.1," H.G.B. Alexander Research Foundation, U. of Chicago, 1988.

E. de Alba and S. Rocha, "BRAP: Reference Guide to PC Version 1.0," ITAM, Mexico City, 1988.

I. Introduction: Basic Principles of Bayesian Analysis

    1.   AZ, Chs. 1,2 and "Optimal Information Processing and Bayes's Theorem," *American Statistician*, Nov. 1988.

    2.   BT, Ch. 1, pp. 1-25.

    3.   J.O. Berger, *Statistical Decision Theory*, 1985, 77-113 and 118-139.

    4.   A. Zellner, "Maximal Data Information Prior Distributions," in AZBIE.

    5.   A. Zellner, "Bayesian Analysis in Econometrics,"* *Journal of Econometrics*, Jan. 1988, 27-50.

    6.   A. Zellner, "Bayesian Methods and Entropy in Economics and Econometrics," in W.T. Grandy and L.H. Schick (eds.), *Maximum Entropy and Bayesian Methods*, Kluwer, 1991, 17-31.

II. Simple and Multiple Regression

    A.   Theory

        1.   AZ, Ch. 3.

        2.   DVL, Ch. 8, Sects. 8.1 and 8.3.

        3.   BT, Ch. 2, pp. 112-126.

    B.   Additional Results and Selected Applications

        1.   M. Baxter, "The Role of Expectations in Stabilization Policy,"* *J. of Monetary Economics*, 15, 1985, 343-362.

        2.   A. Zellner and B.M. Moulton, "Bayesian Regression Diagnostics with Applications to International Consumption and Income Data,"* *J. of Econometrics*, 29, 1985, 187-211.

        3.   A. Zellner and J.F. Richard, "Use of Prior Information in the Analysis and Estimation of Cobb-Douglas Production Function Models,"* *Int. Econ. Rev.*, 14, Feb. 1973, 107-119.

        4.   H. Varian, "A Bayesian Approach to Real Estate Assessment,"* in FZ, pp. 195-208.

        5.   D.E.A. Giles and A.C. Rayner, "The Mean Squared Errors of the Maximum Likelihood and Natural Conjugate Bayes Regression Estimators," *J. of Econometrics*, Oct./Dec., 1979.

        6.   A. Zellner, "On Assessing Informative Prior Distributions for Regression Coefficients," ms., 1973.

        7.   A. Zellner, "Bayesian and Non-Bayesian Analysis of the Regression Model with Multivariate Student-t Error Terms," *JASA*, June 1976, and

---

*Included in Course Packet.

"Bayesian and Non-Bayesian Analysis of the Log-Normal Distribution and Log-Normal Regression," *JASA*, June 1971 and in AZBIE.

8. A. Zellner and W. Vandaele, "Bayes-Stein Estimators for k-Means, Regression and Simultaneous Equation Models," in FZ, pp. 627-641.

9. E.E. Leamer, "Multicollinearity: A Bayesian Interpretation," *Rev. of Economics and Statistics*, Aug. 1973, 371-380.

10. E.S. Soofi, "Effects of Collinearity on Information About Regression Coefficients," *J. of Econometrics*, 43, 1990, 255-274.

11. N.J. Gonedes and H.V. Roberts, "Bayesian Assessment of the Unconditional Mean Square Error of Repeated Predictions from a Regression Equation," *J. of Econometrics*, Sept. 1974.

12. A. Zellner, "On Assessing Prior Distributions and Bayesian Regression Analysis with g-Prior Distributions," in P.K. Goel and A. Zellner (eds.), *Bayesian Inference and Decision Techniques: Essays in Honor of Bruno de Finetti*, North-Holland, 1986, 233-243.

III. Special Problems in Regression Analysis

1. AZ, Ch. 4 and Ch. 5, pp. 145-157.

2. A. Zellner, "Bayesian Analysis of Regression Error Terms," *JASA*, March 1975.

3. K. Chaloner and R. Brant, "A Bayesian Approach to Outlier Detection and Residual Analysis,"* *Biometrika*, 75, 1988, 651-659.

4. D.D. Boos and J.F. Monahan, "Bootstrap Methods Using Prior Information,"* *Biometrika*, 73, 1986, 77-83.

5. V.K. Chetty, "Pooling of Time Series and Cross Section Data," *Econometrica*, 36, 1968.

6. A. Zellner, "Notes on Bayesian Up-dating Procedures for a Random Parameter Model,"* ms., 1985.

7. J.H. Drèze, "Bayesian Regression Analysis Using Poly-t Densities," *J. of Econometrics*, Nov. 1977.

8. A. Zellner, "Estimation of Functions of Population Means and Regression Coefficients: A Minimum Expected Loss (MELO) Approach," *J. of Econometrics*, Oct. 1978.

9. A. Zellner and S.B. Park, "Minimum Expected Loss (MELO) Estimators for Functions of Parameters and Structural Coefficients of Econometric Models,"* *JASA*, Mar. 1979.

10. R. Reynolds, "Posterior Odds for the Hypothesis of Independence Between Stochastic Regressors and Disturbances,"* *Int. Econ. Rev.*, June 1982.

11. E.E. Leamer, *Specification Searches*, Wiley, 1978, Ch. 4.

12. A. Zellner and A. Siow, "Posterior Odds Ratios for Selected Regression Hypotheses," in J.M. Bernardo, M.H. DeGroot, D.V. Lindley, and A.F.M. Smith (eds.), *Bayesian Statistics*, Valencia, Spain: University Press, 1980, 585-603.

---

*Included in Course Packet.

13. A. Zellner, "Posterior Odds Ratios for Regression Hypotheses: General Considerations and Some Specific Results," in AZBIE.

14. A. Zellner and J.F. Richard, "Use of Prior Information in the Analysis and Estimation of Cobb-Douglas Production Function Models," *Int. Econ. Rev.*, 14, 1973.

15. A. Zellner and P.E. Rossi, "Bayesian Analysis of Dichotomous Quantal Response Models,"* *J. of Econometrics*, July 1984, 365-393.

IV. Analysis of Single-Equation Nonlinear Models

1. AZ, Ch. 6.

2. U. Sankar, "Elasticity of Substitution and Returns to Scale in Indian Manufacturing Industries,"* *Int. Econ. Rev.*, Oct. 1970, 399-411.

3. H. Tsurumi and Y. Tsurumi, "A Bayesian Estimation of Macro and Micro CES Production Functions," *J. of Econometrics*, Feb. 1976.

4. J. Bisignano, "Cagan's Real Money Demand Model with Alternative Error Structures: Bayesian Analysis for Four Countries," *Int. Econ. Rev.*, June 1975.

V. Bayesian Time Series Analysis and Asymptotics

A. General Theory

   1. AZ, Ch.7
   2. C.C. Heyde and I.M. Johnstone, "On the Asymptotic Posterior Normality for Stochastic Processes," *J. Roy. Stat. Soc. B*, 41, 1979, 184-189.
   3. C-F. Chen, "On Asymptotic Normality of Limiting Density Functions with Bayesian Implications," *J. Roy. Stat. Soc. B*, 47, 1985, 540-546.*

B. Distributed Lag Models

   1. R.J. Shiller, "A Distributed Lag Estimator Derived from Smoothness Priors," *Econometrica*, July 1973 and in FZ.
   2. A. Zellner and A.D. Williams, "Bayesian Analysis of the Federal Reserve-MIT-Penn Model's Almon Lag Consumption Function," *J. of Econometrics*, Oct. 1973, 267-299.
   3. A. Zellner and M.S. Geisel, "Analysis of Distributed Lag Models with Applications to Consumption Function Estimation," *Econometrica*, 38, 1970.

C. ARMA Models

   1. H. Thornber, "Finite Sample Monte Carlo Studies: An Autoregressive Illustration," *JASA*, Sept. 1967.

---

*Included in Course Packet.

2. P. Evans, "Time Series Analysis of the German Hyperinflation," *Int. Econ. Rev.*, Feb. 1978.
3. J.F. Monahan, "Fully Bayesian Analysis of ARMA Time Series Models," *J. of Econometrics*, 1983, 307-331.

D. ARCH Models

1. J. Geweke, "Exact Inference in Models with Autoregressive Conditional Heteroscedasticity," ms., 1986.
2. J. Geweke, Exact Predictive Densities for Linear Models with ARCH Disturbances, *J. of Econometrics*, 40, 1989, 63-86.

E. Time-Varying Parameter and State Space Models

1. M. West, P.J. Harrison and H.S. Migon, "Dynamic Generalized Linear Models and Bayesian Forecasting," *JASA*, March 1985, 73-83 (with discussion).
2. R. Highfield, "Forecasting with Bayesian State Space Models,"* ms., H.G.B. Alexander Research Foundation, U. of Chicago, 1984.
3. M. West and J. Harrison, *Bayesian Forecasting and Dynamic Models*, New York: Springer-Verlag, 1989.

F. Unit Roots

1. A. Zellner and C. Plosser, "Posterior Odds Ratios for Discriminating Random Walk Models from Stationary and Explosive Autoregressive Models," ms., 1976.
2. L.A. Manas Anton, *Empirical Regularities in Short-Run Exchange Rate Behavior*, doctoral dissertation, U.C. Dept. of Economics, 1986, Ch.2.
3. C.A. Sims, "Bayesian Skepticism on Unit Root Econometrics," *J. Economic Dynamics and Control*, 12, 1988, 463-474.
4. P.C.B. Phillips, "To Criticize the Critics: An Objective Bayesian Analysis of Stochastic Trends," ms., 1990, Yale U., published in *J. Applied Econometrics*, 1991, 333-364.

G. Forecasting

1. R. Litterman, "A Bayesian Procedure for Forecasting with Vector Autoregressions,"* ms., 1980.
2. R. Litterman, "Forecasting with Bayesian Vector Autoregressions--Five Years of Experience," *J. of Business and Economic Statistics*, Jan. 1986, 25-38.
3. P.J. Harrison and C.F. Stevens, "Bayesian Forecasting," *J. Roy. Stat. Soc.* B, 38, 1976, 205-247.

---

*Included in Course Packet.

4. A. Garcia-Ferrer, R.A. Highfield, F. Palm, and A. Zellner, "Macro-economic Forecasting Using Pooled International Data," *J. of Business and Economic Statistics*, 5, 1987, 53-67.

5. A. Zellner and C. Hong, "Forecasting International Growth Rates Using Bayesian Shrinkage and Other Procedures,"* *J. of Econometrics*, 40, 1989, 183-202.

6. A. Zellner, C. Hong and G.M. Gulati, "Turning Points in Economic Time Series, Loss Structures and Bayesian Forecasting," in S. Geisser, J. Hodges, S.J. Press, and A. Zellner (eds.), *Bayesian and Likelihood Methods in Statistics and Econometrics: Essays in Honor of George A. Barnard*, Amsterdam: North-Holland, 1990, 371-389.

7. A. Zellner, C. Hong and C. Min, "Forecasting Turning Points in International Growth Rates Using Bayesian Exponentially Weighted Autoregression, Time-Varying Parameter, and Pooling Techniques," *J. of Econometrics*, 49, 1991, 275-304.

8. C. Hong, "Forecasting Real Output Growth Rates and Cyclical Properties of Models: A Bayesian Approach," U. of Chicago doctoral dissertation, Dept. of Economics, 1989.

9. P.A. Thompson and R.B. Miller, "Sampling the Future: A Bayesian Approach to Forecasting from Univariate Time Series Models," *J. of Business and Economic Statistics*, Oct. 1986, 427-436.

10. R.B. Litterman, "Forecasting with Bayesian Vector Autoregressions -- Five Years of Experience," *J. of Business and Economic Statistics*, Jan. 1986, 25-38.

11. J.P. LeSage, "Forecasting Turning Points in Metropolitan Employment Growth Rates Using Bayesian Techniques," *J. of Regional Science*, 30, 1990, 533-548.

12. F.C. Palm and A. Zellner, "To Combine or Not to Combine? Issues of Combining Forecasts," *J. of Forecasting*, 1992, 687-700.*

13. C. Min, "Economic Analysis and Forecasting of International Growth Rates Using Bayesian Techniques," U. of Chicago doctoral dissertation, Dept. of Economics, 1992.

VI. Multivariate Regression Models

1. AZ, Ch. 8.

2. BT, Chs. 8,9.

3. Lindley, D.V. and A.F.M. Smith, "Bayes Estimate for the Linear Model," *J. Roy. Stat. Soc. B*, 34, 1972, 1-41.

4. P.J. Brown, "Aspects of Multivariate Regression," in J. Bernardo et al. (eds.), *Bayesian Statistics*, Valencia, Spain: University Press, 1980, 249-265.

5. R.M. Hogarth, "Monozygotic Twins Reared Apart: A Bayesian Analysis," in FZ.

---

*Included in Course Packet.

6. G.C. Tiao, W.Y. Tan and Y.C. Chang, "Some Aspects of Bivariate Regression Subject to Linear Restraints," *J. of Econometrics*, Jan. 1977.

7. P.E. Rossi, "Testing Hypotheses in Multivariate Regression: Bayes vs. Non-Bayes Procedures," ms., 1980.

8. R. Kass, "Inferences About Principal Components and Related Quantities Using a Numerical Delta Method and Posteriors Calculated by Simulation," Tech. Report 346, Dept. of Statistics, Carnegie-Mellon U., Sept., 1985.

9. T. Leonard and S.J. Hsu, "Bayesian Inference for a Covariance Matrix," *Biometrika*, 1992, 1669-1696.*

VII. Simultaneous Equation Econometric Models

A. General Theory

1. AZ, Ch. 9.

2. T.J. Rothenberg, "Bayesian Analysis of Simultaneous Equations Models," in FZ.

3. J. Drèze and J.F. Richard, "Bayesian Analysis of Simultaneous Equation Systems," in Z. Griliches and M.D. Intriligator (eds.), *Handbook of Econometrics*, Vol. 1, 1983, Ch. 9.

4. L. Bauwens, *Bayesian Full Information Analysis of Simultaneous Equation Models Using Integration by Monte Carlo*, Springer-Verlag, 1984.

5. J.H. Drèze, "Econometrics and Decision Theory" and "Bayesian Theory of Identification in Simultaneous Equations Models," in FZ.

6. J.B. Kadane, "The Role of Identification in Bayesian Theory," in FZ.

7. A. Zellner, "Further Results on Bayesian Minimum Expected Loss (MELO) Estimates and Posterior Distributions for Structural Coefficients," in D. Slottje (ed.), *Innovations in Quantitative Economics: Essays in Honor of Robert L. Basmann*, JAI Press, 1986, 171-182.

B. Additional Results and Selected Applications

1. V.K. Chetty, "Bayesian Analysis of Haavelmo's Models," *Econometrica*, July-Oct. 1968, and in FZ.

2. A. Zellner, J. Kmenta and J. Drèze, "Specification and Estimation of Cobb-Douglas Production Models," *Econometrica*, Oct. 1966.

3. S. Grossman, "Rational Expectations and the Econometric Modeling of Markets Subject to Uncertainty: A Bayesian Approach," *J. of Econometrics*, Aug. 1975.

4. T. Kloek and H.K. van Dijk, "Bayesian Estimates of Equation System Parameters: An Application of Integration by Monte Carlo," *Econometrica*, Jan. 1978.

---

*Included in Course Packet.

5. J.S. Mehta and P.A.V.B. Swamy, "The Existence of Moments of Some Simple Bayes Estimators in a Simultaneous Equation Model," *J. of Econometrics*, Feb. 1978.

6. A. Zellner, "Statistical Analysis of Econometric Models," *JASA*, Sept. 1979.

7. A. Zellner, "Estimation of Functions of Population Means and Regression Coefficients Including Structural Coefficients: A Minimum Expected Loss (MELO) Approach," *J. of Econometrics*, Oct. 1978.

8. A. Zellner and S.B. Park, "Minimum Expected Loss (MELO) Estimators for Functions of Parameters and Structural Coefficients of Econometric Models,"* *JASA*, Mar. 1979.

9. A. Zellner, L. Bauwens and H.K. van Dijk, "Bayesian Specification Analysis and Estimation of Simultaneous Equation Models Using Monte Carlo Methods," *J. of Econometrics*, 38, 1988, 39-72.

VIII. Comparing and Testing Hypotheses and Models

1. AZ, Ch. 10.

2. A. Zellner, "Statistical Analysis of Hypotheses in Economics and Econometrics," *ASA B&E Proc.*, 1980.

3. A. Zellner and A. Siow, "Posterior Odds Ratios for Selected Regression Hypotheses," in J.M. Bernardo, et al. (eds.), *Bayesian Statistics*, Valencia, Spain: University Press, 1980.

4. M.H. DeGroot, "Doing What Comes Naturally: Interpreting a Tail Area as a Posterior Probability or as a Likelihood Ratio," *JASA*, Dec. 1973.

5. K.M. Gaver and M.S. Geisel, "Discriminating Among Alternative Models: Bayesian and Non-Bayesian Methods," in P. Zarembka (ed.), *Frontiers in Econometrics*, Academic Press, 1973.

6. M.S. Geisel, "Bayesian Comparisons of Simple Macroeconomic Models," *J. Money, Credit and Banking*, Aug. 1973, and in FZ.

7. A.R. Dyer, "Hypothesis Testing Procedures for Separate Families of Hypotheses,"* *JASA*, March 1974.

8. A. Zellner, "Jeffreys-Bayes Posterior Odds Ratio and the Akaike Information Criterion for Discriminating Between Models," *Economics Letters*, 1978.

9. J.M. Dickey, "Is the Tail Area Useful as an Approximate Bayes Factor?" *JASA*, March 1977.

10. P.E. Rossi, "Testing Hypotheses in Multivariate Regression: Bayes vs. Non-Bayes Procedures,"* ms., H.G.B. Alexander Research Foundation, U. of Chicago, 1980.

11. A.F.M. Smith and D.J. Spiegelhalter, "Bayes Factors and Choice Criteria for Linear Models," *J. Roy. Stat. Soc.*, B, 42, 1980, 213-220.

12. J.O. Berger and M. Delampady, "Testing Precise Hypotheses" (with discussion), *Statistical Science*, 1987, 317-352.

---

*Included in Course Packet.

13. R. McCulloch and P.E. Rossi, "Posterior, Predictive and Utility-based Approaches to Testing the Arbitrage Pricing Theory," *J. of Financial Economics*, 1990, 7-38.*

14. A. Zellner and C. Min, "Bayesian Analysis, Model Selection and Prediction," ms., 1992,, 20pp.*

15. E.I. George and R. McCulloch, "Variable Selection via Gibbs Sampling," ms, 1992, 28pp.*

16. D.J. Poirier (ed.), "Bayesian Empirical Studies in Economics and Finance," *J. of Econometrics*, July/Aug. 1991, 304pp.

IX.   Analysis of Selected Decision and Control Problems

1. AZ, Ch. 11.

2. E.C. Prescott, "The Multi-Period Control Problem Under Uncertainty," *Econometrica*, Nov. 1972.

3. H.W. Bowman and A.M. Laporte, "Stochastic Optimization in Recursive Equation Systems with Random Parameters," *Ann. of Econ. and Social Measurement*, Oct. 1972 and in FZ.

4. S. Grossman, "Rational Expectations and the Econometric Modeling of Markets Subject to Uncertainty: A Bayesian Approach," *J. of Econometrics*, Aug. 1975.

5. S. Brown, "Optimal Portfolio Choice Under Uncertainty," doctoral dissertation, Grad. Sch. of Bus., U. of Chicago, 1976.

6. P. Jorion, "International Portfolio Diversification with Estimation Risk,"* *J. of Business*, 58, 1985.

7. E.C. Prescott and R.M. Townsend, "Equilibrium Under Uncertainty: Multi-Agent Statistical Decision Theory," in A. Zellner (ed.), *Bayesian Analysis in Econometrics and Statistics: Essays in Honor of Harold Jeffreys*, North-Holland, 1980.

8. M. Wong, et al., "A Bayesian Data Analysis System for the Evaluation of Social Programs," *JASA*, Dec. 1977.

9. F.B. Stafford, "A Decision Theoretic Approach to the Evaluation of Manpower Programs," ms., Aug. 1975.

X.   Selected References on Bayesian Computing

1. AZ, App. C

2. Kloek, T. and H.K. van Dijk, "Bayesian Estimates of Equation System Parameters: An Application of Integration by Monte Carlo," *Econometrica*, 46, 1978, 1-20.

3. Zellner, A. and P. Rossi, "Bayesian Analysis of Quantal Response Models, *J. of Econometrics*, 25, 1984, 365-394.

4. Geweke, J., "Exact Inference in the Inequality Constrained Normal Linear Regression Model," *J. of Applied Econometrics*, 1, 1986, 127-141.

---

*Included in Course Packet.

5. Tanner, M.A., *Tools for Statistical Inference: Observed Data and Data Augmentation Methods*, Springer-Verlag, 1991.

6. West, M. and J. Harrison, *Bayesian Forecasting and Dynamic Models*, New York: Springer-Verlag, 1989.

7. J. Geweke, "Antithetic Acceleration of Monte Carlo in Bayesian Integration," *J. of Econometrics*, 38, 1988, 73-89.

8. J. Geweke, "Bayesian Inference in Econometric Models Using Monte Carlo Integration," *Econometrica*, 57, 1989, 1317-1334.

9. A.E. Gelfand, S.E. Hills, A. Racine-Poon and A.F.M. Smith, "Illustration of Bayesian Inference in Normal Data Models Using Gibbs Sampling," *J. Am. Stat. Assoc.*, 85, 1990, 972-985.*

10. L. Tierney and J.B. Kadane, "Accurate Approximations for Posterior Moments and Marginal Densities," *JASA*, 81, 1986, 82-86.

11. V.E. Johnson, "Convergence Properties of Quantile Integration for Vector-Valued Parameters," Inst. of Statistics and Decision Sciences, Duke U., 1990.

12. A. Zellner and C. Min, "Gibbs Sampler Convergence Criteria (GSC^2)," ms, July 1992.

XI. Comparisons of Bayesian and Non-Bayesian Approaches

1. A. Zellner, "The Bayesian Approach and Alternatives in Econometrics," in FZ.

2. T.J. Rothenberg, "The Bayesian Approach and Alternatives, II," in FZ.

3. G.M. Kaufman, J.W. Pratt, and A. Zellner, "Comments," in FZ.

4. J.O. Berger and R.L. Wolpert, *The Likelihood Principle*, IMS Lecture Notes-Monograph Series, Vol. 6, Institute of Mathematical Statistics, Hayward, CA, 1984.

5. I.J. Good, *Good Thinking: The Foundations of Probability and Its Applications*, U. of Minnesota Press, 1983 (reviewed in *JASA*, March 1985, 232-233 by J.O. Berger).

6. H. Jeffreys, *Theory of Probability* (3rd ed. 1967), Chs. VII-VIII.

7. B. Efron, "Why Isn't Everyone a Bayesian?" *The American Statistician*, Feb. 1986 with discussion by H. Chernoff, D.V. Lindley, C.N. Morris, S.J. Press, and A.F.M. Smith, and the author's reply. See also discussion in *The American Statistician*, Nov. 1986, 330-331.

8. A. Zellner, "A Bayesian Era," in J.M. Bernardo et al. (eds.), *Bayesian Statistics 3*, London: Oxford U. Press, 1988. 509-516.

---

*Included in Course Packet.

The textbook is G. Judge, et. al, Introduction to the Theory and Practice of Econometrics, second edition (Wiley, 1988). "Handouts" will be distributed in class. Other readings are on reserve in Mann Library. P. Kennedy, A Guide to Econometrics, third edition (MIT Press, 1992), is a useful supplement.

Introduction (0.75 week)[1]

Nature of Econometrics and Economic Data
Econometric Models

Text, Chapter 1 and Section 14.7. [Kennedy = K, Chapter 1]

Notes About Data (handout)

Fox, Econometric Analysis for Public Policy, pp. 33-43.

Bessler and Covey, "On the Search for Econometric Structure ...," Amer. J. Agr. Econ., Oct. 1993, pp. 41-47.

Multiple Linear Regression Analysis (1.75 weeks)

Classical Linear Regression Model
Statistical Criteria for Evaluating Estimators
Ordinary Least Squares Estimator
Properties of OLS Estimator
Coefficients of Determination
Empirical Example

Text, Chapter 5; Section 6.1; and if needed, review Sections 2.3, 2.4, 2.5, 3.1, 3.2, 3.3 and Appendix A. [K, Chapters 2 and 3]

Notes on the Least Squares Estimator and OLS Estimator When Data are in Deviations from Means (handout)

Analysis of Covariance; Hypothesis Tests (1.25 weeks)

Fixed Effects Analysis of Covariance Model
Hypothesis Test for an Individual Parameter (t distribution)
Hypothesis Tests for Sets of Parameters (F distribution)

---

[1] One week equals four fifty-minute lectures.

Text, Sections 10.1, 10.2, 10.3, 3.5.1, 3.5.2, 3.5.3, 6.4. [K, Chapter 14, Sections 4-1, 4-2, and 4-3]

Developing the F Statistic for Hypothesis Tests (handout)

Collinearity and Specification Error (1 week)

On Defining Multicollinearity
Consequences, Diagnosis, and Solutions
Specification Error
OLS, RLS, and Pretest Estimators Compared
Selecting Among Alternative Specifications

Text, Chapter 21, Sections 20.4, 20.3.1, and 20.3.1a. [K, Chapters 5, 6, 11, 12]

Wallace, "Pretest Estimation in Regression: A Survey," American Journal of Agricultural Economics, Aug. 1977, pp. 431-443.

McGuirk, et al. "Misspecification Testing: A Comprehensive Approach," American Journal of Agricultural Economics, Nov. 1993, pp. 1044-1055.

Comments on Model Selection (handout)

Nonspherical Disturbances (1.75 weeks)

Assumptions about Variance-Covariance Structure
Consequences of Autocorrelated Errors
Tests for Autocorrelation
Generalized Least Squares (GLS)
Additional Topics: Alternative Models, Heteroscedasticity

Text, Chapters 8 (Prediction, Section 8.7, discussed separately) and 9. [K, Chapters 7, 8]

Notes on the Variance of the OLS Estimator and Model Specification and Autocorrelated Residuals (handouts)

Mid-Term Exam, Thursday, March 9, 2:30-4 p.m.

Stochastic Regressors (1.75 weeks)

Introduction; Strictly Exogenous Regressors
Asymptotic Distributions and Alternative Assumptions
Distributed Lag Models: Specification and Estimation

Text, Sections 3.3.1c (review), 3.3.3 (review), 6.6, Chapter 13 (except Section 13.3.1), Sections 16.2.3, 16.2.4, 16.3, and Chapter 17 (except 17.4.2b). [K, Chapter 9]

Stock & Watson, "Variable Trends in Economic Time Series," Journal of Economic Perspectives, Summer 1988, pp. 147-174, especially section starting on page 163.

On Showing that an Estimator is Consistent; Note About Unit Roots and Cointegration; Geometric Form Model Notations; Alternative Dynamic Models (handouts)

Systems of Equations (1.5 weeks)

Notation and Alternative Models
Seemingly Unrelated Regression Model, Estimators
Recursive Model
Simultaneous Equations Model

Direct Products of Matrices (handout, to be reviewed if needed)

Text, Chapter 11, and Sections 14.1, 14.2, and 14.7. [K, Section 10.1]

Seemingly Unrelated Regression (handout)

Johnson, Econometric Methods, Third Edition, pp. 467-469 (recursive model).

Examples:

Harlow, "A Recursive Model of the Hog Industry," Agr. Econ. Res., Jan. 1962.

Houck and Mann, An Analysis of ... Demand for U.S. Soybeans ..., Minnesota Technical Bulletin 256, pp. 3-17.

Kahl and Tomek, "Forward-Pricing Models for Futures Markets ...," Food Res. Inst. Studies, 1986, No. 1., pp. 71-85.

Identification and Indirect Least Squares (0.5 week)

Identification in Linear Simultaneous Systems
Indirect Least Squares and Just-Identified Equations
ILS and Over- and Under- Identified Equations

Text, Sections 14.4, 14.5, and 14.6. [K, Section 10.2]

Simultaneous Equation Estimators (2.5 weeks)

Concept of IV Estimator; Its Properties
Selecting Instrumental Variables; ILS and IV
Errors in Variables and Distributed Lag Applications
TSLS Estimator: As GIVE, GLS, and k-Class Estimators
3SLS Estimator
Structural Coefficients, Properties
Problems of Simultaneous Equations Estimators
Tests of Hypotheses

Text, Sections 13.3 and 17.4.2b and Chapter 15 (Section 15.5 covered elsewhere). [K, Sections 10.3, 10.4]

TSLS as GIVE and Klein's Model I (handouts)

Kiviet, "Model Selection Test Procedures ...," Journal of Econometrics, June 1985, pp. 327-362. [Godfrey, Misspecification Tests in Econometrics, Chapter 5 is a good summary of literature.]

Forecasting; Multipliers (as time permits)

Framework for Linear Regression Model
Statistical Properties of Forecasts (OLS Estimator)
Errors in Forecasts and Realistic Confidence Intervals
Relaxing Assumptions of Regression Model
Evaluating Forecasting Ability for Single Endogenous Variable
Alternative Forecast Sources and Comparisons
Forecasting from Simultaneous System
Final Form of Model

Text, Sections 5.9, 8.7, 9.5.5, and 15.5 [K, Chapter 17]

Leuthold, "On the Use of Theil's Inequality Coefficients," American Journal of Agricultural Economics, May 1975, pp. 344-346.

Granger and Newbold, Forecasting Economic Time Series, 2d Edition, Sections 9-1, 9-2, 9-3.

Tomek and Robinson, Agricultural Product Prices, 3d edition, pp. 342-350.

Convenient Computational Approach to Forecasting (handout)

Fomby, et. al. Advanced Econometric Methods, Chapter 23 and 24 (Prediction and Dynamic Multipliers).

Final Examination, Thursday, May 18, 3:00-5:30 p.m.

Ag. Econ. 710
Spring Term 1995

PREREQUISITES, EXAMINATIONS, AND HOMEWORK

1. <u>Prerequisites:</u> Statistics 417 and 601 or their equivalents are the minimum statistical and mathematical foundations needed for course 710. The topics covered in Chapter 2 and Appendix A of the text are assumed to be known.

2. <u>Examinations:</u> A mid-term (25% weight toward course grade) and a comprehensive final examination (40% weight) will be given. Both are closed book.

3. <u>Homework:</u> A set of seven exercises provide experience and give background for the term report (below). The exercises will be graded, mainly to provide feedback, but the best five of those six exercises numbered 2 to 7, will receive a 10% weight in the course grade. Exercise one will be graded, but not counted toward the course grade. Homeworks 2 to 7 will all use a fixed data file based on U.S. meat consumption and prices. Students are free to <u>discuss</u> the homework with each other, <u>but the computations and written answers must be your independent work</u>. To be graded for credit, each exercise must be turned in by classtime on the dates announced when the exercises are distributed.

4. <u>Term Report:</u>

   a. Each student is to specify, estimate and report on a price or demand relationship for pork in the context of a specific research problem. I suggest that you select a specific objective such as comparing alternative models of the same phenomenon, determining whether a "structural change" has occurred in the demand for pork, etc. Braschler is one simple starting point (see references, over).

   b. The report should not exceed 12 double-spaced pages and should be written as if it were being submitted to a professional journal. It must be an independent piece of work.

   c. Please confine your analysis to the data files used in the homework exercises. However, variables may be transformed and trend and dummy variables can be created. A limited number of post-sample observations will be available to evaluate forecasts and/or structural stability. Statistical models and estimation methods should be limited to those covered in course 710.

   d. The report's grade (25% weight in course grade) will be based on correctness and interpretation of the econometrics relative to the stated objective and on the logic and clarity of presentation. The grade, however, will not depend on the seeming perfection of the final statistical results, provided that obvious imperfections are pointed out in your report. If your "final" model seems to have problems, conclude with a discussion of possible further work.

   e. <u>The written report is to be turned in by 9 a.m., Tuesday, May 9</u>. I must insist on this deadline, because I want to have the time to grade the papers personally. Earlier submissions would be appreciated.

234

Cornell University

**COURSE OUTLINE
ARME 711
ECONOMETRICS II
FALL 1994**

G

Instructor:	Tim Mount, Room 110 Warren Hall (255-4512)
Lectures:	Tuesday and Thursday 10:10 - 12:05 110 Bradfield Hall (Office hours by appointment)
T.A.	Cécile Ducrot, Room 304 Warren Hall (255-8107) (Office hours to be arranged)
Prerequisites:	Matrix Algebra Statistical Methods Agricultural Economics 710
Credit:	4 hours
Text:	G.G. Judge, W. E. Griffiths, R. C. Hill, H. Lutkepohl, and T-C Lee, <u>Introduction to the Theory and Practice of Econometrics</u>, Wiley, New York, 2nd Ed., 1987.

1. General Linear Model

a) Estimation
Ordinary least squares (OLS)
Generalized least squares (GLS)
White's Covariance Estimator
b) Testing hypotheses
Single linear hypothesis
Multiple linear hypotheses
Simultaneous confidence intervals
c) Transformations
Converting GLS to OLS
Linear transformations of regressors
Orthonormal regression
Principal components regression
d) Maximum likelihood estimation and nonlinear tests
Information matrix
Asymptotic properties of ML estimators
Likelihood ratio test
Wald test
Lagrange multiplier test
Hausman test

2. **Using Prior Information**

    a)   Statistical decision theory
                Pretest estimation
                Mixed estimation
                Bayesian methods
                Stein procedures
                Empirical Bayesian methods
    b)   Collinearity diagnostics
                Condition number
                Variance decomposition
                Effects of prior information
    c)   Single observation diagnostics
                Outliers and influence
                Alternative measures
                Effects of prior information

3. **Models with Non-Homoscedastic Residuals**

    a)   Variance components models
                Pooled cross-section and time-series data
                Stochastic coefficients
                General linear model
    b)   Heteroskedasticity
                Weighted regression
                Breusch-Pagan test
                White's test
                Modeling variances
                Uncertainty in policy models

4. **Limited Dependent Variables**

    a)   Discrete choice
                Linear probability model
                Logit and probit transformations
                Maximum likelihood estimation
                Tobit models and truncated samples
                Generalized tobit
    b)   Simultaneous systems
                Self selection
                Switching regressions
    c)   Share models
                Linear share model
                Logit share model
                Dirichlet model
    d)   Global properties of demand systems
                Translog
                Almost ideal demand system
                Generalized logit
                Semi-nonparametric estimation

The relevant sections of the text book are referred to by letter and section number.
Supplemental readings are identified with asterisks.

J: G. G. Judge, R. C. Hill, W. E. Griffiths, H. Lutkepohl, and T-C Lee,
    Introduction to The Theory and Practice of Econometrics, Wiley, New York,
    2nd Ed., 1987.

1. General Linear Model

a) Estimation
        J: 2.4, 5.4-11, 8.1-4, 8.6, 13.1, Appendix A
    *Consistent covariance estimator
        H. White, "A Heteroskedasticity - Consistent Covariance Matrix
        Estimator and a Direct Test for Heteroskedasticity", Econometrica,
        48, 1980, pp. 817-838.

b) Testing hypotheses
        J: 2.5, 6.2-5, 8.5
    * Simultaneous confidence intervals
        N.E. Savin, "The Bonferroni and the Scheffe Multiple Comparison
        Procedures", Review of Economic Studies (RES), 1980, pp. 255-273.

c) Transformations
        J: 8.1.2, Appendix A
    * Matrix computations
        Chapter 2.1-4 in G.G. Judge, et al., The Theory and Practice of
        Econometrics, 2nd Ed., 1984, (Big Judge).
        G. H. Golub and C. F. VanLoan, Matrix Computations, Johns Hopkins,
        Baltimore, MD, 1983.

d) Maximum likelihood estimation and nonlinear tests
        J: 2.5, 3.2, 3.5, 6.1-5, 12.3, 20.4.4
    * Maximum likelihood
        Chapter 3 of A. C. Harvey The Econometric Analysis of Time Series, 2nd
        Ed., MIT Press, 1989.
    * Testing hypotheses
        R. F. Engle, "Wald, Likelihood Ratio and Lagrange Multiplier Tests in
        Econometrics", in Handbook of Econometrics, ed. by Z. Griliches and
        M. D. Intriligator, North Holland, 1984 (Handbook).
        J. A. Hausman, "Specification Tests in Econometrics", Econometrica, 46,
        1978, pp. 1251-1272.

2. **Using Prior Information**

a) Statistical decision theory
   J: 20.1-3, 7.1-5
   * Pre-test estimators
       Chapter 3.3 of Big Judge.
       G. G. Judge and M. E. Bock, <u>The Statistical Implications of</u>
       <u>Pre-Test and Stein-Rule Estimators in Econometrics</u>, North-Holland,
       1978.
   * Bayesian approaches to model selection
       Chapter 4.4 of Big Judge.
       E. Leamer, "Model Choice and Specification Analysis", Vol. 1
       Handbook, Chapter 5, 1983.

b) Collinearity
   J: 21.1-5
   * Stein estimators
       Chapter 3.4 of Big Judge.
       Chapter 10 of G. Casella and R. L. Berger, <u>Statistical Inference</u>,
       Wadsworth & Brooks/Cole, Pacific Grove, CA, 1990.
       R.C. Hill and R. F. Ziemer, "The Risk of General Stein-like Estimators in
       the Presence of Multicollinearity", <u>Journal of Econometrics</u>, 1984,
       pp. 205-216.
   * Collinearity diagnostics
       Chapters 3.1-4 and 4.1 of D. A. Belsley, E. Kuh and R. E. Welsch,
       <u>Regression Diagnostics: Identifying Influential Data and Sources of</u>
       <u>Collinearity</u>, Wiley, New York, 1980 (BKW).

c) Single observation diagnostics
   * Alternative measures
       Chapters 2, 4.1 of BKW.
       Chapter 4 of S. Chatterjee and A. S. Hadi, <u>Sensitivity Analysis in Linear</u>
       <u>Regression</u>, Wiley, NY, 1988.
       P. F. Velleman and D. C. Hoaglin, "Data Analysis", Chapter 2 in
       <u>Perspectives on Contemporary Statistics,</u> edited by Hoaglin and Moore,
       Mathematical Association of America, Washington, DC, 1992.

3. **Models with Correlated Residuals**

a) Variance components models
   J: 11.4-7, 10.5
   * Pooling data
       G. S. Maddala, "The Use of Variance Components in Pooling Cross
       Section and Time Series Data", <u>Econometrica</u>, 39, 1971, pp. 341-358.
   * Stochastic coefficients
       D. A. Harville, "Maximum Likelihood Approaches to Variance Compared
       Estimation and to Related Problems", <u>JASA</u>, 72, 1977, pp. 320-338.
       A. P. Dempster, N. M. Laird, and D. B. Rubin, "Maximum Likelihood
       for Incomplete Data via the EM Algorithm", <u>Journal of The Royal</u>
       <u>Statistical Society B</u> (JRSS,B), 72, 1977, pp. 320-338.
       G. Chamberlain, "Panel Data", Vol. 2 of Handbook, Chapter 22, 1984.

b) Heteroskedasticity
J: 9.3-4
* Weighted regression
Chapters 1, 2 and 6 of R. J. Carroll and D. Ruppert <u>Transformation and Weighting in Regression</u>, Chapman and Hall, New York, 1988.
*Uncertainty in policy models
Chapters 3, 8 and 12 of M.G. Morgan and M. Henrion, <u>Uncertainty</u>, Cambridge, NY, 1990.

4. Limited Dependent Variables

a) Discrete choice
J: 19.1-4
* Probit, logit and Tobit
Chapters 2, 3 and 6 of G.S. Maddala, <u>Limited Dependent and Qualitative Variables in Econometrics</u>, Cambridge University Press, London, 1983. (Maddala).
D. C. McFadden "Econometric Analysis of Qualitative Response Models", Vol. 2, Handbook, Chapter 24, 1983.

b) Simultaneous systems
* Endogenous limited dependent variables
Big Judge 18.5
Chapters 7-10 of Maddala.

c) Share models
* Linear logit models
T. J. Tyrrell and T. D. Mount, "A Nonlinear Expenditure System Using a Linear Logit Specification", <u>American Journal of Agricultural Economics</u>, 64, No. 3, 1982, pp. 539-546.
*Estimating demand systems
T. J. Considine and T. D. Mount, "The Use of Linear Logit Models for Dynamic Input Demand Systems", <u>The Review of Economics and Statistics</u>, 66, No. 3, 1984, pp. 434-443.
Chapters 7-9 of R. Bewley <u>Allocation Models</u>, Ballinger, Cambridge, MA, 1986.

d) Global properties of demand systems
* Comparison of alternative functional forms
D. S. Rothman, J. H. Hong and T. D. Mount, "Estimating Consumer Energy Demand Using International Data: Theoretical and Policy Implications", <u>The Energy Journal</u>, 15, No. 2, pp. 67-88, 1994.
*Semi-nonparametric methods
A. R. Gallant and Douglas W. Nychka, "Semi-nonparametric Maximum Likelihood Estimation", <u>Econometrica</u>, 55, 1987, pp. 363-390.

ARME 713
Quantitative Methods II
Spring 1995   G

Instructors: Jon M. Conrad   Tim D. Mount
                        307 Warren Hall   109 Warren Hall
                        Phone: 255-7681   Phone: 255-4512

Course
Description:

This course is concerned with the optimization
and estimation of dynamical systems. Specific course
objectives are to (1) present the basic theory of dynamic
optimization and the econometrics of time series models,
(2) introduce some methods for numerical and
econometric analysis, (3) present some case studies and,
hopefully, (4) equip the student with the basic tools for
applied research on dynamic allocation problems.

Course
Prerequisites:

Econ. 509 and Ag. Econ. 710

Time
Place and
Grading:

The course will employ a lecture/discussion
format. The class will meet from 9:05-11:00 a.m.
on Monday and Wednesday in Warren 260. During the
first half of the semester students will be given
approximately seven problem sets. This part of the
course, dealing with dynamic optimization, will end on
Wednesday, March 15th. A Take-Home Mid-Term Exam
will be distributed on that day. It will be due at the
beginning of class on Monday, March 27th. The second half
of the course will cover the stability and estimation of
time-series models. There will be approximately four
problem sets over this portion of the course followed by an
exam administered during the official exam period. The
grade for the course will be based on the problem sets,
mid-term and final exam.

Course Outline:

PART 1: Dynamic Optimization

I. Deterministic, Discrete-Time Models
    (a) The Method of Lagrange Multipliers
    (b) The Maximum Principle
    (c) Dynamic Programming
II. Deterministic, Continuous-Time Models
    (a) The Calculus of Variations
    (b) The Maximum Principle
    (c) Dynamic Programming
III. Stochastic, Discrete-Time Models
    (a) Certainty Equivalence
    (b) Stochastic Dynamic Programming
IV. Stochastic, Continuous-Time Models
    (a) Wiener Processes and Ito's Lemma
    (b) Stochastic Dynamic Programming
    (c) Stopping Rules

PART 2: Econometric Time Series

I. Difference Equations
II. Time Series Models (ARIMA)
III. Vector Autoregression
IV. Dynamic Structural Models (SEMTSA)
V. Causality and Cointegration
VI State-Space Models (Kalman Filter)
VII. Linear-Quadratic-Gaussian Models
(Stochastic Control)

Required Text: **Part 1** Léonard, D. and N. V. Long. 1992. *Optimal Control Theory and Static Optimization in Economics,* Cambridge University Press, Cambridge.

Dixit, A. K. and R. S. Pindyck. 1994. *Investment Under Uncertainty,* Princeton University Press, Princeton, New Jersey.

Suggested Text: **Part 1** Kamien, M. I. and N. L. Schwartz. 1991. *The Calculus of Variations and Optimal Control in Economics and Management,* Elsevier, New York.

241

Suggested Text: Part II Hamilton, C. L. 1993. *"Time Series Analysis"*, Princeton University Press, California

J.M. Conrad - Reading List

Brock, W. A., Rothschild, M. and J. E. Stiglitz. 1989. "Stochastic Capital Theory," in *Joan Robinson and Modern Economic Theory,* G. R. Feiwel, editor, New York University Press, New York.

Conrad, J. M. and C. W. Clark. 1987. *Natural Resource Economics: Notes and Problems,* Cambridge University Press, Cambridge.

Dixit, A. K. 1989. "Entry and Exit Decisions Under Uncertainty," *Journal of Political Economy,* 97(June):620-638.

Dixit, A. K. and R. J. Pindyck. 1994. *Investment Under Uncertainty,* Princeton University Press, Princeton, New Jersey.

Dorfman, R. 1969. "An Economic Interpretation of Optimal Control," *The American Economic Review,* 59(Dec.):817-831.

Intriligator, M. D. 1971. *Mathematical Optimization and Economic Theory,* Prentice-Hall, Englewood Cliffs.

Kennedy, J. O. S. 1986. *Dynamic Programming: Applications to Agricultural and Natural Resources,* Elsevier Applied Science Publishers, London.

Pindyck, R. S. 1991. "Irreversibility, Uncertainty, and Investment," *Journal of Economic Literature,* 29 (3): 1110-1148.

Ross, S. M. 1983. *An Introduction to Stochastic Dynamic Programming,* Academic Press, New York.

Spence, A. M. and D. Starrett. 1975. "Most Rapid Approach Paths in Accumulation Problems," *International Economic Review,* 16(2):388-403.

242

Bertsekas, D. 1976. *Dynamic Programming and Stochastic Control,* Academic Press, New York.

Engle, R. F. and C. W. J. Granger. 1987. "Co-Integration and Error Correction: Representation, Estimation and Testing", *Econometrica,* 55(2):251-276.

Engle, R. F., Hendry, D. F. and J. F. Richard. 1987. "Exogeneity", *Econometrica,* 55(2):277-304.

Engle, R. F., and B. S. Yoo. 1987. "Forecasting and Testing in Co-Integrated Systems", *Journal of Econometrics,* 35:143-159.

Friedman, M. and A. J. Schwartz. 1991. "Alternative Approaches to Analyzing Economic Data", *The American Economic Review,* 81(1).

Granger, C. W. J. 1986. "Development in the Study of Cointegrated Economic Variables", *Oxford Bulletin of Economics and Statistics,* 48(3):213-227.

Granger, C. W. J. and P. Newbold. 1986. "Forecasting Economic Time Series", *Academic Press,* San Diego, (Second Edition).

Hansen, L. P. and T. J. Sargent. 1981. "Linear Rational Expectations Models for Dynamically Interrelated Variables", in *Rational Expectations and Econometric Practice,* eds. R. E. Lucas and T. J. Sargent, University of Minnesota Press, Minneapolis, pp. 127-156.

Harvey, A. C. 1989. *Econometric Analysis of Time Series,* (Second Edition) MIT Press, Cambridge Massachusetts. (Abbreviated on Reading Assignments as EATS).

Harvey, A. C. 1989. *Forecasting, Structural Time Series Models and the Kalman Filter,* Allan, Cambridge University Press, (Abbreviated as FSTSM).

Hendry, D. F. and N. R. Ericsson. 1991. "An Econometric Analysis of U.K. Money Demand in Monetary Trends in the United States and the United Kingdom: by Milton Friedman and Anna J. Schwartz", *The American Economic Review,* 81(1).

Hendry, D. F. and N. R. Ericsson. 1990. "Modeling the Demand for Narrow Money in the United Kingdom and the United States", *International Finance Discussion Papers*, Board of Governors of the Federal Reserve System, 383.

Judge, G. G., et al. 1985. *Theory and Practice of Econometrics*, Wiley & Sons, New York, (Second Edition).

Kokkelenberg, E. C. and T. D. Mount. 1993. "Oil Shocks and the Demand For Electricity", *The Energy Journal*, 14:(2):113-138.

Nelson, C. R. and H. Kang. 1981. "Spurious Periodicity in Inappropriately Detrended Time Series", *Econometrica*, 49(3):741-751.

Newbold, P. and S. M. Hotopp. 1986. "Testing Causality Using Efficiently Parametrized ARMA Models", *Applied Mathematics and Computation*, 20: 329-348.

Park, J. Y. 1988. "Canonical Cointegrating Regressions", Center for Analytic Economics, CAE Working Paper #88-29, Cornell University, Ithaca.

Phillips, P. C. B. 1987. "Time Series Regression with a Unit Root", *Econometrica*, 55(2):277-302.

Pindyck, R. S. and D. L. Rubinfeld. 1976. *Econometric Models and Economic Forecasts*, McGraw-Hill, New York.

Robertson, J. and D. Orden. 1988. "A Vector Error-Correction Model of Money and Price Dynamics in New Zealand, unpublished manuscript, Virginia Tech, Blacksburg, Virginia.

Sargent, T. J. 1987. *Macroeconomic Theory*, Academic Press, Boston.

Sims, C. A. 1980. "Macroeconomics and Reality", *Econometrica*, 48, 1-48.

Zellner, A. 1979. "Statistical Analysis of Econometric Models", *Journal of the American Statistical Association*, 74:628-643.

Reading Assignments

Part 1: Dynamic Optimization

I. Deterministic, Discrete-Time Models
  - (a) Conrad and Clark: Section 1.2
  - (b) Kennedy: Chapter 1, Léonard and Long: Section 4.2
  - (c) Conrad and Clark: Section 1.3, Kennedy: Chapter 2, Léonard and Long: Section 5.2

II. Deterministic, Continuous-Time Models
  - (a) Léonard and Long: Section 5.1
    Kamien and Schwartz: Part I, Sections 1 and 2.
    Intriligator: Chapters 11 and 12.
    Kamien and Schwartz: Part I, Sections 3-9, 15 and 16.
  - (b) Léonard and Long: Chapters 4, 6, 7, 8, and 9
    Intriligator: Chapter 14.
    Kamien and Schwartz: Part II, Sections 1-10, 14 and 15.
    Dorfman.
    Spence and Starrett.

  - (c) Léonard and Long: Section 5.3
    Intriligator: Chapter 13
    Kamien and Schwartz: Part II, Section 21.

III. Stochastic, Discrete-Time Models
  - (a) Conrad and Clark Chapter 5, Section 5.4.
  - (b) Kennedy: Chapter 3.
    Ross: Chapters I and II.

IV. Stochastic, Continuous-Time Models
  - (a) Dixit and Pindyck, Chapters 1-3
    Appendix to Pindyck (1991)
  - (b) Dixit and Pindyck, Chapter 4
    Kamien and Schwartz: Section 22
  - (c) Brock, Rothschild and Stiglitz
    Dixit and Pindyck, Chapter 5
    Dixit (1989)

Part 2:   Estimation and Control

I.   Hamilton: Chapters 1-2

II.   Hamilton: Chapters 3-5:
      Pindyck and Rubinfeld: Chapters 13-17
      Granger and Newbold: Chapters 3,6
      Nelson and Kang

III. Hamilton: Chapters 10-11
      Granger and Newbold: Chapters 7,8
      Newbold and Hotopp
      Judge et al.: Chapter 16.1
      Sims

IV.   Hamilton: Chapters 15-19
      Harvey (EATS): Chapters 8.6, 7, 9.6-8
      Judge et al.: Chapter 16.2, 7
      Zellner
      Kokklenberg and Mount

V.   Engle, Hendry and Richard
      Engle and Granger
      Engle and Yoo
      Granger
      Hendry and Ericsson
      Park
      Robertson and Orden
      Phillips

VI.   Hamilton: Chapter 13
      Harvey (FSTSM) Chapters 3-4

VII. Bertsekas: Chapters 2-4
      Sargent: Chapter 1
      Hansen and Sargent

ECONOMICS READING LISTS, COURSE OUTLINES, EXAMS, PUZZLES & PROBLEMS
Compiled by Edward Tower, *Duke University & The University of Auckland*, September 1995

The price of each volume is $24. The discount price of the complete set of 25 Economics volumes is $395. A special offer for individuals buying economics volumes: Buy 2 volumes at the regular price, and get additional volumes for $20 each when ordering directly from Eno River Press. Please add $3/order for shipping on all orders. Additional postage charges are: US first class and Canadian air @ $3/volume; other foreign air @ $6/volume.

BUSINESS ADMINISTRATION READING LISTS AND COURSE OUTLINES

Compiled by Richard Schwindt, *Simon Fraser University*, 1995

Volume 1 ACCOUNTING I: Introductory, Intermediate and Advanced Accounting, Financial Accounting, Auditing, 224 pp.

Volume 2 ACCOUNTING II: Managerial Accounting, International Accounting, Financial Statement Analysis and Tax, 212 pp.

Volume 3 MARKETING I: Marketing Strategy, Management and Research, 237 pp.

Volume 4 MARKETING II: Buyer Behavior, Industrial Marketing, International Marketing, The 4 P's, 292 pp.

Volume 5 FINANCE I: Corporate Finance, 194 pp.

Volume 6 FINANCE II: Investments and Financial Markets, 235 pp.

Volume 7 INTERNATIONAL BUSINESS I: Multinational Management and the International Environment, 274 pp.

Volume 8 INTERNATIONAL BUSINESS II: Comparative Management, Regional Studies (Japan, Russia, Eastern Europe, The Pacific Basin), International Business Law, 197 pp.

Volume 9 INTERNATIONAL FINANCE AND FINANCIAL MARKETS, 166 pp.

Volume 10 INDUSTRIAL RELATIONS AND HUMAN RESOURCES MANAGEMENT, 248 pp.

Volume 11 BUSINESS ETHICS, REGULATION AND LAW, 287 pp.

Volume 12 BUSINESS POLICY AND STRATEGY, 246 pp.

Volume 13 DECISION MAKING UNDER UNCERTAINTY, GAMES AND BARGAINING, 208 pp.

Volume 14 OPERATIONS RESEARCH, 286 pp.

Volume 15 ENTREPRENEURSHIP, 176 pp.

Volume 16 MANAGEMENT COMMUNICATION, 200 pp. *Compiled by Mary Munter*

Volume 17 BUSINESS ECONOMICS, 227 pp.

Volume 18 ORGANIZATIONAL BEHAVIOR I: Organizational Behavior And Theory, 233 pp.

Volume 19 ORGANIZATIONAL BEHAVIOR II: Managerial and Social Psychology, Human Resource Accounting, Leadership, Diversity, Skills, Sensemaking, Organizational Development, 240 pp.

Volume 20 MANAGEMENT INFORMATION SYSTEMS AND BUSINESS STATISTICS, 230 pp.

All volumes are priced at $24 each. The complete set is $350. Please add $3/order for shipping on all orders. Additional postage charges are: U.S. first class and Canadian air @ $3/volume; other foreign air @ $6/volume. Payment accepted in U.S. funds only.

Eno River Press
115 Stoneridge Dr.
Chapel Hill, NC 27514-9737, USA

5876

DATE DUE

#952

6-3-57